OAK LAWN PUBLIC LIBRARY
W9-BYL-993

★ Our Army Nurses ★

★ Our Army Nurses ★

Stories from Women in the Civil War

MARY GARDNER HOLLAND

Introduction by Daniel John Hoisington

APR 01 1999
OAK LAWN LIBRARY

Edinborough Press

Edinborough Press
P.O. Box 13790
Roseville, Minnesota 55113-2293
1-888-251-6336

10 9 8 7 6 5 4 3 2 1

Copyright © 1998 by Edinborough Press. All rights reserved including the right
of reproduction in whole or in part in any form.

The text is composed in Janson typeface.
This book is printed on acid-free paper.
Research Associate: Daniel Aaron Hoisington

Cover Art: Anne Bell at Nashville Hospital, 1864 (USAMHI).
Frontispiece from *The Boys of '61* by Charles Coffin.

Publisher's Cataloguing In Publication Data

Holland, Marssner.
Our Army Nurses: Stories from Women in the Civil War.
Edited with an introduction by Daniel John Hoisington.
    p.   cm.
    Includes index.

ISBN 1-889020-04-4

    1. United States–History–Civil War, 1861-1865–Participation, Female.
    2. United States–History–Civil War, 1861-1865–Medical Care.
    3. United States—History—Civil War, 1861-1865—Women.
    I. Holland, Mary Gardner. II. Hoisington, Daniel John. III. Title.

E621.W87 1998
973.7'75—dc20   LCCN 97-60189

Printed in Canada

Contents

Introduction

THIRTY YEARS after the Civil War, Mary Gardner Holland gathered stories from her fellow nurses with the purpose of "opening of the way of communication between nurse and patient." The collection, *Our Army Nurses*, was printed in 1895 and sold through subscription. The strength of this book is that it records the stories of a cross-section of women who responded to the call to preserve the Union. Some contributors provided lengthy essays. Others submitted one or two paragraphs. For a few of the most noted army nurses, Holland copied biographies from newspapers or magazines of the day. In her second edition, published in 1897, she added a long article detailing the work of Catholic sisters.

It was a propitious time for Holland to gather her information. These women, in their fifties and sixties, had reached an age of reflection. Matilda Morris wrote that her daughters "often coax me to tell a story of the war." Margaret Hamilton said that it was a standing joke among her eight children that they have "Civil War for breakfast, dinner, and supper." The anonymous biographer of Margaret Weed noted that she was "inclined to live in the past and think over the scenes of war-times." "Among the sad memories of these years," Sophronia Bucklin said, "there remain some pleasant ones,—the most cherished of my life." Oliver Wendell Holmes Jr.'s sentiment applied to women as well as men: "In our youths, our hearts were touched by fire."

Clara Barton voiced a common concern that their work might be forgotten. In her poem, "The Women Who Went To The War," Barton asked:

> And who were they all?—They were many, my men:
> Their record was kept by no tabular pen:
> They exist in traditions from father to son.
> Who recalls, in dim memory, now here and there one.—
> A few names were writ, and by chance live to-day;
> But's a perishing record fast fading away.

There were additional reasons for these women to preserve the "perishing record." The United States Congress passed the Army Nurse Pension Act in 1892, recognizing, for the first time, women as military veterans. Army nurses were awarded a pension of twelve dollars a month if they could establish a service record of at least six months. Under this act, 2,448 Union army nurses requested pensions. It is unclear exactly how many applications were approved, although one source placed the total around six hundred at the turn-of-the-century.

Many were rejected because they could not provide "competent authority" of their service. As Barton suggests, records were not always kept "by tabular pen." Betsy Cook reported that her pension application was rejected because her commission was unauthorized. Lucy Barron wrote that she had been sworn in by Captain S. M. Davis, "but neglected to be enrolled." Mrs. M. J. Boston remembered,

> When asked for my name, to enter on [the] books, I said: "No,
> I do not want any pay for my services. I only try to do all I can
> for the soldiers." "You had better give me your name," [the doctor] said, "It may be of use to you sometime."

By publishing their story, the women placed their claims into the public record and increased the chance that soldiers, doctors, or fellow workers might come forward to support their claims.

Who were these women? Approximately 5,600 women are listed in Union hospital records as "nurse." If the contributors to this book are a sample, they represent all parts of the north. They generally came from old Yankee stock—several explicitly claiming Revolutionary War veterans as ancestors. It appears as if only one of the writers was an immigrant—Ellen Marsh—and she came from England. Although Holland included two entries describing the work of Catholic sisters, many of whom were of foreign birth, they remain shadow figures understood as a special class. African-American women were excluded from this book. Official records might list them as a "laundress" or "cook," although they performed the same tasks as a nurse. Sojourner Truth and Susie King Taylor are two clearly documented cases of black women who cared for the sick.[1]

Why did they join? Women, as well as men, were swept by patriotic fever following the attack on Fort Sumter. Several contributors cited the equality of the sexes in this matter. Selener Richards wrote, "In those days, the love of country was as strong in the hearts of the loyal girls as in that of their brothers." When Mary Stinebaugh's father objected to her wish to become a nurse, she said, "You have given your boys to die for their country; now you can give your girls to nurse them." "If only I were a man!" exclaimed Mrs. L. B. Downs before she enlisted. Others joined for personal reasons. A quarter of the women represented in this book followed their husbands into the army, sometimes leaving children at home.

The federal government provided a single channel for these volunteers when it appointed Dorothea Dix as Superintendent of Women Nurses in June 1861. Dix was widely respected across the country for her work in the reformation of insane asylums. She had studied the work of Florence Nightingale and hoped to build a similar corps of nurses employing women of good character. She established strict standards to place them beyond reproach. She wrote,

> No young ladies should be sent at all, but some who . . . are sober, earnest, self-sacrificing, and self-sustained; who can bear the presence of suffering and exercise entire self-control of speech and manner; who can be calm, gentle, quiet, active, and steadfast in duty. All nurses are required to be plain looking women. Their dresses must be brown or black, with no bows, no curls, no jewelry, and no hoop-skirts.

Dix's formidable personality made the job interview a memorable event for many women. Mary Gardner Holland applied, telling the Superintendent, "I am plain-looking enough to suit you, and old enough. I have no near relatives in the war, no lover there. I never had a husband, and am not looking for one." Amanda Farnham Felch appeared in a bloomer-type outfit. Dix looked her up and down, and pronounced, "The dress you wear is abominable." As was often the case with Dix, she valued the testimonials to character more than the rules. Felch received a commission and became a trusted aide. Elizabeth Chamberlain Perkins followed the 11th Maine Volunteers as a volunteer nurse. When Dix finally met her at the Hygeia Hospital in Hampton, Virginia, Perkins feared rejection since she was only twenty-two. Again, the "earnest solicitation of the surgeons and nurses" won Dix's support.

Dix kept the selection of her corps outside of the military chain-of-command and maintained haphazard records. She worked with a personal management style, traveled extensively, met with as many nurses as possible, and fought for them when confronted by unsympathetic surgeons. The expanse of the war effort, however, overwhelmed her careful system. Nightingale, by comparison, worked with only thirty-eight women on her Crimean mission.

There were easier routes for women to become an army nurse than to wait for an audience with the Superintendent. While many of the women represented in this book were appointed by Dix or her representatives, Mr. James Yeatman in Saint Louis and Mrs. Mary Livermore in Chicago, one half joined a regiment or simply made their way to a hospital and worked without commission. Clara Barton, for example, obtained a pass, after weeks of lobbying, gathered supplies, and headed to the front lines. When a Union officer questioned Mary Bickerdyke's presence in a military camp, she responded, "I have received my authority from the Lord God Almighty."

Furthermore, Dix's tight control over the appointment of nurses was opposed by many medical officers. In 1863, War Department Order No. 351 officially recognized alternate means of obtaining a commission, permitting surgeons to employ nurses by special appointment of the Surgeon General. Friends told Fanny Titus-Hazen, twenty-four, that she was sure to be rejected by Dorothea Dix. She called, instead, on Surgeon-General William Hammond. "He told me it would be of no use to go to Miss Dix," she recalled, "but if any surgeon in charge of a hospital would give me a position . . . he would endorse my name." These special appointments were generously given, sharply curtailing Dix's powers.

The result was a patchwork. Jane Stuart Woolsey described "the system of women-nurses,"

> There never was a system. Hospital nurses were of all sorts, and came from various sources of supply; volunteers paid and unpaid; soldiers' wives and sisters who had come to see their friends and remained without any clear commission or duties; women sent by State agencies and aid societies; women assigned by the General Superintendent of Nurses; sometimes, the wife or daughter of a medical officer drawing rations.[2]

What did nurses do? The work centered around the primary medical principle established in Florence Nightingale's *Notes on Nursing*: Do no harm and let nature take its healing course. The nurse seldom attended surgery. This was left to male nurses or hospital stewards. Few ever came close to the battlefront, serving instead at army hospitals located in central supply centers such as Nashville, Saint Louis, Washington, Alexandria, Philadelphia, Louisville, or Memphis.

Nurses had three primary tasks. First, they assisted with the "special diet," instituted to carefully regulate what the convalescent soldier could eat. This was differentiated from employment as a cook. When one surgeon requested "Female cooks" from Annie Wittenmyer, she responded, "I employ no cooks, only superintendents of special Diet kitchens." Second, the nurses cared for physical needs, handling distribution of linen and clothing, often managing the supplies provided by the United States Sanitary Commission or the Christian Commission. Third, they assisted with the emotional and spiritual care of the soldier. This book is repleat with stories of deathbed conversations. It is easy to understand the emotional impact that these moments might have. Cecelia White wrote, "I often think how little the people knew of what was going on in the hospital. It seemed very sad to me to see men carried to the deadhouse day after day."

Although the nurses rarely came under fire, they faced great danger in their work. If these stories are a reliable sample, one quarter of the nurses suffered a serious illness during their terms of service, with the results often lingering well after the war. The wards were a breeding ground for disease. When measles swept through troops near Pittsburg Landing, Mrs. Anna McMahon succumbed and was buried in a coffin constructed from old cracker boxes. Jane Worrall wrote, "I contracted the [typhoid] fever in its worst form. . . I barely escaped, and have never been well since." Mrs. M. J. Boston reported the story of a young woman who pricked her finger while pinning a bandage, then contracted blood-poisoning while washing a wound. The woman's hand was amputated, and she eventually died. One wonders if there is a difference between the courage of a soldier marching to the front and a nurse entering a smallpox ward.

There were other risks. "Mother" Ransom related her voyage on the ill-fated ship, *North America*. Carrying several hundred sick and wounded soldiers, the *North America* sank off the coast of Florida on December 16, 1864. One hundred and ninety-four soldiers were lost. Margaret Edgar told of an attack on Hospital No. 1 in Paducah, Kentucky, by troops under General Nathan Bedford Forrest. When confronted by a rebel soldier, she recalled, "I thought my time had come." The hospital, with all its contents, was burned to the ground. When Mary Stinebaugh met refugees on a Mississippi road, a woman warned her that guerillas were planning a raid. The Rebels threatened that "Yanks would lose their heads, women first." Ruth Sinnotte described a fantastic plot by a crew to deliver their ship to the Confederates. She foiled the attempt with the help of a patient on board. "All of the crew, " she wrote, "from the captain to the chambermaid, were so very angry, they would have killed me."

What difference did this experience make? Nursing changed rapidly after the war, and few of these women remained in the profession. Several, including Vesta Swartz, Carol Burghardt, and Nancy Hill, became physicians. Clara Barton, of course, founded the American Red Cross. Some taught in Freedmen's Bureau schools after the war. Others were active in veteran's organizations. Margaret Hamilton, Fanny Titus Hazen, Delia Fay, Hannah Palmer, and Hannah Starbird, contributors to this volume, served as officers in the National Association of Army Nurses of the Civil War. Dr. Vesta Swartz placed their experience in perspective, writing:

> The war for the preservation of our Union...did much to advance the best interests of woman. It created a necessity for her labor in new and untried ways. It gave her an opportunity to prove her ability and also to cultivate that true courage without which the most capable person may utterly fail of success.

Women's work in the war provided an argument in favor of women's suffrage. Mary Gardner Holland made an explicit connection, when she added, as a postscript to the second edition, an essay written by Mrs. Ida Harper for the San Francisco *Argonaut*. Harper, chair of the California State Suffrage Press Committee, argued that women earned the right to vote. "Can any man read this record," she asked, "and continue to say, 'No woman shall have a voice in this government because she cannot go to war and fight?'"

Finally, the work of the army nurse during the Civil War dramatically changed public perceptions about the place of women in medicine. In 1868 Dr. Samuel Gross, President of the American Medical Association, strongly endorsed the development of nurse's training. Women veterans accepted the challenge, and helped to found the Connecticut Training School for Nurses and the Boston Training School for Nurses. In 1903 Mary Livermore noted this change when she addressed the annual convention of the Nurses' Associated Alumnae. She told them, "I find all that is within me rising up in this presence in a semi-reverential attitude. A congregation of trained women nurses. Something that in my earlier days I never expected to see."[3]

That "semi-reverential attitude" might well be reserved for the women whose stories we find in *Our Army Nurses*. These brief biographies are filled with diversity of experience and personality. If we simply classify these women according to gender, race, or class; or, if we hallow them as saintly angels of the battlefield, we miss the richness of their stories, the warmth of their humanity, and the truth of their contribution to history.

—Daniel John Hoisington

A NOTE ON THE TEXT

The text comes from *Our Army Nurses: Interesting Sketches, Addresses, and Photographs of nearly One Hundred of the Noble Women who Served in Hospitals and on the Battlefields during our Civil War,* compiled by Mary A. Gardner Holland. (Boston: B. Wilkins & Co., 1895; 1897). The second edition (1897) included additional material, including a long chapter describing the work of Catholic sisters. The editor eliminated a few extraneous contributions, including a lengthy essay about Clara Barton's post-war work with the Red Cross, a preface by Rev. Edward A. Horton, and an article from the San Francisco *Argonaut* by Ida Harper.

The editor attempted to avoid intrusions on the text. He corrected two obvious errors: Sophronia Bucklin, a well-known nurse, was named "Brecklin;" Lauretta Husington was changed to the correct "Hoisington." Punctuation was modified when it contributed to better comprehension. There was no apparent organization to the original book. This edition placed the nurses in alphabetical order.

ENDNOTES

[1] Jane E. Schultz, "Race, Gender, and Bureaucracy: Civil War Army Nurses and the Pension Bureau," *Journal of Women's History,* 6 (1994), 45-69. Schultz has contributed landmark work on army nurses in a series of journal articles.

[2] Jane Stuart Woolsey, *Hospital Days: Reminiscence of a Civil War Nurse* (Roseville, MN: Edinborough Press, 1996), 36.

[3] Mary A. Livermore, "Nurses in the Civil War," *Proceedings of the Sixth Annual Convention of the Nurses' Associated Alumnae of the United States, June 10, 11, and 12, 1903* (Philadelphia: J. B. Lippincott Co., 1903), 1-6.

A Soldier Remembers

To NO CLASS OF PEOPLE are the soldiers of the late war more indebted than to the Army Nurses. How the eyes of the old veteran fill with tears when, at our camp fires, some old lady is introduced, and the presiding officer says, "Boys, she was an army nurse." For a moment the distinguished officers present are forgotten, and they gather around the dear old lady, eager to grasp her hand and say some kind and loving word in appreciation of her services. I have often witnessed such a greeting at the annual reunion of New Hampshire veterans at the Weirs, when Aunt Harriet Dame has been presented.

The work of the army nurse began as soon as Sumter was fired upon. Within thirty days after the call for 75,000 men, made by President Lincoln, April 14, 1861, the Woman's Central Association of New York had chosen, from hundreds of candidates, one hundred competent women to be trained by the physicians and surgeons of New York as nurses in the army hospitals.

June 10, 1861, Miss Dorothea Dix was appointed, by the Secretary of War, Superintendent of female nurses. She gave herself up, without compensation, to the selection of competent nurses. Secretary Stanton vested her with full power to appoint army nurses in the hospitals, and she cheerfully gave her labor and her fortune to the cause. Nurses selected by her, and others, who followed the several regiments to the front, were found on every battlefield from Bull Run to Appomattox. They were in every hospital, ministering to the sick, wounded, and dying of the Union Army.

An incident of their devotion and angelic loveliness came under my personal observation. At the battle of Antietam my brother fell, mortally wounded. For two days I was unable to obtain any trace of him, as, by change of front, the rebels held the portion of the field where he lay. As soon as they retreated, I found him near an old haystack in a barnyard at the right of Dunker Church. I saw at once that he could live only a few days, and was anxious to get him where he could have medical attendance, and, calling an ambulance, had him taken to a field hospital near Sharpsburg.

As I was kneeling by his side, taking his last message to our dear mother, a voice said, "Is this your brother?" and looking up I saw the sweet face of a woman, and by her side, a sergeant of the Philadelphia Fire Zouaves. That woman was Mrs. Mary Lee of Philadelphia. She had given her only son to his country and had followed him to the field. I explained to her how my brother and I had enlisted together, and that, being in command of the company, and under orders to march at once, I could not stay with him. She said, "I will take his mother's place," and she nursed him until he died; then saw him buried, his grave marked, and in a few days wrote me all the sad circumstances.

When the war was over, I met Mrs. Lee in Philadelphia. She followed the old Second Division, Second Corps, to the end. She wore on her breast a gold Corps badge, presented by the boys of the 72d Pennsylvania. God spared her son, and I have visited the family in their happy home. A few years ago Mrs. Lee passed to a higher life, mourned by all the men in the old Corps, who loved her as a mother.

It would be invidious to mention by name where so many served. Miss Clara Barton served from first to last; "Mother" Bickerdyke, who was called by General Sherman, one of his best generals; Mrs. Mary A. Livermore, who served in the Army of the West; Miss Gilson, who was attached to the transfer service in the Chickahominy campaign and with the Army of the Potomac in the Wilderness; and a host of others, all sacrificing and suffering as much as any soldier in the ranks. The pay of those regularly mustered in the service was twelve dollars per month; but hundreds never waited to be mustered in, only desiring to serve where duty called, without pay or hope of reward.

Many died of exposure and disease contracted in the service. Many returned with health impaired; and some, be it said with shame and sorrow, died in poverty. Until within a few years no official recognition has ever been given them by the Government which they served so well. Some three years since a pension bill was passed, giving them twelve dollars a month, but the record of their service is so imperfect that it is almost impossible to prove a claim, and a large portion go to their graves unrecognized and unrewarded; yet while their names are written on no army roll, and but few books have been published telling the story of their services, their memory will ever live in the hearts of the veterans they nursed with such tender care, and they will never grow weary of telling to their children and children's children the story of the loving, tender, and Christian ministrations of those "angels of mercy."

John G. B. Adams
PAST NATIONAL COMMANDER G. A. R.

Mary G. Holland

HAVING CONCEIVED THE PLAN of the army nurses writing an abbreviated sketch of their war record to put in book form, I undertook the arduous work of securing the addresses of all I could locate and have received letters and photographs of more than can be contained in this book. I trust that the outcome of the work may be an opening of the way of communication between nurse and patient, a desire on the heart of many, covering the period of intervening years since the war.

Many a veteran will here be able to look into the face of his faithful nurse who stood by him in those terrible days of suffering. Friends who have survived the soldier who has passed the last roll-call must look with equal interest upon the faces of those who by force of circumstances took their places to watch and wait, to cheer and comfort the loved husband, father, son, or brother who responded to our country's call.

With some it was hard to decide the question, "Shall I leave my home and dear ones, mayhap never to return?" But while the decision lay trembling in the balance, the battle call sounded, and the martial tread was heard,—tramp! tramp! tramp! Our boys, uniformed in blue, are coming, over the mountains, from the riverside, and through the valleys. Now the thunder of the engine is heard in the distance. It comes nearer, and yet nearer, until the eye of the locomotive rests upon the multitude gathered upon the platform. Grief is too great to allow confusion or bustle. The little groups apart exchange the parting words. The hour has come. The inevitable farewell must now be given,—and the last hand-clasp. The shrill whistle warns a hurried good-bye, and "God bless you!" echoes and re-echoes as the iron steed bears our boys away.

Oh, how many of them, on those fateful days, had in reality given the last "farewell"! Sorrowfully the weeping wife led her little ones back to the desolate hearthstone, to gather them in a fond embrace and tell them of their soldier father,—how he had gone to strike back the rebel arm that would trail our Stars and Stripes in the dust, and dishonor its glorious record.

And the old mother, bending a little with age, with trembling hand lifts the latch that last closed when her son went out to return no more. No pen can depict the sorrows that shadowed the lonely homes our soldiers left during those four years of blood-shed,—four years of suffering and watching for news of the next battle and its results; four years of suffering on the part of our soldiers, tenting in swamps, marching through the mud of Southern soil, on double-quick, to the scene of carnage! The fierce contest has begun,—and they bare their defenseless bodies to the shot and shell of our Southern brothers, whose big guns sweep furrows through our ranks. The gaps are immediately closed, our boys falling dead or disabled.

What more fitting place for women with holy motives and tenderest sympathy than on those fields of blood and death or in retreats prepared for our suffering heroes? We are glad even at this late date to record upon these pages, the names of as many nurses as we have been able to gather. No lapse of years can cool the patriotism that urged them to the responsibilities they took upon themselves, and the same spirit breathes in every line of contribution to this book, that actuated their deeds during the dark days of the Civil War: days that tried men's souls, while women wept in grief and sympathy. All risked life,— thousands met death while the struggle went on that preserved for us the sheltering folds of our flag, that "grand emblem of protection to home and native land." It seems to me that had I died battling for my country's honor, that my right hand would almost leap from its entombed dust to strike back the arm that would dare drag our flag from its high standard of glory,—the grandest emblem of the grandest country that lies under God's sunshine! Let no foe dare molest that flag, and thus insult our country. Such would be compelled to retreat to their own corners in dismay, for the spirit of the old Revolution days burned in the hearts of our country-men during the Civil War and is transmitted to the rising generation. Our boys and girls are taught in many of the schools to salute the flag and swear allegiance to "one country, one flag, one language."

Though my place is small in comparison to that of many heroic women of the war, I feel the assurance that the Recording Angel has borne my name to Him who has said, "As ye have done it unto one of the least of these my brethren, ye have done it unto me." And when the key unlocks to us the mysteries of life, and opens the unknown future, may it be said of all army nurses, "They did what they could," and "Well done, good and faithful servant; enter thou into the joy of thy Lord."

My service in hospitals covered a period of nearly fourteen months. The first gun fired on Sumter fired every drop of my blood. Had it been possible I should have made my appearance at the first battle of Bull Run. I had an aged mother, who depended almost altogether upon me for her support, and that duty deterred me. At one time I said to her, "It seems to me that I must go to the war." I worked for her and for myself during the day, and on Sanitary Commission work evenings. I told her there were married women, with families of half-grown girls, who could not go to the front but could do all I was doing. She had long known my desire to be identified with some more important work, so after considering calmly for a few moments she answered, "Well, my daughter, if you can go under government protection, your mother is willing." "But," I answered, "you cannot spare me." She continued the same reflective attitude and repeated what she had just said, adding: "God will take care of your mother. If you ever go, do all you can, and tell the dying boys of God and heaven."

From that day I left no method untried to go under government protection; but not until early in the spring of 1864 did I accomplish my desire. I had tried to enlist under Miss Abbie May of Boston. At one time it seemed that my plans were well nigh completed to go to Fortress Monroe, where Mrs. Lander was trying to establish a hospital. She failed in her enterprise, and I was doomed to further delay. Later, I procured one of Miss Dix's circulars, and read it again and again. It appeared to me a queer demand. It read like this: "No woman under thirty years need apply to serve in government hospitals. All nurses are required to be very plain-looking women. Their dresses must be brown or black, with no bows, no curls, or jewelry, and no hoop-skirts."

It was fashionable at that time to wear immense hoops. I had worn one for some time, and really felt it a sacrifice to leave it off. Other requirements were agreeable, but I felt I could not walk without a hoop. I said, "Well, if I can't walk without it, I will crawl; for I must go, and I will do the best I can." Soon after this I took up a morning paper and read that the wounded were being brought into Washington so fast that more help was needed at once. I wrote immediately to Miss Dix, saying: "I am in possession of one of your circulars and will comply with all your requirements. I am plain-looking enough to suit you, and old enough. I have no near relatives in the war, no lover there. I never had a husband, and am not looking for one. Will you take me?" In a few days her answer came: "Report at once at my house, corner of 14th Street and New York Avenue, Washington."

She labeled me so nicely that had I been a box of glass, I think I should have gone safely, and gave me instructions to procure transportations at Nos. 12 and 13 Temple Place, Boston.

She first quartered me at Columbia College Hospital, Meridian Heights, Washington. From there I went to the Seminary Hospital, West Washington—all officers. Then to Annapolis. I served mostly in charge of linen rooms, and as matron; doing the principal part of real nursing evenings, and sometimes all night after having attended to the duties assigned me during the day.

My work was very hard, as I did not feel satisfied to fill the places given me and not attend to the wounded men.

I would like to mention a case in the Officers' Hospital at Georgetown, D. C. One evening there were nine wounded officers brought in, and consigned to the convalescent ward, Rebecca Wiswell, of Plymouth, Massachusetts, nurse in charge. This ward was on the same floor where I was acting as matron. I assisted the male attendants in giving the wounded officers their supper. The doctors and Miss Wiswell attended to dressing their wounds. A young man about twenty-three years of age, was laid on a bed across the hall from my room, and nearly opposite. Lieutenant Lee had died on that cot in the morning. It was a distressing death; he was two days dying. His poor mother was with him, and the scene was terrible. The young man placed on the cot that evening was only slightly wounded. A spent ball had entered the left forearm and lodged, but had been removed by the surgeon before bringing him to the hospital. As soon as all were located, a dispatch was sent to his father in Pennsylvania, saying, "In Officers' Hospital, Georgetown, slightly wounded." The return had come before I left the room, "Shall we come to you?" When all had received attention, Aunt Becky, as she was familiarly called, stepped to my side, and as we stood in the doorway, looking over the ward, I asked her how many of the last arrivals she thought would pull through. Pointing to one poor fellow she said, "He may not live until morning," then spoke of two other doubtful cases. I said, "I think that young man behind the door will die." "Oh, no," was her reply; "he is the most slightly wounded of any."

In the morning I went to his bedside, and said, "How did you get on during the night?" "Oh, very well." His voice was sweet as a woman's; his face was beautiful. Large drops of sweat stood out all over his high, white forehead. I could see a change in him from the evening before. I wiped away the perspiration, and fanned him for a few minutes. When I left him he said, "Must you go?" "To breakfast," I replied. "I will come in again soon." All the nurses had preceded me to the table, and Aunt Becky said: "Miss Holland, your premonitions about that young man were correct. He must die." I asked what the shiver meant that passed over him so frequently. "The lockjaw. We were with him half the night after you left, but can do nothing to save him."

Very soon I took my place by his cot and left it only for a few moments at a time to attend to the direction of other duties, as I was then acting matron. His spasms were frequent and severe all the forenoon. Just before noon he came out of one and asked, "Is my case a critical one?" "My dear boy, I fear it is," I said. He went into another, and when he came out of it said, "If anything happens to me send my body home." A moment after he said, "Mother!" loud and clear; then his teeth came together with a crash, and he passed away in that struggle, at just twelve o'clock noon.

I had retired to my room that evening. It was about half past ten when I heard a great wail of grief in the steward's office. Those sounds were frequent, yet every time they touched a tender chord of pity in my heart, and I said aloud, though alone, "Some poor soul has come and found that the dear one is gone." Presently there was a knock at my door. I inquired, and the answer was from the steward's orderly, "Mr. Pollock has come, and the steward wants you in the office."

The poor old father was in a reclining position, with both hands pressed against his face. I stood in the middle of the floor waiting, as I had not the heart to approach such intense grief. When the steward said, "Mr. Pollock, here is the woman who gave your son his last supper," he lifted his face to mine, then fell prone upon the floor. He wound my skirts about his face, not knowing what he did. At length he became a little calmer, and told us that Chester was his only boy. He had graduated from college, and had just entered upon what he had determined a life work as a lawyer, when his country called him to her defense, in which he had given his life. Over and over I told the old father the story of his coming into the hospital the evening before, and of his suffering through the forenoon of that day. He wanted me to go home with him, that the invalid wife and mother might look upon the woman who gave their boy his last supper. He offered every inducement in money and presents, but I could not be spared. I think the boy's first name was Chester; I am not sure. His last name was Pollock, his commission a lieutenant.

For a few days I was quartered at the Lincoln Barracks Hospital, East Capitol Street, D. C. I had a nephew there, William K. Nason, from Maine. He was badly wounded. Miss Dix had sent me there for a week, to do anything that I saw needed to be done. My nephew had his father with him so I was not required to do much for him. I looked up and down the ward to ascertain where I might be most needed. Near the far end I saw a pale face half covered with flies. I went to the cot, and found the poor fellow had suffered twenty days with a fractured ankle bone, then had an amputation between the knee and the ankle. The surgeon, for some reason better known to himself than to any one else, had left the stump open; had not drawn the flesh over the end of the bone, as is usual in amputations, but was to bandage it close, and more closely until healed. After suppuration had commenced, the artery sluffed off, and the night before I found him he had bled fearfully after lights had been turned down. The watchman was passing the foot of the bed, and slipped on the blood; he then called the surgeon, who put a compress on the leg above the knee, burned the end of the artery, and stopped the flow. I had been by the cot but a few minutes, when the surgeon and orderly came in again.

The surgeon threw back the sheet in a careless way, almost roughly, and picked at the end of the artery. The blood spurted, and he made another turn on the compress, saying, "We must hunt for that artery again." The poor boy said in a whisper, the first I had heard him speak, "Can't you wait till morning?" It was morning then; you can understand how weak he was. They gave him a glass of brandy and went at the wound. I thought from the quantities of blood that followed the almost inhuman treatment, that his life would go out ere the trial ended. But he lived through it, and I stayed by him four days. Every morning I took him a quart of delicious blackberries. He ate those, but took no other food. The morning of the fifth day I said: "I must go away this noon, and cannot come to you again. Have you mother, wife, or sister to send for? I fear you are too weak to rally." "No one who could come," he replied. "Give me your address." I wrote it, and he said, "Now put it into the book under my pillow." It was a Testament, and my address was deposited therein. I bade him good-bye, and spoke a little of the heavenly land, then left him.

In about two months I received a letter, saying the only excuse he had for writing to me was that he had not strength to thank me when I left him, and he believed the blackberries I gave him had saved his life. That day he had been on crutches beside his cot for the first time, and but for a minute; hoped he should soon be transferred to his own state. I have forgotten where he lived, but if this should ever meet the eye of John Tucker, I hope to hear from him.

I could add many thrilling incidents to this brief journal, but forbear, that I may give space for the large number of contributions to this book, many of them having barely place for their present address.

Mary A. Gardner Holland

Maria Abbey

ON THE THIRD SUNDAY IN APRIL 1861 at Plymouth Church, Brooklyn, New York, I heard Rev. H. W. Beecher read a call for women as volunteers to work in New York for the good of our soldiers; also a call for volunteers to go as nurses in the war. I responded at once, and was one of a company of six ladies who left New York for the seat of war the first day of May. We reached Baltimore that evening, and Washington the next day at 5 o'clock P.M. We stopped at the Kirkwood over two weeks; then received permission to go into the Union Hospital at Georgetown, where we soon found work enough to do.

As yet there was no organization, and we found it very difficult to do anything systematically; but we were each obliged to do the best we could.

The hospital began to fill after the first battle of Bull Run, and we had no rest then.

Up to that time I had been in good health, but the impure and infectious atmosphere began to tell upon my strength. I failed rapidly, and was obliged to leave on the 3d of September.

A little later I was induced to take a house, which I opened as a private hospital, and maintained it myself for two years. Then I moved, but my means and strength were still given for our suffering soldiers, and my house was open to them, although few could repay me, and I have not received anything for my services.

I left Nashville in September, 1867, a widow, and with broken health. Since that time I have maintained myself, although I am now lame.

Yours in F., G. and L.,
Marie W. Abbey
92 RALPH AVENUE
BROOKLYN, NEW YORK

Susan Babcock

I ENLISTED in the United States service on October 1, 1861, as a nurse under Miss Dix, who was the General Superintendent, and was ordered to the front at Belle Plain, to carry supplies and attend the sick and wounded. Then I returned to Washington, and was ordered to the Georgetown Hospital. From there I went to Fortress Monroe, Virginia, under order of Miss Dix, and remained about three months; then returned to Washington, and was assigned to Stone Hospital, where I remained six months. Then went to Columbia Hospital, where I stayed a year. After that I went to Harewood Hospital for about eight months. The first year I served without compensation. In all, I worked about four years; then was married, in January 1864.

I am eighty-three years old, and although my general health is as good as could be expected for one of my years, my memory is somewhat impaired; so if I were to attempt to write an outline of my experiences, I should not do it justice.

Yours truly,
Susan M. Babcock
SMITHVILLE, NEW YORK

Martha Baker

I WAS BORN IN CONCORD, INDIANA, April 9, 1838, a daughter of Benjamin and Anna Denton. At the age of sixteen I went to Sugar Grove Institute. In 1859, my mother and father both being dead, I was married to Abner Baker.

In February 1862, my husband enlisted in the 40th Indiana Volunteers, leaving me at my brother's with our little girl. After the battle of Chickamauga he was sent to Nashville, in charge of twenty-seven officers. Finding that he was an extra nurse, he was transferred to the 160th Battalion Veteran Relief Corps, and made chief wound-dresser of one ward in the Officers' Hospital. He then wrote for me, and I went from Stockwell, Indiana, January 1864, and was appointed to the Special Diet Kitchen, under the charge of Major Lyons. At that time we prepared food for the Officers' Hospital and No. 2,—about five hundred men.

Just before the battle of Atlanta, a good many of the boys went home to vote, and it cut us short of hands, as we had fifteen hundred to cook for, and but little help. Our strength was taxed to the utmost. Sometimes it was almost impossible to keep up, but with the aid of the Lord, who always strengthens and prepares the back for the burden, we were enabled to do our duty, and speak a few words of comfort to the poor soldiers who were away from home and friends. We were glad to see our boys come back from their furlough, and to think they remembered to bring us some tokens of love from mother or sister. We shall always remember the kindness of the soldiers.

Doctor Green, an especial friend of ours, was put in as assistant surgeon, and he often came for my little girl to go with him to see the patients; he would laugh and say she did them as much good as he did.

I was there during the battle of Nashville. Cannon were placed within one hundred yards of our building. I saw men bayonetted from the breastworks. The cannonading was so heavy it shook the building. There I beheld all the horrors of war, and after the battle, the sad sight of the ambulances coming in with their fearful loads.

With almost breaking hearts, our hands were still busy caring for the wounded. I met two soldier girls who had donned the blue. One, Frances Hook, *alias* Harry Miller, served two years and nine months; the other was called Anna. She was put under our charge until the military authorities could send her North.

I left the service in February 1865.

Yours truly,
Martha A. Baker
RUSHVILLE, MISSOURI

Lauraetta Balch

I WENT ALONE from Boston to Fort Schuyler, New York, October 18, 1862, and was the first lady nurse on the ground. Everything was in a very rough condition,—just thrown together. The barracks were a shelter for the sick and wounded, and that was about all. There were thirty-two wards, with fifty-two beds in each. Miss Williams, or Sister Nettie Williams, as we called her, was at the head of the department. She was a Boston lady, who did good service, devoting time and money to our soldiers. I have regretted that I did not keep a diary, as I have forgotten many who I should be glad to remember. But they were constantly coming and going, and those were busy times; still, I recall many of the nurses, who were beautiful and devoted characters.

As a rule my "boys" were a happy set of sufferers, more especially those who could get about on their crutches; and in their efforts to be cheerful and help others pass the weary hours, they often seemed to forget their own suffering.

I remained in that hospital during the fifteen months of my service, going from ward to ward where there was the most to be done.

I returned to Boston in January 1864.

Lauraetta C. Balch
LOWELL, MASSACHUSETTS

Lucy Barron

I WAS A REGIMENTAL NURSE in our late war, from March 1861 to March 1863, and went from place to place wherever the "boys" were ordered. I was sworn in as nurse by Capt. S. M. Davis, but neglected to be enrolled.

I served at Camp Reed, Erie, two months, then went with the troops to Maryland, where I entered the Regimental Hospital at Baltimore. In May 1862, we went to Harper's Ferry, and I served in the General Hospital there until the surrender in September, when we returned to Washington and I was stationed in many different places that one could hardly call hospitals, for almost every house contained some sick or wounded.

While in West Virginia the rebels took me for a target, but, praise God, they missed their mark, and the bullet whistled above my head. Once they surrounded us, and we could get no supplies for nearly three weeks. At the last we had nothing to eat but hardtack, and not much of that. At this extremity our men fought their way out; the commander of the place surrendered, and was shot for it, as a traitor. I had a severe time among those rebels while I had the typhoid fever, receiving care only from the good Union doctor. We dared not say we were Union, or we might have been killed. When able to travel I returned to the Regimental Hospital in West Virginia where I remained, until I returned to my home. While in the College Hospital, at Georgetown, an affecting scene was enacted. A young soldier was wounded in the shoulder, severing the main artery, and he would die in a few moments if the blood were allowed to flow; but we nurses took turns in holding back the life-stream until he could be baptized; then he said: "I am ready now. You may take away your hand," and in a very few minutes he died.

Lucy (Fenman) Barron
EUREKA, CALIFORNIA

Clara Barton

THE WORK OF MISS CLARA BARTON during the late war, as that of Miss Dix, is too well known to require further comment; but the Red Cross movement, of which she is the pioneer American champion, has been so quietly and modestly managed that our people, as a rule, know little about the Society, although it has been in existence for almost thirty years, and the American Branch for eleven.

The Society of the Red Cross is today one of the most important philanthropic organizations in the world, whose results prove it the most productive and beneficent. Briefly stated, it is a confederation of societies in different countries, having as an aim the amelioration of the condition of sick and wounded prisoners in time of war.

At the beginning of our late Rebellion, Miss Barton was in Washington. When news came that the troops on their way to the Capital had been fired upon, and that wounded men were lying in Baltimore, she volunteered with others to go and care for them. She had entered upon what proved to be her life work. From that time she was to be found in the hospitals, or wherever soldiers were in need of attendance. Soon she was recognized as a woman of great ability and discretion, and could pass in and out at will, where others met with constant hindrance by "red tape."

She met the wounded from Virginia; she was present at the battles of Cedar Mountain, Second Bull Run, Antietam and Fredericksburg;

was eight months at the siege of Charleston, at Fort Wagner, in front of Petersburg and at the Wilderness. She was also at the hospitals near Richmond and on Morris Island. Neither were her labors over when the war ended, but her tenderness and reverence led her to remain in Andersonville six weeks, to mark as many as possible of the thirteen thousand graves of Union prisoners who were buried there.

When this self-imposed task was over, her physician ordered her to Europe for rest and change. But her splendid work on our battlefields was known abroad, and before her health was fully established, she was asked to join the relief corps of the Red Cross during the Franco-Prussian War. Her experience and knowledge were eagerly sought and she did heroic service.

In 1869, when the International Committee learned that she was in Geneva, they called upon her to ask an explanation of the strange fact that while the United States had shown the most tender care for its own wounded, it had held aloof from the Red Cross.

Miss Barton told them she had never heard of the Society nor of the Geneva Treaty while at home, and that she was certain that the United States, as a people, were totally ignorant that proposals such as they alluded to had ever been submitted to the government, and showed her visitors how some single official could carelessly keep the people from any knowledge that such proposals had been made to them. Of course she was aflame with enthusiasm for the movement, and shamed that the United States was not a party to the treaty; and she resolved to give herself no rest until our people were acquainted with the Treaty of Geneva.

After the convention in 1868, in Paris, when the United States was represented by Dr. Henry Bellows, the subject was again presented to our Government by that gentleman, and, singularly enough, met only indifference; however through his efforts a society was formed but it lacked the essentials to success; viz., the sanction and sympathy of government, and soon died. After the war in Europe was over, Miss Barton came home, all invalid, and lay upon her bed for years; and when at last she rallied, it was to begin almost as a child, and slowly acquire even the power to walk.

As soon as she was able she went to Washington and presented the subject of the treaty to President Hayes in 1877, and the cause was set forth by a committee of three women and one man. This effort won no response, but four years later when Garfield was in the chair, the little society received assurances of sympathy from Government. Secretary Windom laid the subject before the Cabinet, and the President and all his secretaries were at once cordially interested. Secretary Blaine wrote a warm letter of approval, and the President, in his first message to Congress, recommended our accession to the Treaty. This was seventeen years after the subject was first presented to our Government. The society of 1877 was reorganized, and became incorporated as the American Association of the Red Cross. But it remained for President Arthur to sign the Treaty, March 1, 1882.

No better occasion to illustrate the work of the Red Cross has ever occurred than at the Johnstown disaster. The President, with fifty aides, arrived on the first train from the East, and with them came everything necessary for people, who were left utterly destitute. Establishing themselves in tents, they began to distribute food, and means were provided to insure the fact that no one would be overlooked.

The confidence in the Society was such that money and supplies continued to arrive and buildings were erected to receive them. The crushed, heart-broken women were organized into committees to assist in the work, and with their help the wants of over 20,000 persons were made known to the secretary in waiting. The white wagons with the red symbol carried supplies for all of these. Barracks were erected, where large numbers were housed and fed; then two and four-roomed buildings were put up and furnished by the Society, and family life began once more. A comfortable hospital was next arranged, and in the autumn turned over to the city. Miss Barton remained five months in that devastated city, and among the most touching tributes ever paid to the Red Cross is a sketch in a Johnstown paper of that date:

"The vital idea of the Red Cross is not charity, it scorns the word, but friendliness, helpfulness. It is a privilege to do for those in trouble; they are neighbors in the good Samaritan sense: in a word, human brotherhood is their creed, and nothing less than the true law of love as given by Jesus Christ their animating principle."

In writing of Miss Barton, Laura Doolittle, says: "Her superb executive ability must have impressed all who met her. She influences and controls men and women not so much because of native gifts of leadership, as because of elevation of character, strong convictions, and high purposes. In person and manner she is gentle and womanly, her voice sweet and feminine; but that she is an unusual, peculiar woman, every one feels who meets her. That which is deeply borne in upon the mind is that she is totally without fear; that the 'custom' which lies upon the rest of us with such a weight, lies not at all upon her; that for some deep reason she is a woman apart. She is a law to her staff, and is worshiped by them.

"A life devoted wholly to the highest objects, a heart single to the service of humanity, time, health and fortune given without stint, and without hope of earthly reward,—history cannot fail to place her high on the roll of those who love God supremely, and her neighbor as themselves.

"In a little casket in Miss Barton's room lie some few jewels, badges of orders, gifts from royal persons, societies, beneficiaries, visible testimonials of love, gratitude, and appreciation; court jewels from the Grand Duchess of Baden; a medal and jewels from the Empress of Germany; a decoration from the Queen of Serbia; the Iron Cross of Merit, given only for heroic deeds of kindness, from old Kaiser Wilhelm, and some other decorations. A beautiful brooch and pendant of diamonds testify to the abound in gratitude and love of the people of Johnstown."

The American Society has its headquarters in Washington in the mansion once used as the headquarters of General Grant. The walls are decorated by flags of many nations, the banner of Switzerland, with its white cross on a crimson field, occupying the place of honor. Miss Barton meets all the expenses of the establishment from her private fortune.

Over this building floats the banner of the Red Cross, telling to all the world that the United States is leagued with thirty-nine other nations pledged to promote the human brotherhood.

Mary Bell

I WAS BORN in Hillsborough, Highland County, Ohio, July 28, 1840. I went from my home in Bellefontaine, Ohio, in September 1863, to begin my work in the war at Covington Barracks, Kentucky. My husband, A. O. Hartley, was hospital steward, and I assisted him in caring for the sick of the regiment at that place. In November we were ordered to Munfordsville, Kentucky, and went into winter quarters there.

A post hospital was immediately established, and I was appointed matron by the surgeon in charge. Here the sick of these regiments, and also the sick and wounded who were brought in to us, received the most careful treatment. Everything was done that would add to their speedy recovery or their comfort.

I had special care of the low diet for the very sick patients, but my care extended to all in the hospital. Many were the letters written for sick and dying soldiers; many the sad messages sent to bereaved ones at home.

We remained there until May 1864; then came marching orders, "To the front." The sick and wounded were sent to other places, and very soon the hospital that had been our home for months, was deserted; but, with other ladies of our regiment, I failed to obtain permission to go to the front, so I came North, and remained until 1865, when I entered the work again at Jeffersonville Hospital for three months.

At Chattanooga, Tennessee, on April 15, 1865, my husband died, from injuries received in the service.

At the close of my hospital work I was commissioned to teach the Freedmen. I taught one year in the Fisk University, at Nashville, Tennessee, and three years in other parts of that State.

Mary E. Bell

Mary Bickerdyke

I SERVED IN OUR GREAT CIVIL WAR from June 9, 1861 to March 20, 1865. I did the work of one, and tried to do it well. I was in nineteen hard-fought battles, in the departments of the Ohio, Tennessee, and Cumberland armies. Fort Donelson, February 15th and 16th, was the first battle to which I was eyewitness; Pittsburg Landing, April 6th and 7th, the second; Iuka, September 20th, the third; and Corinth, October 3d and 4th, the fourth.

In January 1863, we went from Corinth to Memphis, and from January to October 1863, passed 63,800 men through our hospitals.

During the siege of Vicksburg I made several trips from that city with wounded soldiers to the Memphis hospitals.

On the 27th of October, I received orders to report at Chattanooga, and arrived in time to see the battle of Lookout Mountain,—that famous "battle above the clouds." I watched the dreadful combat until the clouds hid all from view. In fancy I can hear General Hooker's artillery now.

Our next fearful struggle was Missionary Ridge. This point was strongly fortified, the rifle-pits were closely arranged, and with the artillery belching forth fire and death, it seemed impossible for our men to take it. The night before the battle was bright moonlight, and all night long the troops marched to their positions. In the morning they presented a solid wall of blue. Never were men more hopeful, and yet it looked so terrible, so appalling,—that dangerous route up the rough and jagged mountain side. I was in the second story of the hotel. My duty was to receive the gifts from the soldiers to their friends, if, to use their own expression, they "bit the dust." These gifts consisted of fare-well letters, watches, money, and any little things they wanted sent "home" if they never returned.

The order to march was given between eleven and twelve o'clock. Amid the din and roar of shot and shell, and the commands of the officers, it was almost impossible to distinguish any particular sound; yet General Osterhaus's thrilling commands could be heard with startling distinctness. It was his artillery that sent the first shell through General Bragg's headquarters.

The men marched up that stony precipice so rapidly that even the officers were amazed. General Grant asked, "Who gave that command?" General Thomas replied, "They gave it themselves." In one short hour that desperate battle was fought and won; General Bragg was in full retreat, and his army closely pursued. Was not the "God of Battle" there?

The Stars and Stripes floated from one end of Missionary Ridge to the other. Seventeen hundred men were killed and wounded in the 10th Army Corps alone. Our wounded were kept at the foot of Missionary Ridge five weeks, and then they were removed to Chattanooga in time for the coldest storm on record; but none of our patients froze to death.

The first of March found us in Huntsville, Alabama, getting ready for the spring campaign. Resaca, early in May, was our first battle,—and a bloody and hard-fought one it was, too. Now comes a constant roar of artillery for one hundred days, until Atlanta was taken, and many were the battles in this campaign. Kennesaw Mountain was where we dislodged Gen. Joseph Johnston. Then came Mt. Hope, Big Shantee, and on, and on, until the fall of Atlanta. Here we had the worst hospitals of the war. Kingston, then Altoona Pass, then on to Marietta, where, while the shooting of both blue and gray went on, in Sherman's army we had at one time twenty thousand wounded soldiers. The exhaustion and suffering of that Georgia campaign can never be told!

Here is where I saw General Kilpatrick and his seven thousand cavalrymen swinging around Atlanta, burning and destroying everything they could lay hands on, swimming the Black Warrior with the enemy close behind them. This stream takes its name from the Creek Indians, who, closely pursued, preferred death to surrender; and plunging into the turbulent waters were drowned: hence the name, "Black Warrior." But General Kilpatrick's work was not in vain. Atlanta surrendered, and we, the army nurses, treated the general and his wornout troops to bread and butter and coffee.

The surrender of Atlanta marked the close of my work in the Georgia campaign.

Mrs. M. A. Bickerdyke

* * * *

The work of "Mother Bickerdyke" is so widely and well known, that the above article from her pen cannot fail to be greatly appreciated; but realizing that one by one our comrades are crossing the river, and that to the rising generation the Civil War is already like a half-forgotten story, aside from the lessons of patriotism it teaches, we have gathered a few of the details of this most remarkable woman's work, and re-tell them, hoping that a measure of her spirit of whole-souled devotion to country and to suffering humanity may find lodgment in the heart of every reader.

After the surrender of Sumter her heart, which had been burdened with a mother's solicitude for the boys she had seen march away, could no longer endure the dreadful suspense, and the still more dreadful confirmation of her fears that daily met her eye as she glanced over the crowded columns of the papers. Her clear judgment did not admit of her failing to realize the horrible sights and the hardships she would have to undergo at the front; but by the force of her indomitable will, the lesser evil would be lost in the greater, and she would unfalteringly tread the path of duty, outwardly unmoved by environments that must have unnerved a less-determined person.

Many stories have been told of the half-frenzied search for friends and relatives among the slain, when tortured love lent an almost super-human fearlessness that enabled the seekers to endure the strain of their ghastly surroundings; but perhaps no single incident in the life of Mrs. Bickerdyke portrays her large-heartedness, in fact the motherly care that she felt for the wounded soldiers, than the following: The victory had been gained at Fort Donelson, and the glad news carried with it great rejoicing; meanwhile the soldiers who had won that victory were suffering more than tongue can relate. Their clothes often froze to their bodies, and as there were no accommodations for so many, hundreds perished wholly without care. Mrs. Bickerdyke had witnessed her first battle with a courage equal to every demand. That fearful day was at last ended, and darkness settled over the deserted field, where the dead still lay awaiting burial.

The night grew darker and darker. The strange, weird silence, after such a days produced an indescribable feeling of awe. At midnight an officer noticed a light moving up and down among the dead, and dispatched some one to see what it meant. The man soon returned, and told him that it was Mrs. Bickerdyke, who, with her lantern, was examining the bodies to make sure that no living man should be left alone amid such surroundings. She did not seem to realize that she was doing anything remarkable, and turning from the messenger, continued her search over that awful field, actuated simply by her love for humanity.

Many wounded of the rebel army, who had been deserted, were the recipients of her care. As a mangled arm was being dressed for one, he felt instinctively the deep sympathy for his suffering, and said, "That arm would not have done such service if I had known what sort of people I was fighting."

Her work was varied: now on the field of battle; now on board a boat, caring for a load of soldiers in transit; now in the hospital; and now engaged in more general sanitary duties. Thus many phases of a soldier's life came under her observation.

Often young boys found their way into the ranks, and it was infinitely pathetic to realize their position, and picture in imagination how they had been loved and cherished at home. Ah, how many of them today fill heroes' graves! One mentioned by Mrs. Bickerdyke was a boy about nineteen years of age, but large and manly for his years. During his infancy his mother died, leaving him to the almost idolizing care of father, brothers, and sisters. He entered the army a happy, half-willful boy, looking upon his position in the hopeful, confident manner of youth.

Slowly, but surely, he was transformed into the grave patriot, ready to give his life wherever it should be needed most; no longer looking forward to battle, but anticipating his first active service with an ever-increasing self-surrender. He was at Pittsburg Landing, in General Prentiss' division, and when they were surprised, about sunrise, he was among the first ones ready to repulse the attack. Soon he was wounded, and while being carried from the field another ball struck him; but he had time to say, "Tell my friends that I died on the field."

While the battle was raging, Mrs. Bickerdyke was attending an officer who had been wounded at Donelson, and could live only a short time. Ah, how it thrilled her heart and awakened her deepest admiration to see how he longed to be with his regiment, when he had already given so much! And when it seemed that our men must be defeated, he cried: "It can't be! Those brave troops will never surrender! They will fight to the last, and conquer! Oh that I were with them!" He was with many of them soon, beyond the tumult of war.

Mrs. Bickerdyke did not see all of the horrors of that field, as her heart and hands were full in caring for the wounded. But in connection with this battle she has said: "The saddest thing in my experience was receiving their last messages, and little treasures to be sent home to their families when death came to relieve them from pain. Such cries as 'What will become of my children?' were hardest of all to bear." Yet few realized how deeply she felt for those around her, for she was so habitually strong and cheerful, inspiring others with the same feeling.

One night she was making her usual round of the ward. The lights were turned down, and many of the soldiers were sleeping, while here and there a restless sufferer counted the lagging seconds, and longed for the morning. Passing along, she ministered to each as occasion demanded, until one asked, "Are you not tired, Mother Bickerdyke?" Not for a moment did she think of claiming sympathy, but replied in her usual brisk way: "What if I am? That is nothing. I am well and strong, and all I want is to see you so, too." In a few moments more she was at her place by the table, to assist the surgeon in an amputation; then received the patient into her own care; and as she gave him a restorative he whispered, "Take a message from me to my poor family; I shall surely die." How her heart ached for him in his weakness and suffering! But there was no change in her calm cheerful manner as she replied: "Now do not talk. You are going to take all your messages to them yourself, for I know you have a splendid chance to get well."

Her only purpose during those trying seasons was beautifully expressed in her own simple words, "I keep doing something all the time to make the men better, and help them to get well," and her name was spoken with gratitude by numberless soldiers.

In September a battle was fought at Iuka. Here Mother Bickerdyke again walked over a blood-stained field to save many a life fast ebbing away for want of immediate aid. She deftly stopped the flow of blood from wounds that must otherwise have proved fatal. The number of wounded swelled to nearly fifteen hundred. The accommodations were crowded, and the wounded were sent to Corinth as fast as their condition would permit.

Mrs. Bickerdyke not only went with them, to alleviate suffering on the painful journey, but did much to prevent waste. Owing to limited time and means of transportation, soiled clothing, and things that were not especially needed to fit up the place to which they were going, were to be left behind. But prudent Mother Bickerdyke had all articles packed closely, and when she saw that they were to be left, exclaimed in surprise: "Do you suppose that we are going to throw away those things that the daughters and wives of our soldiers have worked so hard to give us? I will prove that they can be saved, and the clothes washed. Just take them along;" and the order was obeyed.

A mother kneeling by the cot of her son, who was scarcely seventeen years old, said: "It is no wonder that you are called 'Mother' here, for you treat all these men with such kindness and patience. I owe to you the preservation of my darling's life. It would have broken my heart had I found him dead!" With that thought she burst into a passion of sobs, and buried her face in the pillow. He smoothed her silver hair with one hand (he had lost the other), and tried to comfort her. Such scenes aroused feelings in the heart of Mrs. Bickerdyke for which she could find no expression save in work.

The large hospitals in Memphis had not been prepared in vain, and she was often seen among the patients in the different wards, besides performing her duties as matron of the Gayoso.

She was always planning for more and better food for her sick boys. Fresh milk and eggs were supplied in scant quantities, and were very poor at that. She declared that it was a nuisance to pay forty cents a quart for chalk and water. She wanted something nourishing. Her plan was at first deemed impracticable, but after consideration it was conceded that her judgment was not at fault. The sanction of her plan was gained from proper authorities, and just as Spring was preparing to welcome Summer, she started upon her famous "cow and hen mission." Her object was to obtain one hundred cows and one thousand hens, to be cared for on an island in the Mississippi, near Memphis. The beginning of this mission was distinguished by more than one hundred crippled soldiers accompanying her as far as Saint Louis. There was not one of the poor maimed fellows who did not bless her when she saw them all safely in a hospital there.

As soon as she made her plans known in Jacksonville, Illinois, a wealthy farmer, aided by a few of his neighbors, gave her the hundred cows; and as she proceeded, chickens were cackling all about her. She procured the desired one thousand, and her arrival at Milwaukee was heralded by the lowing of cows and the sprightly song of hens.

She visited Chicago, where she was entertained by Mary A. Livermore of the Christian Commission. It was a Sabbath afternoon, and the family were preparing to attend the marriage of a friend; and although Mrs. Bickerdyke had taken no rest since her arrival, she preferred to join them rather than to retire. The ceremony was a quiet one, performed in the bride's home. A young officer in his bright uniform was the bridegroom; and when he introduced the white-robed girl as his wife to Mrs. Bickerdyke, she was surprised by his telling her they had previously met at Fort Donelson. Then he reminded her of an officer there who had been wounded by a minnie-ball, appealing in vain to a surgeon to save his leg. She induced the surgeon to wait until morning, when it was found that he could recover without losing the limb. "I never can express my gratitude to you" he concluded. "You have been to me a mother indeed."

She accompanied the soldiers to Farmington, whence they removed to Corinth to secure better accommodations. Here she established a Diet Kitchen and a laundry. The great bundles of soiled and blood-stained clothing were sent to the woods, where colored men washed them, superintended by Mrs. Bickerdyke. She rode a white horse, the distance being nearly two miles from camp.

One of her best-known acts is an "interference" that gained for her the title of "General." It was at the time when the Confederates attempted to re-capture Corinth, and attacked the defense October 3, 1862. The hospital work was so well organized that it could be done very quickly, and Mrs. Bickerdyke found some time to study the progress of the battle.

The whole action was rapid and concerted. The Board of Trade Regiment, twelve hundred strong, had marched twenty-four miles to enter the conflict, and only four hundred returned. The steady roar of artillery drowned all other sounds. Toward evening she saw a brigade hurrying forward, and learned that they had been marching since noon, and were about to join in the struggle. The officer in command was requested to let them rest a few moments, but refused. The men were passing the hospital when a strong voice cried, "Halt!" Instinctively they obeyed, and attendants began to distribute soup and coffee; meanwhile their canteens were filled, and each received a loaf of bread. "Forward, march!" came the order in a very few minutes, the time lost being more than compensated by the renewed courage of the men, who had no other chance to rest until midnight. Mrs. Bickerdyke had given the order to halt herself, when she found that no one else would do it, and her "interference" was deeply appreciated; for in spite of her efforts, many died from hunger and thirst during that battle.

She experienced some difficulty in getting transportation for her stores to Resaca, but finally arrived while the hospital tents were being pitched. All around lay the wounded, who, one by one, were being carried to the operating tables, by the sides of which were heaped those ghastly piles of human flesh. Turning from such fearful sights she began to work among the men, binding up a wound here, straightening a limb there, and again bending to bathe a quivering, agonized face.

Day after day the fearful work went on, and day after day Mother Bickerdyke passed in and out among the soldiers, ministering to needs of both mind and body, as only a strong, loving woman could do. She had given herself unreservedly to the works and to such a nature as her retreat would be impossible. Sickness, sorrow and danger of every kind must necessarily come, but she would meet them as the soldiers did,—as obstacles that must be overcome; for the path of duty lay clearly marked out before her and she could not turn aside. For herself she would accept nothing; if her boys could be comfortably cared for she was happy. She was a capital forager, and for the sake of the sick soldier she would brave any danger. She was once present at the Chamber of Commerce in Milwaukee, with the Ladies' Aid Society of the Northwestern Sanitary Commission. The President of the Chamber, in his blandest tones, informed the ladies that the Chamber had considered their request, but that they had expended so much in fitting out a regiment that they must be excused from making further contributions.

Mrs. Bickerdyke asked the privilege of saying a few words, and for a half hour she held them enchained. She described in plain, simple language the life of a soldier,—his privations and sufferings, the patriotism which animated him to suffer and to dare without murmuring. She contrasted this with the love of gain, and such an excuse for making no further donations. "You rich men are living at your ease here in Milwaukee, dressed in your broadcloth, knowing so little of the sufferings of these soldiers writhing in pain, cold, hungry, many of them finally meeting death,—and all that you and your little ones, your wealth and your homes, may be saved to a future republic. Shame on you, cowards!" The Chamber of Commerce was not prepared to be thus rebuked. They reconsidered their action and made an appropriation.

Though Mrs. Bickerdyke was always neat and cleanly in her dress, she was indifferent to its attractions; and amid the flying sparks from open fires her calico dress would take fire, and was often full of little holes. Some one asked if she were not afraid of being burned. "Oh," she replied, "my boys put me out!" With her clothing in this condition she visited Chicago late in the summer of 1863. The ladies replenished her wardrobe, and soon after sent her a box of nice clothing for her own use. Some of the articles were richly trimmed, among them two nightgowns. She traded off the most of the articles with the rebel women of the place for eggs, butter, and other good things for her sick soldiers.

She was soon to go to Cairo, and she thought the nightgowns would sell for more there; but on her way, in one of the towns on the Mobile and Ohio Railroad, she found two soldiers who had been discharged from the hospitals before their wounds were healed. The exertion of travel had opened them afresh. They were in an old shanty, bleeding, hungry, penniless. Mrs. Bickerdyke took them at once in hand, washed their wounds, stopped the flow of blood, tore off the bottoms of the nightgowns and used them for bandages. Then as the men had no shirts she dressed them in the fine nightgowns, ruffles, lace, and all. They demurred a little, but she told them if any one spoke about it to say they had been in Seceshville.

Some soldiers in fresh uniforms waited upon her one sunny morning and tendered her a review. Mrs. Bickerdyke smilingly consented, donned her sunbonnet and permitted herself to be stationed in a rude, elevated position. Then the fine old cows who had supplied them with milk filed past her. Each one had been smoothly curried, their horns had been polished, and their hoofs blackened. The favorites were decked with little flags, and a lively march was played as the queer procession filed past. Many of these cows had marched a long distance with the army. They were a treasure to Mrs. Bickerdyke, as she could make custards and other delicacies for her sick soldiers. This boyish prank, "The Cows' Review," was a pleasant incident which she greatly enjoyed.

When the army was ordered to Washington for the grand review, and the soldiers realized that they were soon to meet the loved ones at home, they became as light-hearted as boys, and the march from Alexandria was a joyous one. Mrs. Bickerdyke accompanied them, riding her glossy horse. She wore a simple calico dress and a large sunbonnet. She crossed the Long Bridge in advance of the 15th Army Corps, and was met by Dorothy Dix and others, who came to welcome her to the capital. This was a triumph such as few women have ever achieved; and during the weeks following she was everywhere treated with great respect and consideration.

The calico dress and sunbonnet were sold for one hundred dollars, and preserved as relics of the Rebellion. This money she spent at once, for "the boys needed so many things."

At last the great war was over. Peace was declared, and the Nation awoke to the fact that it had on its hands a mighty army,—victorious, it is true, but with many of the men destitute, and bearing the marks of the four years' struggle. In a short time that army disappeared in a manner that has been the wonder of every nation.

But where had they gone, and under what circumstances? Those soldiers could never be anything but "her boys" to Mother Bickerdyke, and she could not desert them now, when maimed, and broken in health and fortune, they must go back to the old homes, or wander about in search of new ones. From that time until the present day she has been constantly interested for their welfare. In the old New England homestead, in the sunny valleys of California, or on Western prairies, wherever the soldiers have made their homes, the name of Mother Bickerdyke will be spoken with reverential love, until her boys are mustered out, and their tongues are silent in death.

She is now eighty-two years old, and very smart for one of that age. She keeps a secretary to conduct her large correspondence, coming from soldiers in all parts of the country.

Her son, Professor J. B. Bickerdyke, lives in Russell, Kansas, and with him his honored mother finds a pleasant retreat in which to pass the sunset of her long and useful life.

Mrs. M. J. Boston

I WAS BORN IN PHILADELPHIA, PENNSYLVANIA, July
17, 1837, but at the breaking out of the war in 1861, was living at the
home of my husband's parents, in Baltimore. Father Boston was one of
the "Eagle Artillery,"—one of Baltimore's defenders in 1812. My own
father, James Butler, was also an old defender in 1812, on the United
States ship "Independence." On April 19, 1861, I inquired of both
brave parents on which side they stood. Both answered: "The Government we fought for! Our flag can never be conquered!" My reply was,
"Beneath the same sheltering folds I shall stand, and if I can be of any
assistance to our Union soldiers I will do what I can." Well, the opportunity came.

In June 1863, Gettysburg was to be the scene of fierce struggle and
great preparation must be made. Orders were sent from headquarters
for every hospital to be put in readiness, convalescents were transferred
to other points, and a temporary hospital as secured on Central Avenue; while on account of the railroad coming directly from Gettysburg, a long row of two-story houses close at hand was vacated, and
here the soldiers could be washed and dressed before being sent to the
different hospitals. Then came a call for physicians and nurses. A
brother-in-law had been used up and discharged at Fredericksburg and
a brother would be at Gettysburg; so my heart went out to poor mothers, wives, and sisters whose loved ones would be exposed to shot and

shell in that fierce struggle, and I said, "Yes, I will go, and just as I bind up the wounds of strangers, perhaps some one will care for my dear brother." An appeal for supplies was next published in the daily papers, and received a hearty response. In a few days everything was in readiness, and some one placed over each department. One took charge of the lint, another of bandages, others the giving of supplies. Some of stronger nerve were the nurses. I was on hand to wash and dress wounds, though wholly inexperienced. I am sorry to say there was no one to book the names. Such a thing was not thought of in those hurried and exciting scenes. I worked with others, sewing bandages and preparing places for supplies. At night my very dear friend and co-worker, Mrs. Wallace, and myself went soliciting cake, jellies, and fruits. All promised a large supply when our men arrived, and the promise was faithfully fulfilled.

July 1st, 2d, and 3d, 1863, will never be forgotten by me. Dispatches came: "The great and terrible battle has begun! Many have fallen!" July 4th freight trains loaded with wounded arrived. Oh, what a sorrowful scene it was! Guards were stationed at each of those houses, to prevent sightseers from entering. All workers wore a miniature flag, pinned on the left breast. Three of these were given to each, so if one was lost another was at hand.

A physician came to me on the arrival of the first rain and said, "Can you dress wounds?" "If instructed I can," was my reply. He then sent me for two buckets of water, two sponges, shirt, drawers, handkerchief, stockings, bandages, pins, find lint. Off I went, trembling and nervous at the first sight of the horrors of war, and procured the supplies. "Now, Mrs. Boston, give particular attention to the cleansing of the wound;" and the doctor showed me just how much blue-stone to drop into a bucket of water. The other bucket was for bathing the face and hands and cleansing the person. Our first patient was wounded on the foot; and when the medical treatment was over and a sheet thrown over him, he thanked me so kindly! I had an assistant, who was then to bring a sandwich, slice of cake, and cup of coffee; and while he ate, she was to fan him. I thought the men had eaten "salt-horse and hard-tack" long enough to have something better on their arrival in Baltimore. As we turned away, the doctor said, "Now, Mrs. Boston, I have initiated you into the work." Then to the Soldiers awaiting their turn: "I leave you in this lady's care. May God bless you! Now don't any of you fall in love with her, for she has a husband and children." Everything was said to cheer the poor sufferers. In a few short days blood-poison had done its work, and they were laid to rest. Rebel bullets were poison.

On recovering from my first trial dressing wounds, my nerves were strong, and I washed and dressed them as quickly as possible, day and night. Always on leaving a very weak patient I gave him a glass of brandy or wine, bathed his face and hands in bay rum, and put a sheet over the stretcher. With tears in their eyes they would thank me, and ask me to go to see them. I often promised, and meant to go, but my time was so occupied I could not, though I sometimes heard from them. They would often inquire my name and residence, and give me theirs; but in my haste I kept no list, though I remembered many a long time. They sometimes kept a memorandum, so I have no doubt some have my name now; if not, reading this may freshen the memory of some one who will remember me.

I was called to one who said, "I don't want to be taken to the hospital." "Where are you wounded?" "In the leg." "Can you lift it?" "No." "I will send for the surgeon." "Oh no!" he cried; "send for my brother." So I saw a friend who had her parlor furniture removed, and he was taken there. His brother arrived the next day, and the poor soldier's joy was great at having home attention, and a dear brother at his side. Soon that brother had to take his lifeless body to his parents. I also attended J. Edward Lawrence. He, too, was anxious to have private care, so a good home place was secured. He was wounded in the side, and the doctor had probed, but could not find the ball. "If that man has any family," he said, "notify them at once. He cannot live many hours." I inquired for his wife, and finding out her address, telegraphed for her. Speedily came the reply, "I shall leave immediately." "Mrs. Boston, did you ask the doctor about my case?" he soon inquired; and I had to tell him his true condition, and that his wife was on her way to see him. By the time she arrived his remains were in the cemetery. I invited Mrs. Lawrence to Father Boston's, informed the authorities at West Hospital, secured the necessary clothes for the burial, and on his left side pinned the little flag I had worn; another I tacked on the coffin, so there should be no mistaken identity, and gave the third to his poor broken-hearted wife, who died in less than two years.

Oh, how many times I have been called upon for deeds of mercy! As Mrs. Wallace and I were leaving the cemetery, after Mr. Lawrence's body was put in the vault, a gentleman came to us and said: "Ladies, I belong in Georgia. This body is my brother." Then to Mrs. Wallace, "Won't you stand by the grave to represent my mother" and to me, "won't you come and represent my sister?" So that brother, the minister, the grave digger, Mrs. Wallace and myself stood together a few minutes beneath the beautiful trees in the grounds apportioned to the Confederate dead. I can never forget such scenes, though I forget hundreds of names.

One of our ladies took her daughter with her, who, having pricked her finger while pinning a bandage, contracted blood-poisoning while washing a wound. The hand was amputated, but to no avails and she died.

I assisted a physician in one severe case. A soldier had been without attention for his wounded arm for ten days, and it was in a terribly decomposed condition. As he stood up and I removed the blanket from his shoulders, the odor was something terrible. The doctor cut the flesh from the arm and it fell to the pavement. It soon cleared the crowd away from in front of the hospital. By standing beside the doctor I inhaled the full odor, and was attacked by fainting. The doctor ordered brandy, but I did not take it. A soldier took my place, and I went home a very sick person, but soon returned to my duty, though I continued to feel a stinging sensation in my nose, and it swelled at times.

After all had been removed from the scene of carnage at Gettysburg, orders came to take the names of the workers, but it was too late. Some had already gone home; others did not consider it important, as the work there was done. Then followed a very sick time for me; my nose and face were a sight! The doctor attending me said, "You have contracted blood poisoning, while dressing wounds, and must stay away now."

Nevertheless I went to Patterson Park Hospital, and worked there and for the superintendent in charge. When asked for my name, to enter on his books, I said: "No, I do not want any pay for my services. I only try to do all I can for the soldiers." "You had better give me your name," he said; "it may be of use to you sometime." "No, sir! I don't work for pay or popularity, but I am always ready to do anything I can for a sufferer." So although my name does not appear on the roll in the War Department, it is engraved on the memory of hundreds of wounded men who will never forget those trying scenes. And my prayer is that when the soldiers of the G. A. R. hall have their hearts cleansed by the precious blood of Jesus, when they have taken their last march on earth, and entered victorious the City of God, that army nurses, soldiers, their families and friends, may meet to rest "forever with the Lord."

I am, very respectfully,
Mrs. M. J. Boston
1221 TATNAL STREET
WILMINGTON, DELAWARE

Mary Briggs

MY GRANDFATHER WAS with Washington at Valley Forge and through the entire war. My father was a "Connecticut Yankee," so we children received many lessons on patriotism, and it is no wonder that when our beloved land was threatened, my three brothers enlisted at once in her defense, as did my husband, also, and I applied at once to Miss Dix for a commission as nurse. It was granted June 19, 1861, and in August, I was summoned to Saint Louis to my work. I was then a resident of Madison, Wisconsin, and was the first enlisted nurse from that State, under James Yeatman, president of the Sanitary Commission.

I was assigned to duty at the Good Samaritan Hospital, where I cared for the brave boys, to the best of my ability, until I was sent to Ironton, Missouri, in 1862. From there I went to Harvey Hospital, Madison, Wisconsin, in 1863, where I remained until the close of the war.

Among the greatest comforts of my declining years is the love I feel for my native land; the knowledge that I was counted worthy to aid, if ever so little, in the effort to preserve it, and in teaching my grandchildren and others lessons of patriotism.

My dear husband reached home, but only to die in 1866. Two of my brothers have passed over before me; one from severe wounds received at Atlanta, Georgia, the other from his sufferings in Andersonville.

Thank God I have lived to see slavery abolished and our land free indeed. Now I am waiting the summons to join my loved ones in that land where war is unknown.

I am an invalid, and seventy-four years of age. I cannot say very much for myself, but this is all that needs to be said,—I tried to do my duty.

Mary M. Briggs
720 SAINT CHARLES STREET
ELGIN, ILLINOIS

Eunice Brown

I AM GLAD THAT I BELONG to a band of army nurses and proud that I sprang from a patriotic race. When the Civil War broke out I was anxious to start, but impossibilities hedged the way until June, 1864. I then went from Windham, Portage County, Ohio, to Camp Chase, near Columbus, and at once began visiting the General Hospital, and doing for our sick soldiers such things as reading, writing, etc., in company with Major Albert Longwell's wife. We continued this delightful work until August, when Surgeon Longwell had orders to open a temporary Post Hospital, till the completion of one in the course of construction. Owing to "red tape" we could not draw any delicacies from the Government for our sick; only soldiers' rations were available while we occupied this temporary building nor could nurses draw pay or rations. I was informed of these regulations, and asked if I would take the position of nurse under such conditions. I cheerfully replied that I would.

A three-months' regiment came in at this time, bringing their sick and wounded. There was not a pillow, blanket, or coat for the poor fellows; nor a delicacy, with the exception of a few that we ladies furnished from our quarters. We just had to put the brave men on the bare floor, and when our store was exhausted, feed the sickest from our tables.

They were patient and thankful, and this paid us well,—better than money. They said, "We thought when we got to God's country, we should have something to eat." We applied to the Soldiers' Aid Society, and received word: "Ohio must take care of her soldiers. Our supplies must go to the front." We went with our ambulance among the farmers, soliciting food, only to be told at nearly every house, "If you wish provisions for the prisoners you can have all you want; but not one thing for the "blue coats." With heavy hearts we would return to our boys with only a few supplies, wishing we were not subject to the "powers that be." I struggled along this way until December 24, 1864, when we moved; after which we had full supplies for our sick. I was then mustered into the 88th Ohio Volunteer Infantry, by Surgeon Longwell, under whom I had served all this time, and continued until his death in April 1865. After this I served under Dr. H. E. Warner, successor to Dr. Longwell, till at the close of the war I was mustered out, in July, 1865. I remained on duty until August, when new hands were capable of caring for those who were unable to leave camp. I served as nurse the entire time.

My experiences are varied. My husband, Surgeon James F. Brown, was assigned to duty among the prisoners, numbering five thousand. This gave me a chance to see the care that was bestowed upon the Confederates. Many of the same farmers we had called on brought from their storehouses an abundance which was not needed; for "Uncle Sam" took good care of the rebels, putting them in condition to fight us again. As I visited their commissary, and saw the supplies in untold quantities,—dried fruits by the barrel, sugar by the hogshead, canned and fresh fruits, butter, eggs, meats, etc., in proportion,—I thought of our empty commissary, and my indignation was great. I wished for an equal division.

One day, at my husband's request, I cooked a delicacy for five little sick boys, not over fourteen years old. As I fed them I asked each, "How came you here, so far away from home and mother?" The answer was in a whisper, "We were pressed into the service." They did not dare say this aloud, having been commanded not to tell. Dear little fellows! Ere nightfall three had gone beyond the roar of battle. The others died the next day.

We had men among those prisoners who were loyal to the flag of our Union. This was proved at an exchange of prisoners. Eighteen hundred at one time refused to go on the exchange, saying: "We were pressed into service at first, and if we leave here we shall have to take up arms against the North again. Our prison life is preferable to that; our fare is better than your men get, we are sorry to say."

I witnessed a regiment of prisoners as they left our camp. Not all looked happy, but most looked healthy. The feeble ones were taken in ambulances all had well-filled haversacks, and were clothed well. Each had a double blanket rolled over his shoulder.

Now I will tell you how our men looked when they came into camp. All were ragged, some hatless, many shoeless, more stockingless; not one blanket not even so much as a ragged one, no haversacks, all walking skeletons. Those unable to walk were borne on the shoulders of some a little stronger. Most all prostrated themselves on the ground; some going to the garbage barrels for food before lying down to wait to be assigned to their quarters. I said all were ragged; I mistake there. One, by the name of Bradley, was well clothed, had a good single blanket, and was a picture of health. I asked: "How is this, Bradley, that you have come back in so much better condition than your comrades? Did you have your money concealed?" He replied: "I was stripped like the rest, but after being put in prison, when hungry all I had to do was to step on a stump and make a speech for the South. This always gave me a good square meal, and anything else I wanted. Mrs. Brown, you are told the reason our men fare so hard in the South is a lack of provisions. It's not true, and don't you believe it. There is no scarcity if you have money, or cater to the South."

I can give you no idea of the condition our poor men were in when released from their prisons. One of the worst cases was that of Mr.——, who was of fine physical build and of superior talents, but had scurvy when he returned to us, and his sores were full of vermin. All we could do did not save him and we were thankful when he was at rest.

THE HUCKSTER

I referred to being unable to get supplies for our camp of the farmers in a "Secesh" county. There was a certain huckster, a woman, who called daily at the prison with a load of pies. We appealed to her for her fruit and eggs, offering to pay cash. Her reply was, "No 'blue coat' gets anything from me." About this time a regiment returned to Camp Chase for muster out. The officers went to Columbus for money to pay their men, forgetting to return for three days. The men, famishing on the third day, asked the huckster to sell out to them, saying, "We have no money today, but will pay you tomorrow." She said: "You old 'blue coats'! If you had been fighting for the South you might have had my whole wagon-load of pies. Now you shall not have one." At this the soldiers said, "We'll see!" and gathered round the wagon, some holding the horse. She raised her whip, saying, "Ge up, Jim! Ge up, Jim!" One soldier caught the lash while she still cried, "Ge up, Jim." The dear, hungry boys devoured every pie with a relish, saying: "Mother, how good your pies are! The best we have had for a long time. Call around tomorrow and get your money." Then releasing the horse they said, "Ge up, Jim! " I could not help shouting, "Glory!" and did not feel conscience smitten either. The old lady looked daggers at me and I was glad I was not in range of that whip; but felt sorry for "Jim," on whom she vented her spite.

MY TWO BOY PATIENTS

I want to tell of my two boy patients, named Henry, because I found such remarkable faith in Christ's promises in one, and in the other such patriotism. One morning, in the rounds of my wards, as I opened the door of Ward 2, a pair of beautiful brown eyes met mine. The face wreathed with smiles, and the lovely brown ringlets covering his pillow, made a picture wondrously fair to behold. On my going directly to him he extended a thin, trembling hands, saying, "Good morning, mother!" I said, "I have a little boy patient." "Yes'm." "How came you to call me mother?" "O, the boys told me you would care for me." "Have you a sick father here you came to see?" "No'm; I have no father." "Have you a soldier brother here, then?" "I have no brother, or sister, or mother; she died when I was eight years old. I have no home, either." "You are a little boy now," I said. "How came you here?" "After mamma died, papa was drafted; he was too poor to hire a substitute, and I had no one else to stay with me, so I asked the officers to take me as their drummer boy. I have been in the service three years and three months." "Pray tell me how old you are." "Eleven years and nine months. Three months ago my father was killed in battle at Antietam, and the same ball that killed him, wounded me in the hip. The surgeon says there is so much scrofula in my system that I am a cripple for life."

I said: "My little Henry looks very happy for one with no home or relatives that he knows of. How is this?" For reply he ran his emaciated fingers beneath his pillow, drawing there-from a small copy of a well-thumbed Bible, and holding it up with trembling hand, sparkling eyes, and glowing countenance, he said: "Mrs. Brown, this book tells me, 'When thy father and mother forsake thee, the Lord will take thee up.' If I get well, and try to be good, I shall have a home somewhere here; if I don't get well, I know I have one 'over there.'"

As we had eager listeners, I questioned him more closely, saying: "Dear child, the war will soon break up. Where will you go?" "I don't know, mother. I am trying to be good; God will not leave me without a home." In my astonishment, knowing his mother had been dead over three years, I said, "My boy, who taught you such faith in God?" "My dear mamma, until she died; then my papa."

In the course of time the child limped around the ward, saying one Sabbath morning, "I wish I could go to Sunday school." Two of our ward attendants said, "Get the child ready, and we will take him." These men formed a seat with crossed hands, and I placed him thereon; Henry putting an arm around the neck of each, and they bore the happy child away, while he cried, "Good-bye every one." He was carried this way during his stay in camp, thus getting different ones to church and Sunday school who were not in the habit of going to either. All loved the child, and he led some to Christ: thus fulfilling the scripture, "A little child shall lead them."

At the close of the war, word came from headquarters to put all of our patients not able to leave camp into Ward 1. In going to do this I found the attendants busy obeying the order, some patients packing their haversacks, preparatory to going home. Judge of my surprise when I found our Henry one of them. I said, "Where are you going, child?" I supposed one of the boys was to take him, knowing all wanted to do so. The little one answered, "I don't know, mother, but God will send some one for me; I will go into Ward 1, and wait till he comes." Sequel: The next day our hospital steward, Dr. George Austin, came to me with a gentleman, saying: "This man is seeking for a soldier orphan boy to adopt. He had no son to give for his country's cause, and he wishes to do something in this way. Tell him all you know of Henry." I told him the above, adding: "The child is a great reader, but despises story newspapers, and all trashy works. He thirsts for an education, but will never be able to do much physical labor. He is a remarkable boy in every respect." His eyes filled with tears as he said: "Thank God, I have found the boy I was seeking! Wife and I are childless, but have enough of this world's goods and to spare. Camp Dennison being nearer, we had planned to go there for our boy; but we both dreamed, on the same night, that we should go to Camp Chase instead. I can see God has led us. I am glad the child wants an education; he shall have it. I don't care for his physical labor, only so far as necessary to his health. If the boy is willing to go, with your consent (referring to Surgeon Warner and steward) I'll take him now."

He left with the steward, and after a little I went to the ward and found the child on the lap of the man, with his arms twined lovingly around his neck. On seeing me he came, and with tears trickling over his happy face, he said: "Didn't I tell you, Mrs. Brown, that God had a home for me? I am so glad, so happy!"

As soon as he was prepared for travel, that wealthy gentleman lifted him tenderly and bore our lovely child to a cab; his laughing eyes turned kindly on us as he said, "Good-bye all; I love you." That was the last we heard of him, only that he was happy in his new home. The gentleman and his wife had legal adoption papers made out for him. Owing to sickness I lost their address, but hope this may fall under the eye of Henry, or some one else there, and trust I may hear from him again. I should be very glad to hear from any one of the patients or attendants. I had a noble corps of helpers; all were very good and helpful; not one unkind word did I hear bring my stay. Better cooks or housekeepers I could not have had than I found in those men. Too much credit cannot be given our surgeons and wives; many sacrificed their lives for our sick. Those who did survive have broken constitutions.

My other Henry was from Kentucky, and was sixteen years old. He had a widowed mother and sister, and both were loyal to our flag. Henry obtained his mother's consent to volunteer in his country's service, promising never to desert, and that he would prove true to the last. He was in one battle and was wounded in the lung and brought to our camp with consumption; was sick a long time. I had a quilt sent to me made of a flag, with the request that it be given to the sickest loyal soldier. Henry was that one. I spread it on his cot when he was asleep.

On awakening he was so delighted! He could not express his joy in the thought of dying under the stars and stripes, saying: "Pain will be less now, and, Mrs. Brown, when I am placed in my coffin, will you promise that I shall have the quilt placed over me? Cover my face and body with it. I want my precious mother to know I remained firm to the last. Mother said if I died in the North, my body was to be brought home. When the casket is opened, she will see her boy was true to the flag!" The dear fellow's request was granted, and the mother was proud of her son.

Joseph And His Father

Permit me to add another pathetic incident that came under my personal observation. There was a prisoner named Joseph, returned from Andersonville. He was near death, and wishing to die under the parental roof, asked me to write home for some one to come for him, as he was too weak to travel alone. In an incredibly short time I noticed an aged gentleman trying to climb the steps of the ward. As I sprang to his aid he remarked: "I came for my son Joseph. I started twenty minutes after reading your letter." I escorted this father of eighty years to his son's cot and they clasped hands in happy greeting. Then the old man exclaimed, "There is some mistake; this is not my Joseph!" His disappointment was so great that he would have fallen if we had not caught him. We tried hard to convince him, but the tears kept rolling down his wrinkled cheeks while he repeated over and over, "No, no; my son was a large, fleshy man, six feet two;" and he paced to and fro saying, "No, no; it's not my Joseph." With tears in his eyes the poor soldier began to call up home scenes; still the father could not be convinced, until he said: "Father, don't you remember how I was converted after I enlisted? You were praying for me, kneeling on one side, with your hand on my head, mother on the other side, when the Lord spoke peace to me. My dear mother said, 'Now, father, we can let our only child go.'" At this recital the father said, "Yes, yes; I know now you are my son." The scene drew tears from many an eye. The next morning we prepared cordials and everything necessary for two feeble invalids during a tedious journey, fearing neither would reach home. Joseph died the next day in his mother's arms, and the aged father and mother soon followed him to the "Golden Shore."

Sophronia Bucklin

ON THE 17TH OF SEPTEMBER 1862, I started, unattended, for the seat of war, and three days later arrived at the front. The order given by my commander, Miss D. L. Dix, was awaiting me, so I was immediately taken to the Judiciary Hospital, on Four and Hay Street, and my labor as an army nurse began.

After three months' service I was ordered to the Baptist Church, where I took care of a sick nurse and her ward for a month; then was sent to Point Lookout, at the entrance to Chesapeake Bay, where I remained all through that cold, dreary winter, without fire, caring for wounded men brought from Fredericksburg, from Bull Run, and from Antietam. Oh, what suffering, what heroic courage for this lovely country of ours! No language can describe it!

In March I was sent to Alexandria, Virginia, and remained there until the battle of Gettysburg; there I was the first nurse in the field hospital, and Miss Plummer and myself were the last to leave.

From there I went to Stoneman's Cavalry Hospital, six miles from Washington, D. C., where I remained seven or eight months. In the winter of 1863 and 1864 I had the fever, and a council of the hospital surgeons gave me up to die; but my work was not yet done. After recovering sufficiently I was sent to Whitehouse, to care for the wounded brought from Cold Harbor, and remained there until the army swung round in front of Petersburg. Then we went to City Point, and five months later to the Point of Rocks, and were there when Petersburg was taken and General Lee surrendered, remaining until our beloved Lincoln was assassinated. Then, and not till then, could I get my own consent to return to the home I had left nearly three years before. I could not leave my post while there was one of my country's noblemen to claim my care.

Sophronia E. Bucklin
Cor. Of Tioga And Fall Streets
ITHACA, NEW YORK

Mary J. Buncher

AGREEABLE TO YOUR REQUEST, I will try to give some account of the hospital to which I was called, and in which I served as a nurse during the last year of the war, from October 1864 to September 1865. In the fall of 1864 the hospitals along the frontier had become overcrowded, and a question arose in the minds of the public-spirited men of our State in regard to providing a hospital for the sick and wounded of our own State. Very little time was lost before a well-equipped United States building was established in Manchester, New Hampshire, receiving the name, "Webster Hospital." It would accommodate six hundred patients, and during the time of its existence, sixteen hundred were admitted and cared for; quite a number from Maine and Massachusetts, as well as from New Hampshire.

The working force consisted of Col. Alex. T. Watson, surgeon in charge, and seven or eight assistant surgeons, four medical cadets, and four stewards, five nurses, and an extra woman of all work. Four convalescent soldiers were detailed to render such assistance as we needed. Our assigned work was in the Extra Diet Department, and we were appointed by Miss Dix. The nurses were Mrs. Eliza P. Stone (deceased) and Mrs. Mary J. Buncher, of Manchester (sisters); Miss Mary J. Knowles, Miss Elizabeth J. Dudley, and Mrs. Moore (deceased).

The responsibility rested more especially upon my sister and myself; the duties devolving upon us included the supervision of preparing the diet and stimulants for all the sick and wounded needing special care, visiting them, and administering such comfort and cheer as we could. The other nurses had their full share of the labor of love in preparing all the little delicacies for the sufferers, from whom we all received ample compensation in their grateful expressions of thankfulness. We saw much suffering bravely borne. Thirteen deaths occurred from various causes,—the first five of as many different nationalities. Those were very solemn occasions. Another sad scene came when the convalescents were sufficiently strong to return to the front; also, when more wounded ones were brought to us.

But there were many pleasant things connected with our hospital life. The people of the city and state were deeply interested in the work. The pastors took turns in coming each Sabbath. The large "mess hall" was arranged for an audience room, and we had excellent discourses delivered there. The singing by the soldier boys was fine. Colonel Watson permitted them to have many kinds of amusement, in which all who were able participated. They frequently gave concerts of no mean order, to which many were invited from the city. The young ladies also gave a fair, and the proceeds were devoted to the purchase of a nice little library, which gave the men a good selection of books, and they were greatly appreciated.

Colonel Watson always maintained the same strict discipline as was observed at the front: only special days were allowed for visiting; no one could enter or leave the grounds without a pass; and after the evening guard went on duty we could not go into any of the wards without giving the countersign.

Gifts of all kinds sent to the sick ones were delivered at our quarters, to be dispensed according to the judgment of their physicians. Thanksgiving Day, I remember, a bountiful provision was made for all those who were able to partake.

That year at Webster Hospital will remain a bright spot in memory, notwithstanding the many painful scenes we were called upon to witness. I rejoice that I was permitted to share in the services rendered by so many noble-hearted women to the brave and heroic sufferers, the defenders of our beloved country. I possess many tokens of kind remembrance from those who were under our care,—letters, photographs, etc.,—and as the years go by, they seem more and more valuable. Quite a number of those who were then young men, now occupy very responsible positions.

I have an excellent photograph of the hospital and grounds, taken before the buildings were removed. It was presented to my sister and myself by Colonel Watson, and I prize it very highly.

My dear sister, Mrs. Eliza P. Stone, died seven years ago. Her experience at the hospital was identical with my own; but her sweet Christian character, and strong faith, impressed itself upon the hearts of many suffering and dying ones, and gave consolation to many in their hours of trial.

Mrs. Mary J. Buncher
182 MAIN STREET
NASHUA, NEW HAMPSHIRE

Caroline Burghardt

A NATIVE OF GREAT BARRINGTON, Berkshire County, Massachusetts, of Dutch and Scotch ancestry, my mother being Miss Asenath L. Grant of Norwich, Connecticut, was in New York City at the breaking out of the war, employed as governess to the children of Mr. and Mrs. Parke Godwin, and grandchildren of Mr. and Mrs. William Cullen Bryant.

On April 19, 1861, went into "Bellevue" Hospital, New York, as number five of a class of ten who were accepted by the Board of Surgeons—Dr. Valentine Mott, Chairman. Remained there, in training for a nurse, until June 8, 1861, when a telegram was received from Washington, D. C. for two nurses to be selected from the class and sent, at once, to headquarters.

We arrived in Washington, June 9, 1861, with sealed orders to the Surgeon General and Miss D. L. Dix, who had been appointed by President Lincoln and Secretary Stanton as superintendent of nurses.

The following unsolicited "Certificate of Hospital Service," which was prepared by Miss Dix, (and given to me after she had left us) will give my war service, and I prefer that she should speak for me.

TESTIMONY OF HOSPITAL SERVICES

When an excellent work has been steadfastly conducted for months and years, certified evidence seems unnecessary, and is, under adopted usage, exceptional; but a record so fair and unbroken as that which embraces the labors of Miss Caroline A. Burghardt of Massachusetts, especially claims honorable notice.

*   *   *   *

Her services as nurse in both fever and surgical wards of United States Army Hospitals during the War of the Rebellion, commenced June 9, 1861, and ended September 6, 1865. During this period she was stationed severally in Washington, Antietam, Gettysburg, Fortress Monroe, Winchester, Wilmington, and Alexandria.

Her superior fidelity and skill required her assignment at the most difficult and responsible stations. Always prompt in the discharge of duty; exemplary in conduct, and competent through good judgment, she won the respect and confidence of surgeons, and the gratitude of patients.

Under Providence, hundreds owe lengthened life to her unfailing watchfulness, and bless her for mitigation of pain and anguish through patient cares and cheerful words.

This testimony is given under full personal knowledge of services above recited.

D. L. Dix, free service
Superintendent of Women Nurses,
during the War of the Rebellion

Belle Coddington

BEFORE TAKING UP MY PEN to write this sketch, I climbed to the top of the library, and taking down a large, old Latin book, uniquely bound in hog-skin, and printed three and a half centuries ago, I turned its musty, though well-preserved pages, and found in a large official envelope another old and highly valued relic,—the commission of an army nurse. It reads as follows:—

OFFICE OF WESTERN SANITARY COMMISSION,
St. Louis, March 19, 1864

Mrs. A. Tannehill, having furnished satisfactory evidence of her qualifications for the position of "nurse" in the employment of the Medical Department, U. S. A., is approved.

James E. Yeatman,
AGENT FOR MISS D. L. DIX

Assigned to duty at Benton Barracks, General Hospital, St. Louis, March 19, 1864, upon application of Ira Russell, surgeon in charge.

James E. Yeatman,
AGENT FOR MISS D. L. DIX
Approved: Dr. Miles, Surgeon
U. S. A., MEDICAL DIRECTOR

In the same envelope was another commission dated at Philadelphia, June 1, 1865, and signed by George H. Stuart, chairman of the
United States Christian Commission. As I glanced over these old papers, my thoughts went back of the dates upon them to the strange
events that influenced my life, resulting in my becoming an army
nurse, and a delegate of the United States Christian Commission.

I thought of my wedding day, when I stood at the altar and took
upon myself the sweet and solemn marriage vows; of the five short
months of unalloyed happiness that followed; then the enlisting of
my young husband in the service of his country, how hard I tried to
be brave as I clung to him in parting; then of the eagerly-looked-for
letters,—and at last the one that never came, but in its stead a message in a strange hand telling me of my husband's death, and burial
near Vicksburg, where his regiment had been sent to reinforce General Grant.

To a true woman there is no sweeter word than wife, no sadder one
than widow. In less than a year I had realized in my experience the
meaning of both. The deep feeling of the heart had been touched by
the hand of Love, the tenderest feeling by the hand of Death; and it is
the experience of sorrow that prepares us to minister to others.

After my husband's death there came an intense desire to do something for the sick and wounded soldiers in the hospitals. But not knowing how to proceed to get a position as nurse, I resumed my former
occupation of school teaching. What had once been a delight, now
seemed irksome and distasteful.

My first term of school had closed, when I met a Mrs. Conrad, who
had been engaged in the Keokuk, Iowa hospital. She told me to corre-
spond with Mrs. Wittenmyer, who would give me the information necessary to secure a position in that hospital. I wrote to her at once, and
received a reply telling me to apply to James E. Yeatman, and inclose
testimonials of good moral character, signed by my pastor and the ladies of the Aid Society where I lived.

Following her directions I soon had a letter from Mr. Yeatman, but,
alas, there was no opening at that time; but he informed me that as
soon as more ladies were needed he would let me know.

Months passed in anxious waiting. A winter term of school was begun and finished, and then came the long-looked for commission, and

with it government transportation. I do not suppose an officer in the army, from general down to second lieutenant, ever received his commission with greater delight or enthusiasm. Little time was spent in preparing for my journey, for I was anxious to get at the work, and only a few days elapsed from the time I received my commission until I had reported for duty where I had been assigned.

The Benton Barracks Hospital was one of the largest in the West, and included the Amphitheatre and other buildings in the fair grounds of the St. Louis Agricultural Society. In this large hospital there were often two thousand patients. Dr. Russell, of Natick, Massachusetts, the surgeon in charge, was every way fitted for his responsible position. One historian in referring to him called him "that able surgeon and earnest philanthropist." I shall ever cherish his memory. Only a few years ago, and a short time before his death, I received from him the kindest of letters and a request that I send him my photograph, and all other nurses I might have in my possession, to be put on file in the archives of the Loyal Legion. I am sorry to say I neglected to send them. His home was in Winchendon, Massachusetts, at the time of his death.

Benton Barracks, when I was there, comprised a promiscuous throng,—white and colored soldiers, refugees, contrabands, teachers, ministers, officers' families, etc. It was especially interesting to me to watch the colored soldiers on dress parade. They realized there was a vast difference between slavery and the overseer's lash, and freedmen in the United States uniform, standing shoulder to shoulder with the men who had fought to make them free. It was a little amusing, too, to see a colored soldier marching a white comrade to the guardhouse, as was sometimes the case. They sank to the depths of humiliation themselves when detailed to do duty in the refugee hospitals, for they scorned the "po' white trash." In the hospitals they received the same careful nursing, and everywhere the same humane treatment, as the white soldier. Books had been furnished them, and it was wonderful to see how eager they were to learn. I was deeply touched one day when one of them, an old man, drew from the pocket of his blue coat a Testament, and bowing politely to me, said, "Please, Missus, show me de place where it tells 'bout de many mansions, and Jesus preparin' de way."

The day of my arrival at the hospital I was met by Miss Emily Parsons, superintendent of the nurses. She was one peculiarly gifted and endowed for such a work, and it could be truly said of her, "She opened her mouth with wisdom, and in her tongue was the law of kindness." Her name recalls precious recollections, and I would offer this tribute to her memory. From her I received instructions in regard to my appointment and my duties as matron of Ward D, General Hospital. The next morning she opened the door, and following her, I stood for the first time

> " In the ward of the whitewashed wall,
> Where the sick and the dying lay."

She soon retired, and I entered upon my work.

The duty of ward matron, as specified, was to attend to the special diet of the weaker patients, to see that the wards were kept in order, to minister to the wants of the patients, and to give them words of good cheer, both by reading and conversation, and to assist them in correspondence with their friends at home. Before I had made the rounds in my ward the first morning, my courage was put to the test I approached a cot, and talking with a sick man found he had the small-pox. His cot was only a few feet from my room, which joined the ward. The partition was not a plastered one, but boards placed on end, barn fashion, with strips nailed over the cracks. The air was virtually the same in both ward and nurse's room. Could I lie down and sleep, knowing that every breath I took was freighted with this terrible contagion? I felt somewhat relieved, however, when, before the day was over, the patient was removed to the pest hospital. Poor fellow! I soon heard of his death.

I became accustomed to disease in its various forms, and even small-pox patients were attended with as much care while they remained in the ward, as any others. Though I did escape the small-pox, I could not resist the measles, but had the orthodox United States type of the malady. One thing I could not become accustomed to, and a heart-sick feeling came over me always when I saw the undertaker's carriage pass along with its load of coffins going to the National Cemetery; and as I have stood in those cemeteries and looked over the acres and acres of graves, as close as they could be made, where were lying our boys in blue, my feelings were indescribable.

Appreciation is grateful to all, and the army nurse received it without measure from those to whom she daily ministered. To hear a soldier say as he bade her good-bye to join his regiment, after having been nursed back to health, "You have saved my life," was the richest compensation she could have received.

We had in connection with the hospital one of those special Diet Kitchens, originated by Mrs. Wittenmyer, which furnished delicate articles of food so grateful to the sick. It was a delight to me, after having gone the rounds with the surgeon of my ward, to go to this kitchen with my approved lists and see them filled, then hear the poor boys say as they tasted the tempting food, "This makes me think of home." It was the hands of Miss Phoebe Allen of Washington, Iowa, that served us so faithfully in the Diet Kitchen for awhile. Then we folded those hands to rest, and wept tears of sorrow at her untimely death.

As the Benton Barracks was so far removed from the seat of war, there was very little of an exciting character while I was there. The work of one day was much like that of every other. Once General Price threatened us, and every soldier who was able, in barracks and hospital, was ordered to sleep on his arms. I remember well that night. After "taps" had been sounded and lights were out I went to my window, and looking out into the night, I wondered it if the rebels would really come. After a while I heard in the distance a sound like the tramping of horses' feet and the rumbling of wagon wheels, and I expected every moment that the entire force would be called out to attack General Price and his army. All remained quiet as usual. Still I listened and soon I could see in the moonlight a train of wagons approaching. It was an enemy in very truth,—only loads of sour commissary bread.

In March 1865, I was transferred to the Nashville Hospital, where Dr. Russell had gone, and was serving as surgeon in charge. Before leaving Benton Barracks, the soldiers in the ward where I had been for nearly a year presented me with an elegant silk dress pattern, in token of their good will.

My work at Nashville was much as it had been before. Many of the patients had been in the engagement between Thomas and Hood. It was simply wonderful to see how bravely these men bore their misfortunes. One who had lost an arm was rejoicing over the fact that it was not a leg; while one who hobbled about on crutches thought he was very fortunate indeed not to have lost an arm, or, worse, his head. A colored soldier being asked by a visitor what was the matter with him, replied, "De doctah says I have de dispensation of de heart." He meant palpitation.

There was a large house with beautiful grounds near by,—confiscated property,—and we were allowed to gather the flowers that grew so abundantly. I remember how we would arrange the tricolors, red, white, and blue, upon the little square stands that stood by each soldier's cot, not only bringing cheer to the sick, but calling forth the admiration of the inspecting officers. It was while I was at Nashville that the exciting news of the surrender of Lee's army was received. The cannon thundered forth from Fort Neighly until the ground seemed to shake beneath our feet. Then while the air was still vibrating with the echoes and the soldiers' jubilant shouts, a telegram announced the assassination of President Lincoln.

In June I was recalled to St. Louis to enter the work of the Christian Commission. The Sanitary Commission was about closing its work. The war was ended, but months must elapse before the soldier could return home. The Christian Commission, instead of disbanding, brought all their resources to the great work of supplying the soldiers until they were finally mustered out.

I left Nashville in July, and returning to Benton Barracks I entered the old Amphitheatre again,—the apartments occupied as the headquarters of the Christian Commission. How distinctly the room comes before me. Along the beams overhead were the words, "Mother, Home, Heaven." Scripture mottoes were on the walls. Long tables extended across the room, where soldiers could come to write letters, or read books and papers. On a little platform was a place usually occupied by a lady delegate of the Commission, and above this was the motto, "Let woman's influence be felt in behalf of her country." Here one of the ladies was usually found with busy hands distributing supplies to those who came into the reading room. The badge she wore was a safe passport to the hospital, barracks, or camp. She worked for God and humanity, and wherever she went the blessing of the soldiers followed her.

The work of mustering out was going on as rapidly as possible and as the mighty armies melted away and our soldiers went from camp to home, the demand for workers grew less. At last there came a day when we were needed no longer. Our work among the soldiers was done. December 3, 1865, I left St. Louis, and reached my home at Troy, Iowa, in time to celebrate my twenty-third birthday, which occurred the same month, having been gone almost two years.

One year after my return I was married to Rev. E. H. Coddington. When the war broke out he was a student at the Iowa Wesleyan University at Mt. Pleasant. At the first call to arms he enlisted in Company F, 14th Iowa Infantry. At the battle of Fort Donelson a rebel musket shot shattered his left arm, rendering a shoulder-joint amputation necessary. After being discharged and regaining sufficient health, he entered college again. Then came the call for more men, and again he enlisted in the service of his country, and was commissioned Captain, Company H, 45th Iowa. Serving out his term, he was discharged, and entered college the third time, and graduated with the class of 1866. The following year he entered the ministry, and in December we were married. Though he had not fully recovered from the loss of his arm, and knew he never would, yet he hoped his life might be spared long enough to bring to him the realization of some of his bright hopes and aspiration. So with brave and happy hearts we enjoyed the present, and planned for the future.

Seven years of successful work in the ministry, four years of intense suffering, then came the end. He was not, for God took him. Two little children had preceded him to the heavenly home; two remained to my care and love,—a son ten years old, a daughter five. I saw them grow to manhood and womanhood, and graduate from the same college that graduated their father.

My son entered journalism but applied himself too closely to his work. Last May, his health failed, and his physician advised him to go to Colorado. In November I was called to Denver to see him die, and I brought him home, and laid him beside his father. When my daughter is not away teaching school she is with me. But for her my life would be as lonely and desolate as when I became an army nurse.

Belle Coddington
MOUNT PLEASANT, IOWA

Emily Cone

I WAS ENROLLED AS AN ARMY NURSE September 2, 1863, and served in that capacity one year and nine months, being discharged May 1865. I went from Rockford, Illinois, and entered the Cumberland Hospital at Nashville, Tennessee, where I served under Major McDermott during the first year, and Major Cloak the year following. I had charge of the Laundry Department and the Low Diet Kitchen, for a short time during the absence of Mrs. Woodruff. When I had any spare time I devoted it to the care of the sick and wounded soldiers.

After the battle of Nashville I was on duty forty-eight hours without sleep, caring for the boys that were brought in from the battlefield, which was about two miles distant. The excitement was intense. We expected to be obliged to leave the hospital and flee to the city for protection, and preparations were made to convey the sick and wounded to a place of safety; but fortunately we were not disturbed.

On his way to Franklin my husband's brother was taken sick through exposure at the time of battle, and removed to Huntsville, Alabama where our army was in camp. He sent for me, and that journey I shall *never* forget, owing to the hardships I endured on the way. We went in box cars with about three hundred soldiers on board. I was the only woman among them from Stephenson down, but I must say I was I never treated with more consideration and kindness than by "our dear boys in blue." I remained three days, and during that time buried the brother; then returned to Nashville, more dead than alive myself.

My husband enlisted in 1861, and served with his regiment until 1863. He was injured at Stephenson, and transferred to the Cumberland Hospital, where he remained with me until we were discharged.

Emily M. Cone
Care Of A. H. Maxwell
NEW MILFORD, ILLINOIS

Betsey Cook

IN 1861, WHEN EVERY HEART that beat in unison for the protection of our country and the dear old flag was filled with patriotism, we were living in Augusta, Illinois. My husband enlisted in July, in the 2d Illinois Cavalry, and went to the army, while I returned to my father's in Jackson. In September my husband wrote, asking me if I would go there as nurse in Delanoe's Dragoons. I replied that I would, and soon received an appointment and transportation. I went from Grass Lake to Fort Halt, Kentucky, across the river from Cairo, arriving there about the middle of October. Doctor Kendall was in charge of the hospital, and I served under him all the time I was with the army.

We all lived in tents, and used one for a hospital, until November, when they built cabins for winter quarters. A room was prepared for the sick, and we got along very well till some time in January, when the water rose and covered the ground so that no one could get out at all who did not wear cavalry boots. So we were obliged to leave our comfortable quarters, and move to higher ground. We went up the Ohio River three or four miles, to a place called Camp Pain. I stayed there until the last of February, and then went home to Michigan, where I remained until November of 1862, when I resumed my duties as nurse at Island No. 10. Doctor Kendall was in charge, and glad to have my help, as there was not another white woman on the island until I had been there some time. I took charge of all the clothing and hospital supplies, and prepared the food that was carried to the sick. My husband was detailed there as hospital cook, and they were using baker's bread, which I must say was not very good. Soon after I arrived I asked him if that was the best bread they could get; and when told that was, I said if I could get some flour I would make some bread that I thought would be better. As there was no yeast I tried the old Yankee way of "salt raising." The bread was good, and I made from it some toast to send to the sick boys. The man who carried it to them soon returned, and said they wanted to know if I brought that all the way from Michigan, and if they could have a little more for it was the best they had tasted since they had been in the army. I told him they could have all they wanted, and from that time I made all we used.

About the last of April, Doctor Kendall was relieved, and sent to Columbus, Kentucky, and Doctor Nelson took his place. Soon a large number of contrabands were brought in, and the able-bodied men were drilled there in camp for awhile, then taken to Columbus, and formed in a company. Soon the necessity of forming a colored military hospital was felt, and my husband was relieved from duty on Island No. 10 and ordered to Columbus. I went there in June 1863 and stayed until the last August. My duties were to oversee the cooking and hospital supplies. After a time Doctor Kendall was taken sick, and went home; then all the officers were changed,—my husband ordered to his company, and I returned to my home in Augusta, where I kept house until Mr. Cook was discharged and came home.

While I was an army nurse I had many pleasant and many sad experiences which I should be glad to tell you, but I am old, and it is hard for me to write. A year ago I made application for a pension but it as rejected on the ground that Mrs. Yates was not legally authorized to appoint me. But if I never receive any pay, I have the satisfaction of knowing that I did what I could to help in the great struggle for Union and the flag.

Yours in F., C. and L.,
Betsey A. Cook
LAMAR, MISSOURI

Elizabeth Cope

In 1861, when the Rebellion broke out, I was living on a farm in Iowa, with my husband and four sons, of whom the eldest was eighteen years, and the youngest, one year old. My husband enlisted in August 1861; but before being sworn in he became very ill, and died August 31st. The following year my eldest son enlisted. He was wounded during the battle of Springfield; then followed a long illness, and the doctors sent him home to die, but with the aid of careful nursing he recovered sufficiently to re-enlist, and was sent to Omaha as hospital steward, and served there until the close of the war.

I entered a hospital at Keokuk in July 1862 and served as ironer until November; then I was duly enrolled as an army nurse, and served until June 26, 1864.

I was the only female nurse in the house, and if this falls under the observation of the soldiers who were there at that time, I think many will remember me. I tried to do all in my power for those who needed help, and I am very grateful that my efforts were so highly appreciated.

Mrs. Elizabeth Cope
528 18th Street
Oakland, California

Susan Cox

I WENT INTO THE SERVICE from Knox County, Illinois, and served with the 83d Illinois Infantry at Fort Henry, Fort Donelson, and Clarksville, from October 1862 until June 1864. This regiment was garrisoned at Fort Donelson the greater part of the time I was with them, so my experience was less varied than that of many others.

Once when my husband had gone with most of the company thirty-five miles up the Cumberland River to guard a boat, we were surrounded, and a fight occurred. The Northern women were ordered on board a boat that was to drop down the river. While on the way to the landing the shot and shell were flying all around us, and I saw one of our boys lying dead, having been fearfully mangled.

One of our soldiers was condemned for desertion, and I saw him shot in the presence of the whole command. The men were formed in a hollow square, so that all could see very plainly. He stood in the center with the nine men, who aimed their guns at his breast, and eight bullets pierced his body within a circle of six inches. Nine more guns were in reserve; but ah! they were not needed.

Yours in F., C. and; L.,
Susan Cox
TECUMSEH, NEBRASKA

Harriet Dame

HARRIET P. DAME, daughter of James Chadbourne and Phebe Agnes Dame, was born at Barnstead, New Hampshire, January 5, 1815. (Her parents moved to North Barnstead about the year 1797; they then had one son. Five children were born in Barnstead of whom Harriet was the youngest.) In 1843 she removed with her parents to Concord, New Hampshire, where she resided until the breaking out of the war. That event at once aroused her enthusiasm, and patriotism, and she anxiously desired to aid the Union cause. Not being permitted to carry a musket, she decided to become an army nurse and joined the 2d New Hampshire Regiment, as hospital matron, in June 1861 and remained with the regiment until it was finally mustered out of the service in December 1865, four years and eight months.

The pay of a hospital matron was six dollars a month until 1863, when it was increased to ten dollars per month and so remained during the war. She was in camp near Washington, D. C., until November, 1861, then at Budd's Ferry, Maryland, until April, 1862, and in that month went with the regiment to Yorktown, Virginia, and up the Peninsula. She was inside the trenches at Fair Oaks while the rebels were bombarding them and a shell tore through the tent just as she left it, and another burst overhead while she was cooking some broth. In the ambulance and hospital she was a ministering angel and saved the lives of many men by careful nursing. After that battle, the troops having retreated, she walked a long distance and assisted the sick and wounded on the march. One very dark night she passed in the thick of the woods, not knowing whether she was near friends or foes, and for that reason not attempting to proceed.

At this time she was the only woman in the brigade, and frequently nursed the sick and wounded of other regiments. She was well known to all the soldiers of the brigade and those of other regiments seemed to rival the 2d New Hampshire in the respect shown her.

At the second battle of Bull Run she was taken prisoner, but was given a pass through the lines, in recognition of her attentions to Confederates and Unions alike. She soon rejoined her regiment at Harrison's Landing where she remained until the 15th of August, 1862, when by universal consent she assumed charge of the supplies, sent from New Hampshire for the sick and wounded from the State, and distributed them to the most needy of the different hospitals. During this winter the 2d New Hampshire Regiment was home recruiting; upon its return to active duty Miss Dame rejoined them and was at the battle of Gettysburg. Here she lost all her effects. She remained after the battle in the Corps Hospital until the sick and wounded were removed to the general hospitals.

She then rejoined the regiment at Point Lookout where they were for a few weeks guarding prisoners of war. At this time Miss Dame was worn out by exposure and incessant duty; and it was decided that she should go South to investigate the sanitary condition of the New Hampshire troops stationed near Charleston, South Carolina. She subsequently rejoined the regiment and was at the battle of Cold Harbor. Soon after that battle the original three-year men of the regiment who had not re-enlisted were mustered out. She remained with the re-enlisted and was for a time in front of Petersburg, and then at Chapin's farms near Richmond. About this time the army was so continuously on the march that corps hospitals were established and the wounded sent to them until they could be safely removed to hospitals further north.

Miss Dame was appointed matron of the 18th Corps Hospital in September, 1864, and had supervision of the nurses on duty and of the cooking for the sick and wounded, who at times numbered not less than four thousand. She remained there till the close of the active operations of the war, then rejoined the 2d New Hampshire Regiment at

Manchester, Virginia, opposite Richmond, and went with them to Fredericksburg. They were then sent to Richmond County on the northern neck between the Potomac and Rappahannock rivers. The regiment while there suffered more from sickness and death than at any equal time during us service. On the 25th of December, 1865, the regiment was mustered out of the service, and Miss Dame's army record ended with theirs.

Of her service Gen. Gilman Marsten, for years colonel of the 2d New Hampshire Volunteers, has said:—

"Miss Dame, on the breaking out of the war for the Union, was at the capitol of the State in the quiet of home life. When the drums sounded for the 1st New Hampshire Regiment under the call for three months' service, she began to consider what a woman could do for her imperilled country, and when the next regiment, enlisting for three years on the war, was formed she attached herself to it as a volunteer nurse, and followed its fortunes in defeat and victory until the end of the war except when on special service, at the request of high officials, in the inspection of hospitals including that too often neglected, yet very important section, known as the hospital kitchen. Many an officer who neglected the men under his command felt the power of her honest criticism, whether he knew it or not.

"The sound of hostile guns is well known to her, for her services were not generally in post hospitals; but in field hospitals, and upon the battle ground itself, where danger did not deter, but where the opportunity for friendly help determined her presence.

"In this field work she was the pioneer American nurse, and is entitled to the credit and honor of that service, and to the renown which her heroic example and patriotic devotion confer.

"Time will not permit even a brief recital of her special army work, but I cannot close this general statement of her public life without adding that there was no shadow upon her reputation and no doubt of her disinterested patriotism. She is always a welcome guest at Veterans' Reunions and at the annual Encampment at the Wiers, in my State, no guest receives greater honor. At the headquarters of the 2d New Hampshire, the best guest chamber is always at her service, and is known as her room. No old soldier fails to give her cordial greeting and respectful homage. Could those who have answered the last roll-call speak, they would call her blessed."

With the soldiers, she is entitled to wear the cross of the 18th Corps, which she accompanied; the diamond of the 3d Corps of Hooker's Division; the heart of the 12th Corps, and a gold badge given by the 2d New Hampshire.

Miss Dame was given a vote of thanks by the New Hampshire Legislature and presented with $500 (five hundred). She accepted both, but gave the money towards founding a home for the veterans of her regiment. She is a pensioner of the United States but has always given the money to the poor and needy.

Miss Dame's life has been one act of charity, and when she passes to her reward the world, which has been the better for her living, will have lost one of its noblest women.

Miss Dame says: "I remember an incident of one morning on the Chickahominy. The men came to me and wanted me to make them some tea which I did. It seemed to refresh them greatly. I walked away from the fire and saw a man sitting on a stump at the edge of the woods. His face was in his hands, he acted greatly fatigued. I asked if he were Illinois. He said, 'No,' but he had been in the saddle for a whole day. As he looked up I saw that he was a major general and offered him some tea, which he gladly accepted. I did not know the man, but years afterward in looking at some pictures I came across that of Kearney, and he was the man on the stump."

In 1867 Miss Dame was appointed to a clerkship in the Treasury Department, which position she filled continuously till February 1895, a period of twenty-eight years, when she fell on the icy sidewalk sustaining a fracture of her leg. Though eighty years old her recovery was rapid, and she was soon back at her desk in the Treasury Department.

On the night of November 27, Miss Dame left her home to visit and comfort a sick friend; in crossing a street she was run into by a woman bicyclist, breaking her thigh, thus having been twice within a year confined to a fracture bed. Her recovery was remarkable. She has not since returned to her desk.

Mary Darling

My husband and myself moved from Wisconsin to Missouri in 1860. When the war broke out he was compelled to hide in cornfields until he could join a regiment. But it was not the men only who were in danger; even the women and children had to flee for their lives. He enlisted at Memphis, July 20, 1861 and I went into the regiment in October. They were then home guards but were mustered into United States service in December and went immediately to Hannibal, Missouri. There Doctor Wyman hired me for the Regimental Hospital. I was to have twelve dollars a month (I did not receive a cent, however). I remained there until April. After the troops left, I had to remain until the sick could be moved; then I went on with all the supplies, the wounded having been sent to general hospitals.

As there was no real nursing to do, my duty was to bake light bread for the convalescents, in accordance with the doctor's order; and I often used fifty pounds of flour a day.

When the army was advancing to Corinth, the 6th Division Hospital was started, near the battleground of Shiloh. I remained there until after Corinth was evacuated, making soups, etc., for the sick, besides carrying water half a mile for them to drink. The regiment had to move off without me, but sent a team back twenty miles, saying I could not be spared any longer. After joining them I had a hospital tent, where I resumed my old occupation of nursing and cooking for the sick. I stayed there until after the battle of Corinth, in October. Then the regiment left me and went home to Missouri, on a recruiting furlough, where they remained until November 1862.

In December my husband was taken with the typhoid fever, and was sent to Mound City Hospital, Illinois, where he remained until March 1863, and during all this time I heard nothing from him. Then I received a pass, and word that he was back with his regiment and needed my care. I stayed there until they moved to Memphis, Tennessee, where they remained until the winter of 1864.

I did not go into the hospitals after this, but waited upon the sick in tents. When the regiment went to Vicksburg I returned to Benton Barracks, where I lived until my husband was discharged. He had continued on duty although he did not speak a word aloud for four years after having the fever.

My nursing was over, but I did some cooking at the barracks for paroled soldiers from Southern prisons, who were not able to cook their rations for themselves.

Mary E. Darling
SAN DIEGO, CALIFORNIA

Dorothea Dix

ON THE 17TH OF JULY 1887 occurred the death of Dorothea Lynde Dix; a woman whose memory will be kept green until acts of humanity become so common that they are passed by without comment.

She was born in 1802, and her early life was bleak, humiliating, and painful. Her father not being able to take care of her she soon left his roof and found an abiding place, but scarcely a home, with her grandmother in Boston.

She possessed exceptional energy and ambition, and early determined to fit herself for a teacher. While one side of her character seemed that of all earnest, unenthusiastic worker, the other was exceptionally sensitive, and full of beautiful ideals. She reveled in poetry and worshiped intellectual greatness; but she was above a selfish absorption in these, for poverty and ignorance appealed to her strongly, and she early began to work for poor and neglected children. For these she opened a school in the barn of her grandmother's house, which was the beginning of the beneficent work afterward carried on at Warren Street Chapel, now the Barnard Memorial on Warrenton Street.

Miss Dix also had a small day school, which afterwards developed into a large combined boarding and day school. While she had charge of this school, which required the most assiduous labor and executive ability, she was writing a book that became a familiar friend to many families a generation ago. It was called the "Science of Common Things," and in a comprehensive, easy manner gave a great deal of valuable information about the ordinary things used in the household. It had a place in almost every home, and was a standard reference. One could find in it information about everything from a needle to a nutmeg; and in any perplexity "Common Things" was consulted as an oracle. This little book passed through sixty editions.

Other later books were "Garland of Flora," "Private Hours," "Alice and Ruth," "Prisons and Prison Discipline."

At last, on account of poor health, the school was relinquished, and she became a governess in the family of Dr. W. E. Channing. It was while a member of his family that she went to the island of Saint Croix, and obtained her first glimpse of the evils of slavery.

After her return to Boston, being in better health, she again took up school work, which was pursued with zeal until 1836, when she broke down utterly, and, accompanied by friends, went abroad for rest and change. She had saved enough money to afford her a modest income suited to her wants.

It was not until 1841 that Miss Dix was brought face to face with the horrible condition of things that existed in the prisons and almshouses of Massachusetts.

She visited the jail of East Cambridge, and found a terrible overcrowding of innocent, guilty and insane prisoners. She then visited all the other prisons of the State, finding such a horrible condition of affairs that she addressed a memorial to the Legislature on the subject, giving a graphic description of the abuses suffered by the insane poor.

Her enthusiasm on the subject enlisted the attention of Dr. S. G. Howe, Charles Sumner, and others. Public opinion was aroused by the horrors unveiled by Miss Dix; politicians were overwhelmed, a bill for relief immediately carried, and an order passed to provide State accommodations for two hundred insane people.

Thus her first step was taken. The conviction came to her that all over the United States the same appalling story was true of the wretched fate of the pauper insane. She felt that she must visit state after state, collect facts, besiege legislatures, and arouse public opinion. It was a stupendous work, but this frail woman, with a grasp of intellect worthy of a statesman, accomplished it. Massachusetts, Rhode Island,

and New Jersey all show her work today. Pennsylvania followed. She made long journeys North and South, East and West, always carrying hope for the unfortunate. In nine years she had carried for reforms the Legislatures of Indiana, Illinois, Kentucky, Tennessee, Missouri, Mississippi, Louisiana, Alabama, South and North Carolina and Maryland, besides establishing an asylum at Halifax, Nova Scotia, and Saint John, New Brunswick. For several sessions she petitioned Congress to grant a large tract of land for the benefit of the insane, but after years of work upon the subject the bill was vetoed by President Pierce.

After this disappointment Miss Dix again visited Europe, and on her return became interested in the work of saving shipwrecked mariners on Sable Island, which had long been called the Graveyard of Seamen. While Miss Dix was visiting the place a wreck occurred, and she saw how inadequate to save life were the means at hand. Through the co-operation of several citizens of Boston, Miss Dix sent life-boats and other life-saving paraphernalia to Sable Island. The day after these arrived a large ship was wrecked on the island, and by means of this apparatus one hundred and eighty souls were saved.

In 1854–55 she investigated, not without opposition, the condition of insane hospitals in Scotland, and found in them a repetition of what she had seen here. She at once began moving the great and cumbrous engine of English law to reform these abuses, but it was not until 1857, after years of labor and opposition, that the object was accomplished. Her attention was then called to similar abuses in the Channel Islands. After thirteen years of agitation a large public asylum for the humane and scientific treatment of the demented was built.

She also inspected the asylums in Rome, finding so much to condemn that she obtained an audience with Pope Pius IX. She was received with the greatest kindness, and her revelations intently listened to. Later the Pope visited the asylum, and found so many shocking things that, at a second audience, he thanked Miss Dix that she, "a woman and a Protestant, had crossed the seas to call his attention to these cruelly ill-treated members of his flock."

On her return to America, until the breaking out of the Civil War, in 1861, Miss Dix devoted herself to hospital work, aiding new institutions and directing older ones. In all, she founded thirty-two hospitals, besides two in Japan, that owe their inception to her influence.

During the war she devoted herself to hospital work. She was super-intendent of nurses, having the entire control of their appointment and assignment to duty. At the close of the war she was instrumental in raising the funds for a great national monument for dead soldiers at Fortress Monroe.

In the latter days of Miss Dix's career it may be said that no benevolent project ever lacked her support. It might be as simple a thing as a drinking fountain in a densely populated district in Boston, or collecting money for the suffering from some great conflagration. Work for others was still her mission and though she was loaded with praise and honor for the great things accomplished, she was as unostentatious as a child, and looked always for the results, and never at her own efforts. She was revered like a patron saint by many who had reaped the benefit of her care.

She dropped at, last, with the harness on, while ready as ever to work for others. Her mind was clear to the last, and she was always interested in what had been her life work.

In her commemoration is the Dix Ward in the McLean Asylum at Somerville, the Dixmont Hospital of Pennsylvania, and the Dorothea L. Dix House on Warrenton Street, just opposite the Barnard Memorial, which was the first fruits of the seed sown by Miss Dix in 1821.

Mrs. L. B. Downs

W HEN THE WAR OPENED I was at my home in Brattleboro, Vermont, and becoming at once intensely interested and eager, I longed with my whole heart to enter the field as a nurse.

Two obstacles barred the way to an immediate realization of my desire,—these were my good father's consent, and my failure to meet the requirement of age. With the intensity of youth I used often to exclaim, oh! if only I were a man, or forty years old!

As time went on I made various attempts to enter the service, but not until after the establishment of the United States Hospitals in the several States was I successful in obtaining an appointment. My actual term of service covered the short space of four months, from April to August in the year 1865, at Dale, United States Hospital, Worcester, Massachusetts. But although few in number the weeks were full of work and incident and felt very grateful that I was permitted to have the honor and privilege of lending a hand in my beloved country's need.

Mrs. L. B. (Jenison) Downs
NEWTON, MASSACHUSETTS

Jane Dunbar

I SERVED IN A HOSPITAL ON AN ISLAND in New York Harbor about four months. Mr. Church was the steward, and Doctor Smith the surgeon in charge. I had received a letter from the steward saying that my husband was very sick, and in response to my inquiry received a dispatch to go at once. I reached the hospital the first of August, 1864, and as there were about eight hundred soldiers there I found plenty of work to do.

When I had been there about a month the surgeon requested me to cook the extra diet for the sickest men, and I continued that work three months. The woman who did it before I went there had forty dollars a month. I was not paid, and I boarded myself until my money gave out, then I drew rations with the rest. I think I never worked so hard in my life.

At length the hospital was needed for the city poor, so the soldiers were removed to McDougal Hospital; and as I was not needed there, I returned to my home. This was in December; so when I applied for a pension I found that I lacked two months of the required time of service.

While I was in the hospital a band of ladies came every week to bring dainties for me to distribute among the sick ones. At the time the Southerners undertook to burn some of the buildings in the city of New York, two women came to examine our hospital, but thought they could not burn it very readily. Two of the soldiers who heard them talking followed them to the city and had them arrested. There was a great deal to do, and I had to go up and down three or four flights of stairs constantly; but it was hard to leave, too. When I first went there the soldiers asked me if I was going to stay; and when I said I would, some of them cried. It looked very hard to see so many sick and wounded.

I am now sixty-five years old, and broken down, but am still able to be around a part of the time.

Yours in F., C. and L.,
Jane E. Dunbar
Sparta, Wisconsin

Lois Dunbar

My war record is one of hard labor and severe trials. I went from Michigan City, Indiana, to Saint Louis on November 10, 1861. Doctor Hodges was the surgeon in charge. There were one thousand patients; Mrs. Harriet Colefax and I having three hundred under our immediate charge most of the time when the wounded were brought off the boats from Fort Donelson. I thought we should never be able to do our duty by so many, but we worked as only women can; and my experience there is something I shall never forget. I picked my way among them as they were brought in, often where it was hard to find standing room, and rendered what aid I could to the worst cases. One poor fellow died on the way, his spurs still on when we found him.

In April 1862, Governor Morton sent a request for Mrs. Colefax and I to report at Evansville, Indiana, as there were a great many there who were very sick, and no nurses. Doctor DeBruler was surgeon in charge of Hospital No. 2, and I was sent there, but Mrs. Colefax went down the Mississippi. I was placed in full charge, and was really commanding officer and nurse, besides having five other hospitals to look after. In September 1862, I received a commission from Miss Dix. The surgeons had wanted me to be inspector of all the hospitals there, but Doctor DeBruler objected, as he needed me; and, besides, I felt that I could be of more use as a nurse. Twice I went down the Ohio and Mississippi Rivers after the sick, and at Satartia, on the Yazoo, was under

fire from the rebels, but our gunboats soon disabled them. We had a
small battle, and took a church which we fitted up for a hospital. We
took some on the boat, gathering up three hundred on the return.

I was at Young's Point the time of the bombardment of Vicksburg.
On that trip my feet were so badly blistered that I had to be carried in a
chair from the landing to the hospital. I was just exhausted, and fainted
when taken to my room, but was soon ready again for duty.

I have had men die clutching my dress till it was almost impossible
to loose their hold. I have often taken young boys in my arms when
they were so tired they could not rest in their beds and held them as I
would my own little boys. I never went to the ward with a sad face but
always had a smile and a cheery word for all. The doctor said that he
knew when I was ahead of him, for the patients had such pleasant
countenances.

I had "saddle-bag pockets," and used to carry little delicacies for
them to eat, for they would get so hungry. At last they used to say,
"Our nurse carries a cook and store in her pockets." My efforts were
nobly seconded by one of the cooks. He seemed never to tire of doing
little extras,— baking potatoes, boiling eggs, making crackers, and
many other things. And how anxious they were for the "loaves and
fishes." Ah, poor fellows, they needed them badly enough!

Once when we were looking for Morgan and his guerrillas, a poor
man came to me and requested that I go to my room at the first alarm,
and said he would stand by my door, and they would have to go over
his dead body to enter. But the pitiful part of it was that he had no use
of his legs,—had to shove his feet along; one arm was disabled, and he
had been shot through the chest. It moved me to tears, and he said,
"Do not be afraid; I will die fighting." Well I knew he would. No such
patriots as ours could be found. Perhaps I should add that the reason I
understood minor surgery so well, was because I had a thorough course
of instruction under Doctor Jameson, who gained great experience in
the Crimean War. I also had a manual that treated the surgery during
that war; so I could, and did assist in many amputations.

My name was then Lois Dennett; but at the close of the war I was
married to one of my first patients, whom I saved after five doctors had
given him up. I left the hospital in September 1864.

Kate Duncan

I SERVED ONE YEAR AT PATTERSON PARK HOSPITAL, Baltimore, Maryland, beginning in September 1862. My husband was wounded in the neck and went home. He was sick eighteen months; then I went with him when he returned to duty. The first six weeks I nursed in Ward 15. They had seventy men,—the worst cases of typhoid fever. I sat up every other night, gave medicine, washed and fed the patients, etc. Doctor Knowles did not like women, and although the surgeon in charge put me there, he did not use me very well for a time. But he soon trusted me to give medicine and see to everything, and made me sit up nights, because he would not trust the male nurses. This was too hard for me, and the surgeon changed me to Ward 1 of surgical cases. Autand was the name of the French surgeon in charge of that ward. His watch-chain was hung with medals from the Crimean War. He had me assist him on his morning rounds, dressing wounds, and did not think anything was too bad for me to see. I had to dress four cases, each with an amputated arm, one wounded through the neck, two through the hip, and one who was wounded nine times, in the lungs and different parts of the body; yet he recovered, and went home at last.

I was there when the battle of Gettysburg was fought and did not have my clothes off for a week after the wounded began to arrive.

Kate M. Duncan
EMMETSBURG, IOWA

Elizabeth Ellis

Your letter addressed to my mother, Mrs. Elizabeth E. Ellis, was forwarded to me, as she was called to her reward three years ago. I am sorry I cannot give you as full an account as I should like, but will do the best I can, as I would like her work to be known.

My father, too, served three years and a half, and finally lost his life on the ill-fated "Sultana."

Mother volunteered, and was duly enrolled as an army nurse, January 14, 1863. She was then twenty-eight years old. She served at Woodward Post Hospital, Cincinnati, Ohio, for fifteen months, when, owing to ill health, she was honorably discharged. She went from Talmage, Ohio, and served under Dr. Henry Johnson, at least a part of the time.

I know her heart and soul were in the work, and she never lost her interest in the old soldiers, but during her last years was the means of securing pensions for some who were under her care in the hospital.

In F., C. and L.,
Mrs. Nettie E. Wink
KNIGHTSTOWN, INDIANA

Mary Ellis

I ASSISTED MY HUSBAND TO RAISE A REGIMENT, the 1st Missouri Volunteer Cavalry, of which he was made colonel, with the understanding that I should accompany him to the field, which I did; going in my own carriage, and taking with me a colored man and woman. I carried my own tent, and everything I needed, so that I was no expense to the Government.

The regiment went into camp at Saint Louis the 1st of August 1861. Soon the measles broke out, and I began my services as nurse there, and continued them until after the battle of Pea Ridge, March, 1862. In camp, on the march, or in the hospital,— when we had one,— there was no part of the work of a nurse that I did not do, even to assisting in surgical operations, particularly at the battle of Pea Ridge, where I stood at the surgeon's table, not one or two, but many hours, with the hot blood steaming into my face, until nature rebelled against such horrible sights and I fainted, but as soon as possible I returned. Our regiment was in the cavalry charge at Sugar Creek, and many of our men were killed and wounded. I was there with my carriage on the field, and brought in the first wounded to the house that was made to do duty for a hospital, and continued to care for the needy until April 1862.

Once, in October 1861, one of our officers was left with the rebels, and was very sick. It was at the close of a hard day's march and his captain came to me to know what could be done. I went on horseback alone, with the determination to find him, and care for him, if possible, and had the pleasure of being the means of saving his life.

In November the regiment surgeon gave a sick man an overdose of narcotics, and I found him lying by the wayside. I took him into my carriage, and sent to the front for his captain. As soon as possible I got him into a house, and laid him on the floor, where to all appearances the man died. I heard the doctor explaining why he died, but I could not believe that life was extinct. I tried to revive him, the doctors meanwhile making light of my efforts. Soon the man caught his breath, with a convulsive movement, while the five doctors turned and left the room. The captain and I soon had him all right, and in two weeks he reported for duty, and served until the close of the war. This act called down on my poor head the bitter enmity of the doctor; and, later, when he was either dismissed or court-martialed, he blamed me for it, though unjustly. The affair was no secret; hundreds knew what the doctor had done, and that I saved the man.

Some time near the middle of October 1861, it was my privilege to carry an important dispatch from General Hunter to General Price. The guerrillas and bushwhackers were so plentiful that the cars on the Northern Missouri Railroad could not run. The telegraph lines were all cut off, and any Union soldier or stranger unlucky enough to be caught beyond the camp was shot immediately. I received the dispatch from General Hunter at 9 A.M. and placed it in the hands of General Price at Jefferson City, at 5 P.M. the same day, having ridden forty miles.

By request of the chief of the Government Detective Force I acted as detective.

At last I was taken sick, and was carried to Saint Louis. It was two months before I was able to stand, and I did not recover sufficiently to return to camp. I was not mustered in or appointed by any one. My service was entirely voluntary and I have never received any pay. On the contrary, I spent thousands of dollars in raising the regiment and caring for the sick.

It would be useless for me to attempt to write an extended account of my experiences. It would only stir up memories of a pleasant home with my husband and son. I had but this one child, and I willingly gave him to my country's service; she sent him back to me crippled and maimed for life. Two years ago he went to join the great army on the shores of eternity; and oh! I want to go to him,—and as I am quite old, it must be soon. I am a physician but my work is done; I am not able to leave my room.

Yours respectfully,
Mary A. Ellis
1026 WEST WASHINGTON STREET
INDIANAPOLIS, INDIANA

Annie Etheridge

AMONG THE MANY NOTED WOMEN whose names adorn the pages of history, associated with the late War of the great Rebellion, none stand higher than this heroine, whose services were the first in the field and did not end until peace was restored.

Annie Etheridge, as she was known during the war, is a native of the State of Michigan. In May 1861, she, in company with nineteen other ladies, volunteered as nurses to accompany the Second Michigan Infantry under command of Colonel Richardson. All the others soon returned, finding the hardships of field service too great for their endurance. She alone remained and served until the close of the war, when she marched with the soldier "boys" through Washington, who carried the torn and smoke-begrimed flags that had, after so much blood and carnage, become the emblems of lasting peace.

"Our Annie," as she was called by the soldiers, participated or was in the field at the front when the battle raged hardest, flitting from one soldier to another as he lay bleeding or dying on the ground. During these four years she was in every battle of the Army of the Potomac, except those of South Mountain and Antietam, where the division to which she belonged was temporarily detached from the army and left in front of Washington.

Her work was in the field hospitals and on the battlefields, but it was in the latter service that she accomplished the greatest amount of good and displayed a heroism and devotion to her work that have not been excelled in the annals of the war. Often in the very thickest of the fight she never flinched for a moment in her self-appointed task. Seeking out the wounded who had been overlooked or not reached by the surgeons, she bound up their wounds with the skill and promptness of a practical surgeon. On one occasion the soldier whose wound she was dressing was struck by a shell and literally torn to pieces.

Her dress was often pierced by bullets, but she fortunately escaped unhurt except a slight wound on the left hand received at Chancellorsville. She unquestionably saved hundreds of lives of wounded men who would have perished but for her timely assistance. On the march she usually rode a horse, but at night by the bivouac she wrapped herself in her blanket and slept upon the ground with all the hardihood of the veteran soldier, yet thus sharing all the exposures and hardships of the common soldier with whom she freely mingled. She always maintained the modest reserve and delicacy of the true lady. The soldiers held her in the highest esteem, not one of whom but would have periled his life in her defense. She was presented with the Kearney Cross of the Legion of Honor by General Birney himself, in recognition of her noble services and bravery.

All this service was performed without any pay from any source whatever. Many of the heroines of history, whose names have been celebrated in song and story, at most performed a few deeds of daring and sacrifice; but this heroine has a record of four years of daring, suffering and self-sacrifice displayed on more than a score of battlefields, of the highest qualities of exalted courage. She remained with the Second Regiment until it was ordered to the Western Department, but she remained and became attached to the headquarters of the Third Brigade, First Division, Third Corps, until the death of its lamented commander, General Berry, at Chancellorsville, May 3, 1863. She then joined her fortunes to the Third Michigan Infantry, remaining until the consolidation of that regiment with the Fifth Michigan and with the consolidated organization until the final muster out at Detroit, July 1, 1865.

It would require a large book to record her experiences in the battles in which she was on the field amidst the shot and shell but she seemed to carry a talisman that insured her life. Does it not prove that truth is stranger than fiction?

The official records state that Anna Etheridge has been with the Third and Fifth Regiments, Michigan Veteran Volunteers Infantry.

* * * *

A Quote From Mrs. F. T. Hazen.

After one of the numerous skirmishes, Annie was missed. The boys who loved her so well, immediately reported to Sheridan that Annie must have been taken prisoner. Sheridan answered, "No, I do not think so, she must be attending to our wounded;" but immediately mounted his horse and rode as near the enemy's lines as possible; using his field-glasses he discovered Annie in their camp.

He rode back to the boys and, pointing in the direction from which he had come, said, "Boys, Annie is there." Without further command or order there was a general rush to the rescue. A triumphant rescue it was, for they returned not only with Annie, but the boys who had been taken prisoners with her.

Delia Bartlett Fay

Mrs. Delia Bartlett Fay was one more of the noble women who gave service in our country's need on battlefields, in hospitals, and the Christian Commission work. She volunteered her services to the 118th Regiment, New York State Volunteers. Her husband, Willie Fay, enlisted in Company C of this regiment. They proceeded at once to Plattsburg and were stationed at the old stone barracks, to await further orders. Their first move from there was to Fort Ethan Allen, near Washington, the object being to strengthen the defense of the National capital; there the regiment remained until 1863. The camp was called Camp Adirondack, as the men of the regiment were largely from the Adirondack region. The regiment did duty at all Government buildings; the men also did camp and picket duty.

From this place the regiment was ordered to Suffolk, where they engaged in their first action. Mrs. Fay was present at this siege, which lasted several days. Many a poor victim of shot and shell breathed his last under the tender care of this noble, self-sacrificing woman, sometimes just where they had fallen. She knew no fear of the rebel fire when her services were needed to hold up the fainting, battle-scarred hero. Many were the tender messages intrusted to her keeping for delivery to loved ones at home. After the siege at Suffolk the regiment was ordered to Yorktown, and were kept on the move for the purpose of surprising the enemy and to attack them from unexpected sources.

About last of June the regiment was again ordered to Suffolk, where the 115th and two companies of the 99th regiment had an engagement with the rebels in which a large number were made prisoners. During all the marches Mrs. Fay shared the lot of the soldier, marching the same number of miles, carrying her load at all times, and sometimes the load of some sick boy, who would have been compelled to drop out by the wayside but for friendly aid; and as soon as camp was struck she would go about preparation of sick diets, to tempt the appetite of the sick and wounded.

Mrs. Fay had great influence with the colored people. She obtained abundance of stores, which would have been beyond the reach of any other one of the regiment. It can be said of Mrs. Fay that her cheerfulness and heroism under all trying conditions gave life and animation to the homesick and weary ones. She was on one occasion detailed to go on a scouting expedition to locate the rebel forces. She was very successful, and reported her information to the satisfaction of her captain.

While the regiment was at Camp Barnes, near the city of Norfolk, they encountered a staunch rebel,—Doctor Wright. He had repeatedly avowed that if he ever saw a white man drilling the negroes he would shoot him on the spot. One day when he was on his way from his house to his office, he saw his man. A lieutenant had been detailed to drill a company of negroes. The old doctor retraced his steps to his house and procured his revolver. His daughter asked what he was going to do. He explained in a few words. The daughter said: "That is right, father; shoot the dirty Yankee. They dare not do anything to you." He proceeded again to where he had seen the lieutenant, and deliberately shot him dead. Doctor Wright did not escape; he was captured not ten paces from where he fired the fatal shot, was tried by court-marshal, and sentenced to be hung in six days. While in prison a very clever piece of strategy was concocted by his daughter, which nearly resulted in his escape. The daughter visited the prison every day, always wearing a large bonnet, closely veiled.

One day when she came out from his cell the guard thought he detected a change in her appearance. She had passed the first guard; here were two more to pass before she could be free. She had nearly reached the second when the first guard rushed up behind her and divested her of her bonnet and veil; the action exposed to view the doctor's face. After all hope of escape was abandoned, the daughter was married in the cell of her father the day preceding the execution. The next day he was led to the scaffold, the noose placed about his neck, then asked if he had anything to say. He said he had not, only that he did not regret what he had done, and would do it again under the circumstances.

Throughout the three years of her service, Mrs. Fay did her part as only a true and kind nature can do; and after the fall of Richmond, she, with her husband, journeyed homeward in the same steamer that they went to service in three years before.

Amanda Felch

AMANDA M. COLBORN WAS BORN in West Glover, Vermont, November 12, 1833. Her father was a farmer in moderate circumstances, and having only one boy, a share in the outdoor work was often given to Amanda. This early training proved of inestimable value to her, when a large reserve of physical strength was so necessary to enable her to endure, with comparative ease, the long marches where hundreds of men were overcome, during the Peninsular, Gettysburg, and other campaigns. At twenty-three years she was married, and it was as Mrs. Farnham that she became well known in the Army of the Potomac.

In the summer of 1861, left alone with her little boy and in poor health, she returned to the old home to find the family in great trouble. Henry, her brother, had enlisted in the 3d Vermont Regiment, thereupon she left her child with her parents, and followed her brother; partly to relieve the great anxiety respecting the only son, partly from a desire to help in the struggle just at hand. Enlisting at Saint Johnsbury, about July 5, 1861, she was enrolled as a member of the 3d Vermont Regiment, and appointed hospital matron.

They were mustered in July 11th, left the State on the 23d, arrived in Washington the 26th, and the next day went six miles up the river to Camp Lyon, near Chain Bridge, on the Maryland side of the river. About this time something occurred that later became a theme for romance and poetry. Willie Scott, a private in Company K, 3d Vermont, was found sleeping at his post, tried, found guilty, and condemned to be executed, but at almost the last moment was pardoned by President Lincoln. Mrs. Farnham had known the boy from a child, and took a deep interest in his case. Seven months later at Lee's Mills, on the Peninsula, when he was shot, she assisted at his burial.

During the fall and winter, sickness and death from disease assumed such alarming proportions that a special corps of noted physicians was sent to advise and aid the medical officers now in the field; but the mortality was not checked until spring. During this period Mrs. Farnham worked almost constantly.

In December 1861, she was dropped from the rolls as matron of the 3d, for the Government would no longer recognize the position; but she still continued her work, and until the Wilderness campaign in 1864, occupied a different position than most female army nurses, as she did not do regular ward duty, but went from one regiment to another, wherever she was most needed. Day or night it made no difference, she always responded to the call, and would stay until the crisis was passed, or death had relieved the patient of his suffering.

It was to the boys, like her brother, that her heart went out with greatest sympathy. Writing letters for such was a daily practice, and when there was no hope she would record the dying request and take care of some keepsake to be sent to friends at home. Before a battle it became a common thing for soldiers, especially of the Vermont troops, to intrust her with money or other valuables for safe-keeping until an event occurred after which she dared no longer accept the responsibility. During the battle of Chancellorsville she had an unusual amount of money, which she carried in a belt on her person, and other things of value in a hand bag. After getting into quarters on our side of the river she put up a tent, as it was raining, and, for the first time in several nights, took off the belt and put it with the bag on the ground under the mattress. Probably this was all seen in her shadow on the tent-cloth, by some one watching for that purpose. She had just fallen asleep when she became conscious that some one was trying to get in; but the flap strings had been drawn inside and tied tightly around the pole, so that plan was abandoned, and the robber passed around the tent. Fully aroused, Mrs. Farnham now crept from the blankets, and finding her revolver, awaited results. Her first thought was to give an alarm, but she knew that the thief could easily escape in the darkness and return later. As no entrance could be found, he cut a long slit in the tent, to reach through. Up to the time that the knife began its work she had not realized how serious was her situation; she hesitated no longer, but, aiming as well as she could in the darkness, fired. An exclamation and the sound of hurried footsteps was all she heard. The next morning news came that one of the new recruits was sick, having been wounded by the "accidental discharge of a pistol in the hands of a chum," and she did not ask to have the case investigated.

In March 1862, the command went to Fortress Monroe to enter upon the campaign of the Peninsula, through which she marched with the troops, shared their hardships and fare, and was actually on the field at Lee's Mills, Williamsburg, Golding's Farm, Savage Station, Glendale, and Malvern Hill, and in the "seven days" retreat from Richmond, back to Harrison's Landing, where they remained till sent to Washington, in August. She not only walked in the rain from Malvern Hill to Harrison's Landing, through mud knee-deep, but also helped soldiers by the way. In August she went home with some sick and wounded soldiers, and did not return until the battle of Antietam. Arriving at Washington on Sunday the 14th, and finding where the army was supposed to be, she tried to get a pass to the front that day, but failed. The next morning she went to Secretary Stanton herself, and received not only her pass, but also an order for an ambulance. She arrived at Antietam the afternoon of the 17th, and immediately went to work among the wounded of French's Division, there performing her first and only surgical operation. A soldier had been struck in the right breast by a partly spent ball, but with force enough to follow around the body under the skin, stopping just below the shoulder blade. Taking the only implement she had, a pair of sharp button-hole scissors, and pinching the ball up with the thumb and finger, she made a slight incision and pressed the ball out.

It was shortly after this, while at Hagerstown, that she met Mr. and Mrs. Baxter, and promised to do all she could to see that the supplies they sent were given to the most needy. The command remained here until the latter part of October 1862, then started for "on to Richmond" for the third time. December 13th came Fredericksburg, with all its horrors; the Vermonters suffering severely, and Mrs. Farnham, who was stationed at the Bernard House, worked with the wounded without rest until getting back to the old camps at White Oak Church, where the winter passed very pleasantly.

In May 1863, the campaign opened at Chancellorsville, and the brigade lost nearly three hundred in killed and wounded,—Mrs. Farnham doing her usual efficient work. The army had to retreat to its old camps, to remain until the march to Gettysburg. When there, through the influence of Mrs. Baxter, she was permitted to keep a two-horse team, to take along supplies on the march. When in camp the boys could usually procure for themselves what they needed, but on the march they often suffered severely. Such articles as shirts, socks, etc., coffee, sugar, condensed milk and canned goods, she carried, and gave where most needed.

It was a weary march from the Rappahannock to Gettysburg, made more so by the night marches, always so trying. The last day they went thirty-four miles over a stone road, and under a burning sun. It is now simply a matter of history that the Sixth Corps marched from Manchester to Gettysburg from daylight until 4 o'clock P.M., and it was the greatest feat in marching ever accomplished by any troops under like conditions. Mrs. Farnham went with them, and most of the way on foot, giving up the spare room on her wagon to worn-out soldiers who could not find room in the crowded ambulances. A ride for an hour for one, and he could walk on again for a time, giving his place to another. Thus many more were able to keep along than would have been without such help. When she found a poor fellow with blistered feet, she gave him a pair of new socks to take the place of the holes, all that was left of his own. The story of her work all night after such a day, has been told many times: how a guard was placed over a certain pump at the request of the ladies of the house, as they feared the well would go dry, and they be obliged to go to Rock Creek, a quarter of a mile distant, for water,—little caring how far the exhausted soldiers had to go. Some of the boys, knowing Mrs. Farnham was near, got her to pump for them; and when complaint was made the guard said his orders did not include women, so she could get all the water she wanted. In this work, and caring for the wounded of Sickles Corps, who filled all the barns and outbuildings on the place, she remained all night long.

Few of the Sixth Corps were wounded at Gettysburg, but she was busy among others, until the division left there. In following up Lee, and at Funkstown, the Vermont Brigade suffered severely. Among those killed was an old acquaintance, and she obtained permission to take his body and two others home. She was absent two weeks, joining the army near Warrenton. From that time until Grant was preparing to make the final move against Richmond, she was quietly occupied with regular duties, and until May expected to go to the front with the troops as before; but Stanton ordered that "no women, no matter who they are," should be allowed in the army longer. A petition praying that she might go was presented but he was obdurate, writing on the back, "Mrs. Farnham's request has the highest recommendations, but is incompatible with the public service." So ended all her preparations of the winter for the summer's campaign. Hardly three days of grace remained in which to dispose of her team and other personal property so it was at great personal loss that she left the army about the 1st of May 1864. She was in Fredericksburg on the 9th, where twenty thousand Union troops were lying; and for about the first time, she was a regular army nurse, appointed by Miss D. L. Dix. She remained until discharged in June 1865.

She used to like to tell of her first interview with Miss Dix. From the time she entered the army, Mrs. Farnham had worn a dress similar to the ladies' cycling costume of the present,—full pants buttoning over the tops of her boots, skirts falling a little below the knee, and a jacket with tight sleeves. This dress she had on when she called to present her papers and request. Miss Dix glanced at the papers then looked Mrs. Farnham over from head to foot until the situation was becoming embarrassing. Finally she arose, saying: "Mrs. Farnham, the dress you wear is abominable, a most abominable dress, and I do not wish any of my nurses to dress in that manner; but you came highly recommended, and I have long known of your work, but I didn't know you wore such a dress. However, you can wear it if you choose." Then she wrote an order for her to report at Fredericksburg. From that time until after the war closed, she was one of Miss Dix's trusted nurses, and was charged with duties and commissions at the front that she would trust to no one else; and though they met many times when Mrs. Farnham wore the same dress, it was not mentioned again.

Elida Fowle

Of all the women who devoted themselves to the soldiers in our late Rebellion, perhaps none had a more varied experience than Elida B. Rumsey, a girl so young that Miss Dix would not receive her as a nurse; a fact for which hundreds had reason to be grateful.

Undaunted by seeming difficulties, she persisted in "doing the next thing," and so fulfilled her great desire to do something for the Union soldiers. Yet it was not to these alone that her kindly ministrations extended; for wherever she saw a soldier in need her ready sympathies were enlisted, little caring if the heartbeats stirred a coat of blue or gray.

Miss Rumsey was born in New York City, June 6, 1842. Upon the removal of her parents to Washington, where the "Secesh" element was strong in '61, her patriotic spirit was so enthused that she determined to help in some way; and relying upon her own resources, she entered upon a career that gave her an almost national reputation, and endeared her to thousands of hearts.

She was engaged to John A. Fowle of Jamaica Plain, Massachusetts, who was employed in the Navy Department, at Washington, but devoted all his spare time to philanthropic enterprises—and their work was supplementary from the first. In November '61 she began to visit the hospitals and sing to the soldiers, who found relief and courage in the tones of her strongly sympathetic voice, and watched eagerly for the young, vivacious face that almost daily appeared in the wards, always bringing sunshine and leaving renewed hope. It was the knowledge of how little the boys had to look forward to from day to day, while all the time under such depressing influences, that first inspired the thought of supplying them with pictures and books. Then, too, much stern condemnation was passed upon the convalescents for playing cards and telling idle stories, and Miss Rumsey believed a better way would be to displace evil by good.

The "Soldiers' Rest" was a name very inappropriately given to a place near the Baltimore & Ohio depots where prisoners were exchanged, or sometimes stayed over night when they had no where else to go. Miss Rumsey had a strong desire to see what kind of men had been in Libby Prison, and when the first lot had been exchanged she went down to see them off as they were going home on a furlough. They looked utterly disheartened and demoralized by disaster and suffering; and their enthusiasm was all gone.

Some one recognized the young lady, and called for a song. To gain attention and give her a moment's preparation, Mr. Fowle stepped to her side and said, "Boys, how would you like a song?" "Oh, very well, I guess," came the reply in spiritless tones. She sang the "Red, White, and Blue." Soon they crowded around her with more interest than they had yet shown since leaving prison; but comparatively few could see her. At the close of the song they called for another, and a pile of knapsacks was thrown on the ground.

Standing on this rude rostrum she sang "The Star-Spangled Banner." Her natural enthusiasm was intensified by the surroundings, and the desire to inspire the boys with the courage they had all but lost. Her voice was full of power, and her whole attitude instinct with patriotism, as she brought her foot down on the imaginary rebel flags (words written by Mr. Fowle on the first captured "rebel flags," then on exhibition in the rotunda in the Capitol),when, raising her eyes, she met those of a Southern officer in a pen just beyond, waiting to be transferred. It was but a momentary interchange of unspoken thought, but a moment surcharged with deep, sympathetic feeling on the part of each; and the impression could not be lightly forgotten. In less time than it takes to tell it, that strange experience was over. Our boys, now restored to their former earnestness, rent the air with cheer after cheer.

From this time her voice, hitherto used only for the enjoyment of her friends, was devoted to her country.

One of the first things definitely accomplished was the establishment of a Sunday evening prayer meeting in Columbia College Hospital, in an upper room in Auntie Pomroy's ward. That room was crowded night after night, and overflow meetings were held in a grove near by. The interest steadily increased, the boys often doing double duty in order to be present, and they were continued as long as it was safe; but the enthusiasm of the soldiers could not be repressed when Miss Rumsey's sweet voice stirred their souls and rekindled the noble, self-sacrificing spirit that had brought them to such a place, and cheers shook the very walls. The soldiers planned what they wanted her to sing from week to week. She threw into the songs all her great desire to bring the boys back to their better selves, and help them to feel that they were not forgotten nor alone.

All this time her plans had been assuming outward form. Now, having received a grant of land from Government, a building was erected, and the "Soldiers' Free Library" founded; Mrs. Walter Baker giving the first hundred dollars and the greater part of the remainder was earned by Miss Rumsey and Mr. Fowle giving concerts, at two of which they had the Marine Band, by order of the President. As far as known, this was the first library ever founded by a woman, and that by a mere girl scarcely eighteen years old. Perhaps no better idea of the institution can be given than by an article from one of the newspapers soon after the new building was occupied.

"Fast Day I took a walk to the Soldiers' Free Library and Reading Room; and, Messrs. Editors, if I ever felt proud of being an old Massachusetts man, my pride had no fall today. Six months ago Miss Elida Rumsey, whose sweet voice has so often been heard in the Choir of Representatives' Hall, conceived the idea of establishing a free library for the soldiers. For this purpose she gave several concerts, the avails from which were devoted to the erection of a plain one-story building 65 x 24 feet, at a cost of about one thousand dollars. The use of the land, on Judiciary Square, was donated by Congress.

"The reading-room is modestly fitted up with seats which will accommodate two hundred and fifty persons. It has a melodeon, on which soldiers practice at will, though every Wednesday evening regular instruction is given in music and singing by Mr. and Mrs. Fowle, and religious services are conducted by the chaplain twice each Sunday. I may as well state here that Miss Rumsey was married a short time since to Mr. John A. Fowle, of the Navy Department, formerly from Jamaica Plain, Massachusetts. He is thoroughly devoted, heart and soul, to the sufferers of the war.

"About fifty different papers are sent regularly by publishers, free of charge. Boxes of books are daily arriving for the library, which already exceeds three thousand volumes. One box from Jamaica Plain came while I was there,—a donation from a Sunday school, comprising many of the new works of the day. The reading-room is open all day, and the library four hours each day. Secretary Stanton has detailed a convalescent soldier who is always on duty to keep the room in order, deliver books, etc.

"One room is devoted to storage of medicine, delicacies, stationery, socks, shirts, etc., and is under the charge of Mrs. Fowle. Here the soldiers can procure Testaments (donated by the Massachusetts Bible Society), hymn books, pamphlets, newspapers, letter paper, envelopes, etc., all free of charge.

"One object interested me deeply,— a box from Dorchester containing one thousand small cotton bags, each filled with tea or ground coffee, with a few lumps of sugar, ready for immediate use. Every convalescent who leaves for camp has a few of those packages placed in his knapsack by Mrs. Fowle."

Having spoken of Miss Rumsey's marriage, we add another sketch, also taken from a paper at that time.

"Mr. and Mrs. Fowle first met in the reception room at the House of Representatives. Today, March 1, 1863, after the conclusion of Doctor Stockton's remarks, a scene never before witnessed in the halls of Congress took place, in the form of a marriage ceremony; the parties being Mr. John A. Fowle and Miss Elida B. Rumsey.

"Mr. Fowle is from Boston, Massachusetts, but at present a clerk in the Navy Department. He is known as connected with movements for the aid of soldiers in the hospitals, and for the establishment of a free library for the soldiers. Miss Rumsey is from New York, her father at present residing in this city. She also has given much attention to the patients in military hospitals. During the present Congress she and

Mr. Fowle have in part composed the Choir of the House. For this cause it is said that certain Senators and Representatives desired that the marriage should take place in the Representatives' Hall. A good deal of publicity had been given the affair, and the floor and galleries were packed. About four thousand people were present. The marriage ceremony was performed according to the rites of the Episcopal Church, by Rev. Mr. Quint, pastor of the church which Mr. Fowle attended in Jamaica Plain, and now chaplain of the Second Massachusetts Regiment.

"The bride was dressed in a plain drab poplin, with linen collar and cuffs, and wore a bonnet of the same color, ornamented with red, white, and blue flowers. A bow of red, white, and blue ribbon was fastened upon her breast.

"After the ceremony had been completed and the benediction pronounced, the couple were receiving congratulations, when a soldier in the gallery shouted, 'Won't the bride sing the "Star Spangled Banner?"' and she did, then and there, in her bridal dress, with never more of fervor in her beautiful voice."

President Lincoln had intended to be present, but at the last moment he was detained; but with "Auntie Pomroy," in his carriage, he sent a magnificent basket of flowers. The city gardener, Mr. Nokes, also sent a basket; and these, with the following note, "Accept as a slight testimonial this check of one hundred dollars from the door-keeper and assistant, Mrs. Ira Goodnoe," were all the presents or payment she ever received for her services. On their return from their bridal trip, the soldiers of Columbia Hospital requested the privilege of reversing the order, and giving a concert themselves to the newly married couple. When the company were assembled, six pieces of plate were presented to the bride and groom; a present from the officers, nurses, and soldiers. But knowing that she would never accept a sacrifice from those for whom she was laboring, no soldier was allowed to give more than twenty-five cents.

Also a large Bible from the soldiers of Judiciary Hospital.

Mrs. Fowle has an almost inexhaustible supply of racy anecdotes and pathetic stories that she knows so well how and when to tell. She has, also, a collection of army relics, among them one of the first rebel flags captured. On this flag she has stood many times while singing

"The Star Spangled Banner." Perfectly fearless in the face of thought-less criticism, she went on her errands of mercy for three years, doing anything that needed to be done. Mr. Fowle had established the mak-ing of crutches and canes for the soldiers, free of charge, and these were stored in one part of the library. Mrs. Fowle (then Miss Rumsey) would frequently go to the Navy Yard after them with her ambulance, and ride back perched on the top of the load.

Knowing that there would be urgent need, and fearful suffering, she determined to go to the second battle of Bull Run. Taking a load of supplies and some four hundred loaves of bread, she and Mr. Fowle started in the ambulance. Having no Government pass it was a hazard-ous undertaking and she experienced some difficulty had getting through the lines. The last guard peremptorily refused to let her go any farther; when, springing from the ambulance, she fell on her knees before him and begged her way through. Thus while Miss Dix and her faithful nurses were detained three miles away, she was inside the lines and ready for action. When almost on the battlefield they came to a little negro cabin, and resolved to use it for a hospital. It was a tiny af-fair, but on opening the door they found that it was already occupied. A terrified crowd of negroes had sought shelter there. Almost wild with fear, they could scarcely obey the order "Be off," but were soon on their way to Washington. Their preparations had not been made any too quickly, for now the wounded men began to arrive.

The little cabin would hold about fifty, and as Mr. Fowle did what he could for one, he was removed, and another took his place. When the stores had all been distributed, Mrs. Fowle determined to go in and help care for the wounded. Just as she stepped inside she glanced down. The floor was completely hidden with blood. She covered her face with her hands and turned away, overpowered for a moment by the thought of walking through that warm human blood. Then came a strong reaction; then no fear of shrinking from duty: she firmly en-tered, and helped to bind up those fearful wounds until the close of that famous Sunday night when the army retreated.

Only two men died during the day that they cared for,—one whose name and regiment were unknown and the other from New York. But though death was not common, there were other scenes as fearful. Once as she was washing the wounds in a pail of water thick with blood, some soldiers begged for it to drink: the water they used had to be carried over two miles.

Mrs. Fowle carries a scar on her face,— a relic of war times,—and its story defines her whole attitude during the Rebellion: a large carbuncle, the result of blood-poisoning, while washing wounds on the battlefield. At last the doctors said it must be lanced. Having a horror of a knife, and with nerves already quivering from the sights around her, she did not feel equal to the ordeal. Still knowing it must be done, she said, "Let me go over to the Judiciary Hospital and see the boys who have had their legs and arms amputated, and I can bear it." A chair was placed in one end of the ward, and calmly seating herself after looking for a moment at the long rows of cots, she told the surgeon to go on.

These scenes have been selected at random from among the everyday experiences of her three years' service. In closing, I will again quote from a newspaper of that period.

"At the Patent Office Hospital last May a soldier lay on his dying bed; he was a mere boy, only seventeen years of age, from the State of New York. Typhoid fever had brought him low, and then consumption marked him for its victim, and day by day he wasted, growing weaker and weaker, until at last he could only whisper. The dear little fellow was conscious he was about to die, and was prepared to go. A young lady of this city, who spends all her time in labors of love for the sick and wounded soldiers, took a special interest in his case, and at the twilight hour she would often visit him, and at his request her sweet voice would be heard at his bedside, singing to him of "Jesus" or "Heaven."

"One evening just as the sun had set she found him failing rapidly; he wanted to hear a hymn, and whispered, 'Sing, "Nearer Home."' It was a favorite, beginning thus,—

One sweetly solemn thought
Comes to me o'er and o'er.

and Tommy liked to hear it set to the sweet tune of 'Dennis.' Under such touching circumstances it was difficult to sing; the tears must flow, and the utterance be choked; but the lady tried, and there, surrounded by a little band of his soldier friends, and faithful nurse, Miss Lawrence, of Albany, New York, she sang the first, second, and third verses,—then stopped, for a great change was taking place in Tommy;

he was dying; he was 'going home,'—was leaving 'his cross of heavy grief, to wear a starry crown.' 'Twas a scene that all present will never forget.

"Some weeks later the hospital was closed, and opened again in September. A few Sabbaths ago the same lady, standing where the soldier died, sang, by request, a little ballad composed by Mr. Fowle in memory of Tommy Reese. A large audience heard it, and not a dry eye could be seen."

THE DYING SOLDIER BOY
Tune, Annie Laurie.
By John A. Fowle

Sing me a song before I go, said the dear and dying boy:
"Me Nearer Home" is the one I love; Oh, sing of heavenly joy!
Sing, for I'm going home, over the crystal sea;
I'm going to join the angel throngs, and spend eternity.

With faint and trembling voice we sang, of laying my burden down;
We sang the sweet, sweet words, wearing my starry crown.
And then the soldier smiled, as his spirit soared above:
He left his cross of heavy grief, to spend a life of love.

Brave boy, we mourn your fate, your life was nobly given;
Far from home, and far from friends, you gave up earth for heaven.
No stone may mark the spot, where our soldier boy is laid,
But in our hearts he has a place,—A spot in memory made.

Our country mourns for heroes brave, who died to save our land;
Our hearts,—how oft they bleed, for many a noble band.
But at their hallowed graves, we all shall Pilgrims be;
We'll shed a tear for those who've died for Right and Liberty.

Mrs. Fowle resides at 337 Boston Street, Dorchester, Massachusetts.

Emma French-Sackett

Having a desire to minister to the needs of our suffering soldiers, I went from Denmark, Iowa, to Chicago in company with Mrs. Colton and reported to Mrs. Livermore, not knowing whether we should be sent to the front amid the battlefields, or where our lot would be cast. February 1, 1864, we were sent to Jeffersonville General Hospital, where I was assigned to Ward 18, which was crowded with sick and wounded, so there was no lack of work to do. And although sad the office we performed, our hearts were filled with pleasure in the work we were doing. It was ours to minister to the wants of mind and body; and when the poor soldier boy had breathed his last, to write to his parents, wife or sister, telling of his last hours, and giving the messages for loved ones at home. And as we folded the letter enclosing a lock of the dear one's hair, we prayed that the white-winged messenger might break the news gently. In this way an interesting correspondence has been continued with those whom I have never seen, as they cling to every item, and long for more incidents of their dead.

I remember one boy, only fifteen years of age, who had his arm amputated. Gangrene set in, and he had to endure another amputation; then death relieved him of his suffering. Poor boy! You little knew what was in store for you when you enlisted. And poor mother! Your fondest hopes were blasted. Another brave soldier from Minnesota had left one leg on the battlefield, and lay upon his cot day after day, mourning for home and loved ones, until his life went out. A pale-faced lad, shot through one lung, lay 'twixt life and death for a long time, then rallied, and the last I knew he was still alive.

One day a letter was brought to our ward for a former patient, who had been transferred to the gangrene ward. I carried it to him, and when his name was called he responded with uplifted hand, while the tears ran down his cheeks, so glad was he to get a word from home. How bitter was the disappointment of a sister who came to the hospital to see her brother, only to learn that he had been transferred to Cincinnati, and that she must continue her search.

So one after another these incidents crowd upon the memory. Sad were the scenes when friends came to see their loved ones, to find that those they were seeking had been buried a few days before. On the morning of the 15th of April, when we beheld the stars and stripes at half-mast, and the words "Lincoln is dead," passed from lip to lip, all was hushed. The stillness of death prevailed, and we questioned, "What next?" for it seemed a terrible crisis. A few of the boys made disloyal remarks and the guardhouse was the penalty.

As the war neared its close, colored men were brought to do guard duty, and we held a freedman's school for a few hours each day in a chapel near. So eager were they to learn, that it was a pleasure to teach them.

Our last work was filling out discharge papers for the soldiers, who were eager to get home, now that the war was over; and therefore when they were given that work, soon hunted up their own papers and were at liberty, leaving Uncle Sam to find new clerks, which he did among the army nurses.

Our services were appreciated by those among whom we labored, as testimonials held by more than one of my colaborers would prove. One day upon entering my ward I was halted, but instead of being confronted by sword or bayonet, a purse was put into my hand, accompanied by a nicely-worded address, as a token of the regard and gratitude of my patients. The original address is treasured among my keepsakes. I was always treated with respect and kindness while in the service, and those to whom I ministered seemed to me more like brothers than strangers.

I went by the authority of Miss Dix, and served under Miss Buckel for nearly eight months, then received my discharge September 23, 1865, and returned to my Iowa home, having no regrets that I had been an army nurse.

Yours In F., C. And L.,
Mrs. Emma French—Sackett
MIDDLE RIVER, IOWA

Alice Frush

WHEN THE WAR BROKE OUT I was living in a little
town called Greencastle, about eleven miles from Chambersburg,
Pennsylvania. My father was a great Union man, and threw our house
open as headquarters for the officers. The generals quartered there
were Dana, Smith, and Fitzhugh, and they had their staffs. We did all
we could for the comfort of the soldiers, and when the call came for
nurses, I was one to volunteer. I served three years; first in the hospital
at Hagerstown, Maryland, then at Greencastle. I left to become the
wife of Sgt. M. L. Frush, of Company B, 6th Virginia Cavalry.

During my hospital service I was on the battlefields of Antietam
and Gettysburg, after the fight, helping the wounded and caring for
the dying. Many of the injured men were carried to our little town of
Greencastle, and we sisters did what we could for them, picking lint,
knitting stockings, etc. I was then Mary Alice Smith, and but eighteen
years of age.

I served under Gen. David Detrich, in Greencastle, but do not remember who was surgeon in charge at Hagerstown. When I was not
engaged in the hospitals I was out with an ambulance, gathering provisions for the soldiers. My father had a large warehouse, and we fed
them there.

Upon my marriage, in December, 1864, I left the service, but was
not discharged, so I have no papers.

One little incident in closing. When Lee's army passed through Greencastle, *en route* for Gettysburg, my sister Sadie and I waved the American flag in front of them and were heartily cheered by the "boys in gray."

Yours in F., C. and L.,
M. Alice Frush
222 SCOTT STREET
YOUNGSTOWN, OHIO

Elizabeth Gibson

ON THE FIRST DAY OF OCTOBER 1861, I received orders from Washington, through Miss Dorothea Dix, to report for duty at Saint Louis, immediately. Upon my arrival I was detailed to duty, October 2d, in the surgical ward of Fifth Street Military Hospital, Saint Louis, where I served, under Dr. John T. Hodgen, twenty-one months. Then patients and nurses were removed to Jefferson Barracks, Missouri, twelve miles down the river. Dr. John F. Randolph, of the regular army, was in charge there. My detail of service to that hospital was dated July 24, 1863. October 26th I received orders to report for duty at Harvey General Hospital, Madison, Wisconsin, and October 13, 1865, received my discharge from hospital service, and returned to Cincinnati; my discharge being signed by Dr. Howard Culbertson, who was in charge at the Harvey Hospital.

To write a sketch of that four years would require more space than you could give but I must say this: I count it a high honor to have been an army nurse, and a great privilege to have ministered to the noble men of the volunteer army. I was also especially blessed in having for head surgeons such noble men as Doctor Hodgen and Doctor Culbertson. Both lives were shortened by their devotion to suffering humanity.

Mary A. Livermore spent a part of one day in the surgical ward of the Fifth Street Hospital, and has given a vivid description of the sufferings of the men who were wounded at Fort Donelson. She has also told how she finally nerved herself to endure the horrible sights and sounds, and so be enabled to alleviate the suffering; and her experience was that of hundreds of sensitive women who entered the hospitals during the war. In this ward that she describes, I was on duty forty-two nights in succession, and at any time afterwards when critical cases needed a woman's watchfulness.

In the four years of service I fainted only once, but many and many a night I have thought I could not live until morning, so intense was my sympathy with the soldiers; and not until I join the "silent majority" shall I be free from bodily suffering caused by my war experiences.

I was allowed to go to the battlefield of Shiloh, because I could dress wounds; also to Vicksburg during the siege. From Shiloh our boat took four hundred and thirty-nine men. They were the last on the field, and many of them were mortally wounded. From Vicksburg the boat carried less than from Shiloh, but on the return trip we had the experience of being fired upon by the rebels. The gunboat that was guarding us soon scattered them, however, and we were not molested again.

Yours in F., C. and L.,
Elizabeth O. Gibson
849 APPLETON STREET
APPLETON, WISCONSIN

Helen Gilson

HELEN L. GILSON OF CHELSEA, MASSACHUSETTS
had been for several years head assistant in the Phillips School in Boston, but ill health obliged her to leave it. She had been teaching the
children of Frank B. Fay, Mayor of Chelsea. On the breaking out of the
war she had an ardent desire to become an army nurse, but did not suc-
ceed until June 1862, when she took a position on one of the hospital
boats of the Sanitary Commission, just after the evacuation of
Yorktown. She continued on hospital boats between White House,
Fortress Monroe, Harrison Landing, and Washington. She reached the
field of Antietam, September 18, 1862, a few hours after the battle, and
remained there and at Pleasant Valley till the wounded had been gathered into general hospitals. In November and December 1862, she
worked in the camps and hospitals near Fredericksburg, at the time of
Burnside's campaign. In the spring of 1863 she was again at that point,
at the battle of Chancellorsville, and in the Potomac Creek Hospital.
When the army moved she joined it at Manassas; but finding that her
special diet supplies had been lost on the passage, she returned to
Washington and went on to Gettysburg, arriving a few hours after the
last day's fight. She worked here till the wounded had been sent to Base
Hospital. In October, November and December 1863, she worked in
the hospitals on Folly and Morris Islands, South Carolina, when General Gilmore was besieging Fort Sumter. Early in 1864 she joined the

army at Brandy Station, and in May went with the Auxiliary Corps of the Sanitary Commission to Fredericksburg, when the battle of the Wilderness was being fought. William Howell Reed, of Boston, who joined the Auxiliary Corps at this point, in his work "Hospital Life in the Army of the Potomac," thus describes the condition of things at Fredericksburg:—

"The buildings were rapidly appropriated by the medical director as temporary hospitals, including public edifices, private dwellings, storehouses, sheds, and churches. But the wounded were arriving in such numbers that many were laid on the streets and sidewalks to wait for shelter, five hundred in one train being laid out in the open field. One of the buildings taken was the Marie Mansion."

It was here he first met Miss Gilson:—

"One afternoon just before the evacuation, when the atmosphere of our rooms was close and foul, and all were longing for a breath of our cooler Northern air, while the men were moaning in pain or were restless with fever, and our hearts were sick with pity for the sufferers, I heard a light step upon the stairs; and looking up I saw a young lady enter, who brought with her such an atmosphere of calm and cheerful courage, so much freshness, such an expression of gentle, womanly sympathy, that her mere presence seemed to revive the drooping spirits of the men, and to give a new power of endurance through the long and painful hours of suffering. First with one, then at the side of another, a friendly word here, a gentle nod and smile there, a tender sympathy with each prostrate sufferer, a sympathy which could read in his eyes his longing for home love, and for the presence of some absent one,—in those few minutes hers was indeed an angel ministry.

Before she left the room she sang to them,—first some stirring national melody, then some sweet or plaintive hymn, to strengthen the fainting heart,—and I remember how the notes penetrated to every part of the building. Soldiers with less severe wounds, from the rooms above, began to crawl out into the entries, and men from below crept up on their hands and knees, to catch every note, and to receive of the benediction of her presence—for such it was to them. Then she went away. I did not know who she was, but I was as much moved and melted as any soldier of them all. This is my first reminiscence of Helen L. Gilson."

It became necessary to evacuate the town, and the wounded were sent away. The steamer, with the last of the wounded and the members of the Auxiliary Corps, left just in season to escape the guerrillas, who came into the town. Mr. Reed says: "As the boat passed down the river the negroes, by instinct, came to the banks and begged, by every gesture of appeal, not to pass them by. At Port Royal they flocked in such numbers that a Government barge was appropriated to their use. A thousand were stowed upon her decks. They had an evening service of prayer and song and the members of the corps went on board to witness it.

When their song had ceased, Miss Gilson addressed them. She pictured the reality of freedom; told them what it meant, and what they would have to do. No longer would there be a master to deal out the peck of corn, no longer a mistress to care for the old people or the children. They were to work for themselves, provide for their own sick, and support their own infirm; but all this was to be done under new conditions. No overseer was to stand over them with the whip, for their new master was the necessity of earning their daily bread. Very soon new and higher motives would come; fresh encouragements, a nobler ambition, would grow into their new condition. Then in the simplest language she explained the difference between their former relations with the then master and their new relations with the Northern people, showing that labor here was voluntary, and that they could only expect to secure kind employers by faithfully doing all they had to do. Then, enforcing truthfulness, neatness, and economy, she said:—

"'You know that the Lord Jesus died and rose again for you. You love to sing His praise, and to draw near to Him in prayer. But remember that this is not all of religion. You must do right, as well as pray right. Your lives must be full of kind deeds toward each other, full of gentle and loving affections, full of unselfishness and truth: this is true piety. You must make Monday and Tuesday just as good and pure as Sunday is, remembering that God looks not only at your prayers and your emotions, but at the way you live, and speak, and act, every hour of your lives.'

"Then she sang this exquisite hymn by Whittier:—

O, praise an' t'anks,—de Lord he come
To set de people free; etc.

After working among the wounded at Cold Harbor the boat went on to City Point. Miss Gilson, with Mrs. General Barlow, at once went to the front of Petersburg, where the Second and Eighteenth Corps had been fighting. She returned to the Base Hospital at City Point, and remained several months.

Mr. Reed thus describes Miss Gilson's work at the Colored Hospital at this place:—

"Up to this time the colored troops had taken but a passive part in the campaign. They were now first brought into action in front of Petersburg, when the fighting was so desperately contested that thousands were left upon the field. The wounded were brought down rapidly to City Point, where a temporary hospital had been provided. It was, however, in no other sense a hospital, than that it was a depot for wounded men. There were defective management and chaotic confusion. The men were neglected, the hospital organization was imperfect, and the mortality was in consequence frightfully large. Their condition was horrible. The severity of the campaign in a malarious country had prostrated many with fevers, and typhoid, in its most malignant forms, was raging with increasing fatality.

"These stories of suffering reached Miss Gilson at a moment when the previous labors of the campaign had nearly exhausted her strength; but her duty seemed plain. There were no volunteers for the emergency, and she prepared to go. Her friends declared that she could not survive it; but replying that she could not die in a cause more sacred, she started out alone. A hospital had to be created. This required all the tact, finesse, and diplomacy of which a woman is capable. Official prejudice and professional pride had to be met and overcome. A new policy had to be introduced, and it had to be done without seeming to interfere. Her doctrine and practice always were, instant, silent, and cheerful obedience to medical and disciplinary orders, without any qualification whatever; and by this she overcame the natural sensitiveness of the medical authorities.

"A hospital kitchen had to be organized upon her method of special diet; nurses had to learn her way, and be educated to their duties; while cleanliness, order, system, had to be enforced in the daily routine. Moving quietly on with her work of renovation, she took the responsibility of all changes that became necessary; and such harmony prevailed in the camp that her policy was vindicated as time rolled on. The rate of mortality was lessened, and the hospital was soon considered the best in the department. This was accomplished by a tact and energy which sought no praise, but modestly veiled themselves behind the orders of officials. The management of her kitchen was like the ticking of a clock,—regular discipline, gentle firmness, and sweet-temper always. The diet for the men was changed three times a day; and it was her aim to cater as far as possible to the appetites of individual men. Her daily rounds in the wards brought her into personal intercourse with every patient, and she knew his special need. At one time nine hundred men were supplied from her kitchen."

"The nurses looked for Miss Gilson's word of praise, and labored for it; and she had only to suggest a variety in the decoration of the tents to stimulate a most honorable rivalry among them, which soon opened a wide field for displaying ingenuity and taste, so that not only was its standard the highest, but it was the most cheerfully picturesque hospital at City Point.

"This Colored Hospital service was one of those extraordinary tasks, out of the ordinary course of army hospital discipline, that none but a woman could execute. It required more than a man's power of endurance, for men fainted and fell under the burden. It required a woman's discernment, a woman's tenderness, a woman's delicacy and tact; it required such nerve and moral force, and such executive power, as are rarely united in any woman's character. The simple grace with which she moved about the hospital camps, the gentle dignity with which she ministered to the suffering about her, won all hearts. As she passed through the wards the men would follow her with their eyes, attracted by the grave sweetness of her manner; and when she stopped by some bedside, and laid her hand upon the forehead and smoothed the hair of a soldier, speaking some cheering, pleasant word, I have seen the tears gather in his eyes, and his lip quiver, as he tried to speak or to touch the fold of her dress, as if appealing to her to listen while he opened his heart about the mother, wife, or sister far away. I have seen her in her sober gray flannel gown, sitting motionless by the dim candlelight,—which was all our camp could afford,— with her eyes open and watchful, and her hands ever ready for all those endless wants of sickness at night, especially sickness that may be tended unto death, or unto the awful struggle between life and death, which it was the lot of nearly all of us at some time to keep watch over until the danger had gone by. And in sadder trials, when the life of a soldier whom she had watched and ministered to was trembling in the balance between earth and heaven, waiting for Him to make all things new, she has seemed, by some special grace of the Spirit, to reach the living Christ, and draw a blessing down as the shining way was opened to the tomb. And I have seen such looks of gratitude from weary eyes, now brightened by visions of heavenly glory, the last of many recognitions of her ministry. Absorbed in her work, unconscious of the spiritual beauty which invested her daily life,—whether in her kitchen, in the heat and overcrowding incident to the issues of a large special diet list, or sitting at the cot of some poor lonely soldier, whispering of the higher realities of another world,—she was always the same presence of grace and love, of peace and benediction. I have been with her in the wards where the men have craved some simple religious service,—the reading of Scripture, the repetition of a psalm, the singing of a hymn, or the offering of a prayer,—and invariably the men were melted to tears by the touching simplicity of her eloquence.

"These were the tokens of her ministry among the sickest men; but it was not here alone that her influence was felt in the hospital. Was there jealousy in the kitchen, her quick penetration detected the cause, and in her gentle way harmony was restored; was there profanity among the convalescents, her daily presence and kindly admonition or reproof, with an occasional glance which spoke her sorrow for such sin, were enough to check the evil; or was there hardship or discontent, the knowledge that she was sharing the discomfort too, was enough to compel patient endurance until a remedy could be provided. Through all the war, from the seven days' conflict upon the Peninsula, in those early July days of 1862, through the campaigns of Antietam and Fredericksburg, of Chancellorsville and Gettysburg, and after the conflicts of the Wilderness, and the fierce and undecided battles which were fought for the possession of Richmond and Petersburg, in 1864 and 1865, she labored steadfastly on until the end. Through scorching heat and pinching cold, in the tent or upon the open field, in the ambulance or on the saddle, through rain and snow, amid unseen perils of the enemy, under fire upon the field, or in the more insidious dangers

of contagion, she worked quietly on, doing her simple part with all
womanly tact and skill, until now the hospital dress is laid aside, and
she rests, with the sense of a noble work done, with the blessing and
prayers of hundreds whose sufferings she has relieved or whose lives
she has saved, being,

"In the great history of the land,
A noble type of good
Heroic womanhood."

From City Point she went to a hospital at Richmond after the
evacuation, and remained until June 1865.

During the following years, she spent some months in Richmond,
working among the colored and white schools, but with declining
health she returned to Massachusetts and died in April 1868, and was
buried in Woodlawn Cemetery, Chelsea. A beautiful monument with
an appropriate inscription was erected over her grave by the soldiers,
which is decorated each year by Grand Army Posts and Women's Relief Corps.

Nancy Gross

IN FEBRUARY 1890, Representative Seth L. Millikin, of Maine, introduced into Congress a bill granting a pension to Nancy M. Gross, of Bucksport, a nurse in the Second and Sixth Regiments. The bill was referred to the Committee on Invalids' Pensions. The evidence submitted was such that a most favorable report was given, and the bill passed without opposition, giving to the deserving lady a pension,—a help and comfort in her declining years. Mrs. Gross filed a large number of letters gladly written by the comrades who were familiar with her brave career.

The following is one of many—

"I would most respectfully call your attention to the fact that Mrs. Nancy M. Atwood-Gross went out with the Sixth Maine Regiment Volunteers as a nurse, and served in that capacity in the field and hospital, caring for our sick and wounded with untiring zeal, and participating in our long and weary marches by day and night, through the dark days of the Rebellion; often standing by the side of some dying comrade who gave his life for the country we so much love, blending her tears and prayers that those comrades be enrolled in the great army of which God is the supreme commander. Believing that this good woman's health was impaired by this arduous duty, and untiring energy and zeal to render assistance to her country in those days of bloodshed and hardship, we ask that the Government, now in the zenith of its prosperity, render her a compensation for her services from 1861 to 1863, believing her most deserving. Respectfully,

Louis P. Abbott
Late Co. E, 6th Maine Volunteers.
Now District Chief Engineer Boston Fire Department."

Mrs. Gross writes:—

I was born in Montville, Maine, in 1834, the daughter of John Verplast, a farmer.

When the war broke out I was a widow with one child, and living in Bangor, where I was earning my living as a seamstress. I had had considerable experience in nursing, and, with good health and strength, I felt it my duty to do what I could to help the Union cause by ministering to the sick and wounded. Accordingly I enlisted as a field nurse, under the name Nancy Atwood, and left Bangor for the front, under Colonel Knowles, in May 1861. The only other nurse in the regiment was a Mrs. McDonald, from a neighboring town,—Corinth, I think.

We were in Hancock's Corps and went into camp at Chain Bridge, Virginia, where I remained until after the first battle of Bull Run. During this time we were in close proximity to the rebels' line. Times without number the camp was thrown into confusion by skirmishes, and we were driven into the swamps. The weather was severe, and my tent was often flooded or blown away. There was much sickness in the regiment. The measles broke out, and I was continually employed among the afflicted.

At the first battle of Bull Run I had my first experience with wounded men. My brother was injured, and I was transferred to his regiment, the 2d Maine, and entered the field hospital at Fort Cochrane, on Gen. Robert Lee's farm, on Arlington Heights. Here great hardships were endured, many of the wounded from the battle of Bull Run having been brought there; and I worked almost day and night to lessen their sufferings. Mrs. Hartsun Crowell, of Bangor, Maine, was the only nurse besides myself in the hospital.

We were in this camp about five months, when the regiment advanced to Hall's Hill, where the winter was spent. Here, in addition to my duties as nurse, my trade as a seamstress came into play, and I repaired or made over hundreds of overcoats and blankets for the men. On the 14th of March 1862, the regiment was ordered to Alexandria, and I was transferred to the Seminary Hospital at Georgetown, D. C. Here I remained nearly a year; then my health began to fail, and I received an honorable discharge.

This is the story of the brave Maine woman, briefly and modestly told; but the boys who wore the blue can read volumes between the lines. Her address is

Nancy M. Gross
BUCKSPORT, MAINE

Margaret Hamilton

I WAS BORN IN ROCHESTER, NEW YORK, October 19, 1840, and being an only child I was well cared for, and knew very little of life's care until the death of my dear mother in 1857. After that I became very restless and unhappy; and as I had always been religiously inclined, I thought I should like to become a Sister of Charity, as I had been trained in their schools, and thought they did a great deal of good among the sick, the poor, and the orphans. I met with great opposition from my father, who could not bear the thought of giving me up to that life; but finally my pleadings won his consent and in 1860 I entered the Orphan Asylum, an aspirant for the Order of Sisters. This was a favor granted to my father, as a mark of respect, for he had been a good friend to the church and the asylum.

After three months' probation I was sent to the Mother House in Emmitsburg, Maryland where I remained six months under their instruction, learning their methods. Finding me qualified, they gave me the habit of the Order, and sent me to the Orphan Asylum in Albany, New York to teach a class.

Here I will state that one is not required to make final vows until she has been in the Order five years.

This was the autumn of 1861,—a critical time in the history of our country; when peaceful homes had to part with loved ones who went forth to battle, that the United States might live undivided, one great and glorious nation. Almost every letter from home brought news of this or that one of my relatives who had enlisted, and I began to regret that I was unable to do anything for the cause. But early in the spring of 1862, an order came from the Mother House for three other Sisters and myself to go to the Satterlee United States Military Hospital in West Philadelphia. I shall never forget the great feeling of true happiness I experienced when the order was made known to me; but I dared not let any one know how I felt, for fear they might not send me if I seemed too anxious to go, as that is a part of the discipline. However, I determined that if I was not sent I should leave the Order, and offer my services in the great struggle.

We went early in May 1862 and found a few other Sisters at the hospital; among them a niece of General Beauregard—a Miss Boulina from Louisiana. She was a student in the academy attached to the Mother House, and became infatuated with the Sisters; so she joined them, very much against the wishes of her family, who were far from being reconciled to her nursing Union soldiers. She herself did not relish it, and after working about eight weeks we suddenly missed her, and never learned what became of her.

We were appointed by Secretary Stanton. Dr. I. I. Hayes, the Arctic explorer, was the surgeon in charge assisted by Dr. James Williams and many others; among them Dr. John S. Billings, of medical fame, who at present resides in Georgetown, D. C. This hospital was built to accommodate five thousand patients, besides the corps of surgeons, nurses, etc., and was opened the 1st of May 1862.

I remember that we fared poorly for some time, as the commissary department had not been established; neither had we conveniences to work with. Doctor Hayes bought our first "rations," sending his regrets that we should have been inconvenienced in that respect.

A day or two later hundreds of our brave boys arrived from the Chickahominy Swamps. Dozens of them were already dead when taken from the ambulances, and many others were just breathing out their brave lives. The ward surgeons, medical cadets, and the commissary department arrived with them. Now began in earnest the work of real hospital life. The first week after the arrival of these wounded and fever-stricken boys, we had scarcely time to eat, rest, or sleep. Our corps of nurses was insufficient for the demand made on their time by the terrible sufferings of the sick and dying. Many of the Sisters were unable to endure the hardships of such a life, and were taken from us, so that our work was greatly increased. From constant standing and walking I soon was afflicted with blistered feet, from which I suffered greatly, but my services were unremitting. I shall never forget one of my next experiences. I had heard of the proverbial "grayback," but my first intimation of his actual presence was an itching sensation. I looked to discover the cause, and saw ever so many of them preying upon my flesh. I was "all of a shiver," and so disgusted that I thought I would leave. But my better nature and common sense came to my rescue, and consideration for my personal comforts was put aside as I thought what the soldiers were suffering so bravely and patiently for the dear country we all loved so well. After this, be the duty ever so hard or unpleasant, I did it cheerfully. During the battles that followed in 1862, 1863, and 1864, our hospital was constantly filled.

At the battle of Gettysburg more soldiers were received from the field than ever before; the wards were overcrowded, and tents were erected on the grounds to accommodate two thousand, the most of these being colored troops, who, when convalescent, made it lively with camp-meeting hymns and prayers, which greatly amused some of the boys, but caused others to use unmentionable words.

The weather was extremely warm and the vast number of the wounded made careful attention to their wounds impossible; and upon their arrival at the hospital many wounds were full of vermin, and in many cases gangrene had set in, and the odor was almost unbearable. The demand on our time and labor was so increased that the number of nurses seemed utterly inadequate, and the hospital presented a true picture of the horrors of war. The poor boys were maimed and mangled in a terrible manner. Readers, try to impress these truths on your memories, and never forget what the soldiers of the Rebellion sacrificed and suffered that this nation, born of God, might live, and that her glorious flag should be respected by all the nations of the earth, both on land and on sea, and that the terrible curse of slavery should be abolished.

I remember one poor fellow who had been struck by a bullet in such a way as to take out both eyes, without touching the brain. He recovered, but only to live out his days in a realm of darkness.

Amid such scenes of dreadful suffering, borne so uncomplainingly, my life as an army nurse was passed. Yet it is with feelings of thankfulness to God that I recall those times, and know that I was permitted to give almost three years of the best of my life to the country I love, and to her brave defenders.

We received a large number of wounded after the battle of the Wilderness, and, among them was a young woman not more than twenty years of age. She ranked as lieutenant. She was wounded in the shoulder, and her sex was not discovered until she came to our hospital. It appeared that she had followed her lover to the battle; and the boys who were brought in with her said that no one in the company showed more bravery than she. She was discharged very soon after entering the ward.

On my return from the National Encampment in Washington, September 1892, I had the great pleasure of visiting Doctor Baldwin, who served in the Satterlee Hospital from June 1862 until the war ended. He was a man of sterling worth and a warm friend of the soldiers. It is needless to say that we had a most enjoyable time talking over the days of the war. We spoke of the great fright we had when General Early made his raid on Chambersburg, and fired it; and how the brave boys who were just getting about, forgot their weakness and were ready to take up arms; how the places of business were all closed in Philadelphia, as the owners were off to defend the city.

After leaving the service, on account of poor health, I was married to a soldier of the 19th Maine Volunteers, and of this marriage eight children were born, seven of whom are now living, and they are a great blessing and comfort to me. I have taken pleasure in instructing them in the great principles of patriotism, and it is a standing joke among them that they have "Civil War for breakfast, dinner, and supper."

I left the Catholic Church, and have been a Baptist for fifteen years. I am trusting only in Christ. And I now send up a prayer to our Heavenly Father to preserve in my children true loyalty to our country,—the dearest and best in the world.

Yours in F., C. and L.,
Margaret Hamilton
70 ELM STREET
WAKEFIELD, MASSACHUSETTS

M. V. Harkin

I LEFT FOND DU LAC on the 12th of February 1862, and arrived in Madison the same day. The next day, I went to the State House, where my commission as a volunteer nurse awaited me; and on the 14th went into a hospital, where I received my first lessons in nursing. My mother, Mrs. Sarah A. McKenna, and myself, with several other nurses, were attached to the 17th Wisconsin Volunteer infantry, and we were all very eager to go to the front. While we were in Madison the barracks caught fire, and two soldiers were burned to death. In March we started for Saint Louis. All along the line the ladies were out in full force to welcome us, and at every station men, women, and children vied with each other in seeing who could do the most for the soldier ladies. In Chicago they treated the boys to cake, coffee, and fruit, while we nurses were almost smothered with flowers.

In due time we arrived in Saint Louis, and as we went into Benton Barracks, the brave 14th Wisconsin Volunteer Infantry marched out, cheering us as they passed.

How little the noble fellows realized of the fierce struggle in which they were about to participate! And how many who were now so full of life and hope, would soon lie low on the bloody field of Shiloh!

In the meantime we were getting our hospital in order. Soon we had plenty of work, for the measles attacked the boys, and we lost several. One Fond Du Lac boy, Charles Daugherty, had the measles in a very light form, and the doctor thought there was no danger; but the young man expected to die, and calling me to him one evening, said: "I am going now. I wanted to help my dear country in her strait, but I know it is ordered otherwise. Let my friends know that I died thinking of them, and of my brother Johnny, who is on a gunboat. He will never reach home. I am all ready, and willing to die." I told him that the doctor said he would recover. He replied: "Not so. Go, now, and come again in half an hour." I went for the doctor, who at once saw a great change, and tried in every way to restore him, but he was sinking rapidly, and in an hour he was dead.

Another case that I shall always remember was that of a poor Indiana boy, "the only son of his mother, and she was a widow." Oh, how he struggled for his life! He would say: "I cannot die, for who will take care of my poor mother? She is old, and she has only me." But in spite of our care the noble fellow died, after undergoing terrible suffering, and I wrote the sad tidings to his mother.

At last the news came that there was every prospect of a fight at Pittsburg Landing, or Shiloh, as it is sometimes called, and the 17th was ordered to be ready at a moment's notice. Our worst cases were sent to the General Hospital, and everything was put in order. Then we were commanded to embark for Pittsburg Landing. There was wild cheering and waving of hats. All were anxious to go, and good-byes to Benton Barracks and Saint Louis resounded on every hand. There was a poor old woman selling apples, and as she tried to cross the plank to go on board the steamer, she missed her footing and fell. Alas! there was no hope of rescuing her, for the great wheel dashed her under the water, and she was lost to our sight forever.

This event cast a gloom over us for some time, and to intensify the feeling a man walked overboard in his sleep the first night, and was drowned. Along the Tennessee shore we watched for a masked battery, but, fortunately, we were not disturbed.

When we reached Savannah we could hear the noise and fuss of the hospital that they had close by the shore.

Here we heard of the battle of Shiloh. The next morning we sighted the Landing, and disembarked about noon.

Our soldiers were detailed at once to help bury the dead, the steamer was used as a hospital, and we were set to work. The doctors pitched hospital tents, also. Here we saw some of the horrors of war. There were wounds of every description, and many a brave young life went out on the amputation table. The battlefield looked as if it had been ploughed in deep furrows; for every inch, north and south, had been contested stubbornly; and the white wood was laid bare on every tree, as if it had been peeled by hand.

After all of the brave dead had been buried in "their graves in company," and the ground made as clean as possible, we began to send North those who were able to move; some to Paducah, some to Savannah, and others to Cairo. We had great hardships to contend against. There was great lack of hospital stores, and we were all on short rations. On account of the masked batteries we found it hard to get supplies, and for one week all we nurses had to eat was hardtack. Not one of us would touch the small store that we had for the sick, and we were nearly starved at the end of that time, when a large steamer brought an abundance of provisions, sent by Wisconsin for her soldiers. Then followed long, weary days, and night watches with poor suffering men. There was almost every form of sickness, and we had to do all the cooking, and we had to keep the soldiers clean and the hospital in order.

Soon a sad time came to us. Mrs. Anna McMahon, a noble nurse, was taken with the measles. We watched over her with the deepest anxiety, for we felt that we could not spare one of our little band; but after five days of suffering she raised her languid eyes and asked, "Have I done my duty?"

The doctor assured her that she had; then with a weary sigh she said, "Good-bye; I will go to sleep." She slept, but it was never to wake. That was a sad day for us. We could not procure a coffin, but a soldier carpenter took some cracker boxes, from which he made as decent a one as possible. We wreathed it in flowers from the battlefield, and buried her beneath three large trees that grew on the bank of the Tennessee River. A rude board head-piece, bearing her name, was erected, and we left her there to take up our work as best we could. As the weather grew warmer sickness increased. The water was not very good, and the men lacked such food as would keep them in good health. The ground on which they had to sleep, with just a blanket wrapped around them, was damp and reeking with vile odors, and it was no wonder that so many died. Could the young who now eye the old soldiers so coldly, look into the past, and see how they marched away to fight for their country and for unborn generations, could they see the suffering and hardships that were borne almost without a murmur, they would give the soldiers a larger place in their hearts than they occupy today. But it is beyond the comprehension of any one who was not actually present.

We had moved about half way from the Landing to Corinth, when a call came for two nurses at the General Hospital. My mother and I went, and when we returned, at the end of a week, we found Mrs. Thurston, another of our nurses, sick unto death. Many, many were the tears that we shed for her, and the soldiers, too, were not ashamed to weep. May the sods lie lightly over her sweet face! Sleep well, beloved friend.

At this place the soldiers of the 15th Michigan Volunteer Infantry had laid out a nice graveyard, and at every grave a board was erected, bearing the soldier's name and regiment. Near this spot we had found a young man who must have been one of the outside pickets at the battle of Pittsburg Landing, and been captured and tied to a tree. We had him taken down and buried, but never learned his name or command. He was one of the "missing."

At Corinth things were much better. We had a large house for a hospital. It is wonderful how much quicker a person will get well when surrounded by the comforts of a home, although every day we were looking for a battle.

Here I came very near making the acquaintance of a Southern prison. The troops were stationed about three miles from Corinth, and the little town was all quiet. There were not many patients in the hospital, and no dangerous cases, so I asked the doctor's permission one day to go for a ride. He warned me not to go far, as there was danger; but I was well mounted, and feeling that there could be no danger, I wanted to enjoy my liberty to the utmost. So away I went, with my little orderly at my side. I soon turned onto a pleasant road, shaded with beautiful trees, and leading almost north.

My horse was fresh and eager to go, and we dashed on. At last we saw soldiers; but they were our own men, and of course I was not afraid of them. As I flew past, as fast as my horse could go, I thought I heard voices calling, but paid no attention, and rode on for as much as two hours; when I came to a large ravine, that cut the road in two. I stopped, looked down into the dark gully, then raised my eyes to the opposite hill, where I saw a rude farm house, and a white cow grazing in the field. I thought I would cross the gully and see if I could buy a drink of milk. I had gone about half way down the hills when at the bottom I saw five men in the well-known "butternut" uniform. My breath almost left my body as the foremost said: "Halt! You are my prisoner." He walked toward me, and in another minute would have had my horse by the bridle. "I will die first," was my thought as I jerked the rein and my dear old horse turned with a jump. "Shoot the spy!" they shouted. I was in truth flying for dear life. They fired three shots after me, but I must have gone like the wind for I heard no more from them. When I reached the picket lines the little orderly was almost sure I was "gobbled," as they called being taken prisoner. The officer gave me a scolding, and told me how three of our men were killed there a short time before. I found my father and mother very anxious about me, and I myself was almost sick with fright.

Soon a soldier was taken with smallpox, and put in a tent by himself. My mother and I took turns caring for him. The poor fellow took cold in the tent, and became deaf, but recovered his health, and we procured his discharge.

As the very warm weather came on my own health was poor, and my mother wanted me to go home. I could not go as long as I could stand at my post; but at last I was threatened with typhoid fever, and as my mother was to accompany some sick to the North, she persuaded me to go with her, promising that I should go back with her the next time; but I was not able, and she returned to Corinth without me; then went to Memphis, where she did good work in Overton Hospital. Dear mother died August 15, 1893. She was a member of George A. Custer Relief Corps, No. 78, Ashland.

Yours in F., C. and L.,
M. V. Harkin
MARSHFIELD, WOOD COUNTY, WISCONSIN

Fannie Harper

In the winter of 1862 and 1863 I was called to the hospital at Le Sueur to see my husband, who was seriously ill with erysipelas. The doctors had given up hope, and no one expected to see him out again; but I took care of him from that time and he came out all right.

There were twenty-four sick soldiers, and no woman to nurse them; so I volunteered, for they were sadly in need of some one. I remained about five months, during which there were five deaths. The sickness was mostly pneumonia and typhoid fever; one died of heart disease. The hospital steward died on his way home on a sick furlough, and was laid to rest in Mound City.

I had a little son born in April 1863. He was baptized by our chaplain, Ezra Lathrop. I went with the command when it was ordered to Memphis, Tennessee, where I entered the field hospital. During the warm weather there was a large amount of sickness and death, sometimes two or three funerals a day, though our quarters were very comfortable, and our boys received good care; besides which, the Christian and Sanitary Commissions brought many luxuries for the soldiers.

How well I remember when Forrest came with his men to take Memphis! He was met by a strong force of the "boys in blue," and driven back; but they made a raid on our hospital, and killed lots of our sick in their bunks.

Later I had fever and ague, and left just before the battle of Nashville. I did not return, as the war had closed before I regained my health.

I belonged to the hospital of the 10th Minnesota Infantry, First Brigade, First Division, 16th Army Corps, commanded by General A. J. Smith.

Yours very truly,
Fannie A. Harper
ROSEMOUNT, MINNESOTA

Margaret Hayes

ON THE 17TH DAY OF FEBRUARY 1863, I left my home in Mendota, Illinois, for Chicago. Arriving there we went to the Sanitary Commission rooms, and were cared for by Mrs. Livermore, who gave us our commissions, put us up a lunch, gave us each a pillow and a small comfortable, as there were no sleeping cars in those days, procured transportations, and started us that same evening for Memphis, Tennessee. Another lady went with me, who was as anxious as I to do something for the "boys in blue."

We arrived safely, and I was immediately assigned to the Adams General Hospital, No. 2 (which had just been opened to receive the sick and wounded from Arkansas), in Ward 2, Room B, where there were seventy-two men. I think the ward master was one of the kindest men I ever knew. Poor fellow! He went through the war, and returned to his home with the regiment, but only to die soon after his arrival. There was a medicine man and a wound-dresser, and six nurses were detailed from among the convalescents. My especial duty was to cook the extra diet, see that the patients received it, wait upon those who could not feed themselves, look after the comfort of all, and, in fact, make myself generally useful. A part of the time I had two wards. The boys appreciated whatever I did for them very much, and presented me with a valuable gold watch, which I still hold as one of my choicest treasures.

I remained at the Adams until January 1865, when I was transferred to the Gayoso, and was discharged from there at the close of the war.

I often think of my "boys," and wonder where they all are. The old ones are mustered out, the young are now gray and old, and would not know me or I them if we should meet. I have even changed my name. I was Mrs. Maggie Meseroll then; they called me "Sister Maggie."

By first ward surgeon was Dr. Taylor of Cambridge, Massachusetts; next, Dr. Cole of Saint Louis; then came Dr. Lard, and Dr. Keenon, who died while in charge succeeded by Dr. Study. At the Gayoso were Dr. Burke and Dr. Stold, Dr. Joe Lynch, and Maj. B. J. D. Irvin.

I could tell many incidents if I could see to write them, but I am so blind that I have not been able to read since 1882.

Yours in F., C. and L.,
Margaret Hayes
SOUTH LOS ANGELES, CALIFORNIA

Nancy Hill

Nancy M. Hill, daughter of William and Harriet (Swan) Hill, was born in West Cambridge (now Arlington and Belmont), Massachusetts. Her forefathers were in the battles of Lexington, West Cambridge, and Bunker Hill. She was educated in the public schools at West Cambridge and at Mount Holyoke Seminary, South Hadley, Massachusetts.

There was a great call for educated women to go as nurses, during the War of the Rebellion, in the hospitals at Washington. Ladies from Cambridge, Boston, and other places offered their services at Armory Square Hospital, under Dr. Bliss, who was surgeon in charge. These ladies were specially appointed by Surgeon-General Barnes. The pay of the volunteer nurses was to go into a hospital fund, to buy extras for the soldiers, which Government did not provide.

There was a vacancy in Ward E in this hospital, and Miss Hill was summoned. She went in April 1863 and remained until August 1865, after the close of the war. Armory Square Hospital was a barrack hospital of eleven buildings, besides tents for the convalescents, capable of holding a thousand men. Each lady had charge of a ward under a doctor. There were fifty-two beds in each ward, but often extra cots were added. This hospital was nearest the boat-landing and the railroad depot, and received the worst cases. They were often brought all the way from the boat on stretchers, as they could not stand the jar of the ambulances.

When the battles of the Wilderness were going on, all hospital supplies and sanitary stores had been sent to the front, and there were none in Washington. Miss Hill wrote to her mother about it, and she had the letter read next morning in the four churches in Arlington. Immediately the congregations were dismissed, and all went home, to return to the Town Hall bringing table-cloths, and linen, and cotton sheets,— the best they had. The ladies and gentlemen worked all day long making and rolling bandages and picking lint. Before nine o'clock that night two large dry-goods boxes, the size of an upright piano, were on their way to Washington by Adams Express, who took them free of charge.

The Soldiers' Aid Societies of both Arlington and Belmont were very generous in their contributions. As fast as they sent boxes away, they began to fill others to send,—and so it was with all the volunteer nurses; friends at the North sent bountiful supplies of whatever was needed.

After General Grant took command of the Army of the Potomac, the hospitals were crowded with severely wounded men. He followed up the foe so fast it was blow upon blow. Every day the wounded came, and every day men who could be moved with safety were sent to Baltimore or Philadelphia to make room for others. It was a common thing to count forty amputation cases at a time, when looking up and down the ward that summer, and so it continued until the end of the war.

After the hospital closed, Dr. Bliss advised Miss Hill to study medicine. Acting on this suggestion she began reading under Dr. Marie Zakryewska, the *Alma Mater* of all lady physicians of Boston and vicinity. Afterwards she became a medical student at the New England Hospital for Women and Children at Roxbury, Massachusetts. She was graduated at the medical department of the Michigan University, at Ann Arbor, in the year 1874. She then came to Dubuque, Iowa, and opened an office, and has been in active practice of medicine ever since.

Dr. Nancy Hill
DUBUQUE, IOWA

Lauretta Hoisington

I WAS ENROLLED UNDER THE NAME of Lauretta H. Cutler. I went from West Williamsfield, Ohio, May 1864, and entered the service at Hospital No. 1, Chattanooga, Tennessee, commissioned by James E. Yeatman, acting agent of Miss Dix. I remained there in Nos. 1 and 2 until I was released in June 1865.

During the first few weeks I worked in the kitchen, visiting the wards a little while each day; then I became a regular nurse. No. 1 Hospital was composed partly of framed buildings, formerly used as a hospital by Bragg; the remainder of tents. If my memory serves me well, its capacity was six hundred and when I went there it was full of sick and wounded soldiers. Here it was that I first began to learn the lesson (that difficult lesson that all nurses had to learn) to govern, or, I would better say, battle against my feelings, and work with a will for the sufferers. I also learned how little could do in comparison to what was needed to be done, and often I could do no more than give a kind look or word to show that I would do more if it were in my power.

Alas! how degradingly cheap is human life in time of war, when our fathers, husbands, brothers, and sons must deliberately kill each other, and call it a victory. I recall a young soldier who was brought in with an unjointed shoulder,—pale, excited, and delirious. As I approached his cot he said: "O mother, I have just been home, and saw you on the lawn with the young folks, but you would not speak to me. Now you are here, can't you give me some lemonade?" But when I took it to him he cheerfully gave it to another, who was in a dying condition.

It is only those who have experienced life in a hospital, who can get a clear picture from a description in words. It must all be seen and felt to be known; even then, in my case, at least, much has faded from my memory in the lapse of thirty years.

I look to my diary half in vain, for much of it is filled with orders from the surgeon, like this: Division 1, Ward 3, bed 35, milk; bed 33, milk and fruit. Ward 8, bed 10, beef tea, toast, and peaches; bed 15, arrowroot. Ward 2, fever case, raspberry vinegar. Ward 5, bed 6, mush and milk; bed 1, oysters.

There were many letters to write, and sanitary things to distribute,—writing paper, stamps, and comfort bags.

There was one called the typhoid fever ward. I went there, and carried cooling drinks and brushed out the flies. I often looked up their comrades in some regiment, or sometimes relatives, whom I would find, perhaps, in the erysipelas ward, with faces so swollen that they could not see; then carried messages between them. At length I caught the fever, but the intelligent care I received saved my life. Then I was allowed to spend a few weeks on Lookout Mountain, with my first colaborer, Miss Babcock, who had been assigned to duty there. On my return I was ordered to No. 2, at the request of Surgeon Collins. The prisoners' ward was here. They had their prayer meetings, and prayed to the same Saviour for their cause, just as our men did. But oh, the horrors of war! May such things never be seen again.

Once we had a large quantity of grapes sent to us; and these my orderly and I distributed to all who were able to eat them. I distributed many pocket handkerchiefs which were thankfully received, sometimes with tears; for you who read this will remember that those handkerchiefs were "home-made," and so were doubly valuable to the boys.

In the camp were various diseases, smallpox among the rest. Some poor fellows were homesick, and this malady one must experience in order to know how easily it may become fatal. I remember one such case. The surgeon said: "I cannot rouse him. Do what you can." His eyes seemed set, his limbs cold, and fingernails somewhat dark. Working upon the supposition that he was home-sick, I commenced to talk of home, his mother, and other loved ones. He listened, but could not speak for some time. Finally I asked him what his mother would give him in such a sickness as this. After several attempts he said, brokenly, "Brandy and peaches." I assured him he should have them; then requested the nurse to heat bricks and put around him; his hands and feet were well rubbed, and I gave him whatever he thought he would have had at home, and he was saved.

Later, another poor boy was brought in from the convalescents' camp; he was near his end from the same cause. His request in broken German was for "The Lord's Supper." He said, "Please give it to me, for I cannot die without it." After some delay, and much anxiety I succeeded in having it administered to him.

Thanksgiving Day, 1864, we had a Thanksgiving dinner. This was like an oasis in the desert to us all. Among the guests were several military officers of high rank. Our own Ex-President Harrison (then a young man), being the brightest, was called upon for a speech, and introduced as the grandson of a former President. In reply he said, "I dislike to be introduced by a reference to relatives who are dead: the inference is that, like a potato, the best part of me is underground." How well I remember my anxiety to have the parade over, so the boys in the wards could have their dinner.

Dear reader, I have tried to tell you some few things about the work, but a thousandth part of the patient, uncomplaining suffering in field and hospital can never be told. That such scenes may never be reenacted is the earnest prayer of an army nurse.

Mrs. L. H. Hoisington
(Formerly Nurse Cutler)
BOX 126, ROCHELLE, ILLINOIS

Clara Hoyt

ON THE 16TH OF SEPTEMBER 1864, in response to a
call from Miss Dix, I bade adieu to home, kindred, and friends, in
Gravesville, New York, and wended my way toward the scene of
battle, to share in the horrors attendant on grim war, as a volunteer
nurse. A few days later I arrived at Washington, and as Miss Dix was
away, I was sent by her order to the Columbia College Hospital, for
rest and instruction until her return. After eight days I received word
to report at headquarters, and was immediately sent to the 18th Army
Corps Hospital, Point of Rocks, Virginia. Arriving there I was assigned to duty, October 6, 1864, by Dr. Fowler, and remained there
until the close of the war.

It would be impossible for me to describe what I passed through.
Oh, the pain, the groans, the dying struggles. Nothing but the stron-
gest devotion to country and flag could have enabled me to endure it.

Many of the present generation have too little sympathy with the
defenders of our Republic,—too slight a realization of the significance
of the four years of strife, the clouds and darkness through which the
nation passed, ere liberty was proclaimed, and the flag floated free.

Clara B. Hoyt
LARNED, KANSAS

Elizabeth Hunt

AT YOUR REQUEST, I WILL GIVE a few items of my experience in hospital life, although I cannot now remember all of them. At that time my home was in Salem, Iowa. The hospital I worked in was at Keokuk, Iowa. There were three hospitals in the city. The one I worked in was called the Main Street Hospital. It was a large eight-story building. I worked in the Fifth Ward. There were a great many patients, and I deeply sympathized with those poor heroes who had risked their lives to protect our homes.

I was employed by Dr. Hughes (now deceased), who had charge. There was a great demand for nurses, and I took my place in May 1862 and left in August. My ward had ten cases of small-pox, and none of the other nurses were willing to wait on them, for fear of the disease. I told the surgeon I would stay. My people were very much alarmed but I had friends in the city who said they would care for me. Soon I was taken very ill with the varioloid form, and was removed from the hospital; but my health was so impaired I was unable to return to the service, and I have never been well since. I made application for a pension but as I was not in the service six months, it was not granted. This seemed to me a little unjust, for I should probably have remained a year or two had I not been stricken down by caring for small-pox patients.
Elizabeth P. Hunt.
BLOOMINGDALE, INDIANA

Elizabeth Hyatt

IN 1861 MY HUSBAND ENLISTED at Chilton, Wisconsin, in Co. K, 4th Regiment, Wisconsin Volunteers, and joined the other companies at Racine in June. I went to bid my husband good-bye before he marched to Dixie, and found plenty of work there to do in camp and hospital. Some of my neighbors were sick, and I did not wait for an invitation, but cooked, nursed, and did whatever I saw to do until the regiment received orders to go South; then packed my grip to go home. But when I went to bid the doctor good-bye, he said: "Oh no, Mrs. Hyatt, you can't go. Don't think of such a thing. You are just the kind of a woman we need." He asked me to walk over to see the colonel with him. The matter was soon decided, and I went to Baltimore with them. I received a certificate, and served in Patterson Park Hospital, in Ward 11, where I had twenty-two soldiers under my charge.

In Ward 12 was a nurse who roomed with me. She was one of the blue kind, always down-hearted, with never a smile on her face; always expecting trouble. Well, she went over to our room and neglected to call for me, so I thought I would go to her ward and cheer her boys a bit. I went in and looked around, just as if I expected to find her there. Then I said: "Boys, do you know what that firing means? Has your nurse told you?" "No, she never tells us anything. What is it?" "Why, Jeff Davis is captured, the South is whipped, peace is declared, and the war is over; so every man who is well enough to travel, will be on his way home as soon as he can pack his knapsack. So, boys, hurrah for home and loved ones!" A shout as went up! The ward-master came to see what was the matter. I told him I thought I would go in and cheer them up a little. He said, "Well, I think you have done it with a vengeance, by the looks of the room." They had thrown their bedclothes, knapsacks, boots and pillows around, and what a looking place it was! I ran down and told my boys all about it, and they had a hearty laugh. The nurse had heard the noise, and knew something wrong was going on in her ward, so hurried back; and what a sight she beheld. It took her two hours to straighten things around in order. She came to see me with such a sad face, but found No. 11 a very cheerful place,—every man was smiling. She said, "Mrs. Hyatt, I will pay you for this." I assured her that she did not owe me anything; that I would do it any time, as it was not one bit of trouble, and it would do them lots of good.

After this I accompanied the regiment for a time; but when it was ordered to Ship Island, I concluded to return to Patterson Park Hospital. I left the "Constitution" at Fortress Monroe, saw the fight between the "Monitor" and the "Merrimac," then went to Baltimore, where I resumed charge of Ward 11, in March 1862. In August I went to Virginia, to try to see my brother. While passing Mt. Vernon the bell tolled, the gentlemen raised their hats, and talking ceased. I went to Warrenton, and ate supper with rebel guards. The next day I dined with Union officers, and there was not a rebel to be found in the place.

I started for Fairfax Court House, but the railroad was torn up, so I called on General Banks for a horse. He sent one to me, and as I could ride very well I soon reached Centerville, where the battle had been fought. Here I found Colonel Andrews with ambulances, but many of the drivers had left the teams to go on the field. I tried to carry water to the wounded, but I felt so sick that I was about to leave the place, when Colonel Andrews asked me if I could drive a team. When I assured him that I could, he asked me to drive an ambulance to Fairfax Court House. There were four wounded men, and before I started, another, slightly wounded on the head, begged to go too. I had him strapped on the seat. The road was smooth, and I told the men if they could bear it to let me trot the horses forty minutes, I could pass the long train, avoid the dust, and could have them unloaded before the others arrived and took the most comfortable places. They told me to drive on.

I turned out and cracked the whip. The horses started on a good round trot. Every ambulance passed, the driver would call to me to stop trotting and drive slowly, or I would kill the men. I paid no attention until one called me a "Secesh." Then I told the man who was strapped on the seat to call them something. He did, and shaking his fist, told them to keep still or they would smell powder.

When I had left the train a mile behind I halted, and gave the men a drink. I cheered them what I could, telling them I would go to Washington and try to get them furloughs to go home, then drove on. When the men were comfortably settled and fed, I started on the return, and soon met the train. The drivers called to know how I got through, so for fun I told them I hadn't a live man left. How they did swear, and call me a rebel. I made no reply, for I was in a hurry to get another load. They apologized when they found I was the 4th Wisconsin woman. They said they had talked with the men, who enjoyed the ride, and were very glad I was plucky enough to keep on.

I called on the Provost Marshal for a place to sleep. He sent me to a room on the second floor, where there were three telegraph operators. I partitioned off a room with a long table in it, then asked if there were no other women to occupy that big place with me. He sent for one, and I soon went to sleep. The next day I went to Washington with the sick men, but could not procure furloughs. Then I returned to my twenty-two boys in Ward 11. They were very glad to see me, and begged me not to go away again. They said it was lonesome, and no one told them any news. I remained there until December 1862.

Ah, how many sad things happened! One night at six o'clock I left one of my boys ever so much better than he had been. The next morning a man met me with the news that Willie was dead. I went to the dead-house to see him. A doctor told me the boy was poisoned. A soldier in the ward said that a woman came in with chocolate, and that Willie drank a cupful, but none of the rest would. I felt very badly. That was the only death in my ward. I nursed the soldiers carefully, cheered them all I could, and would see that they had plenty of good food, even if I had to put my hand in my own pocket to pay for it.

Elizabeth A. Hyatt
NORTHVILLE, WAYNE CO., MICHIGAN

Martha Jennison

I<small>F</small> I <small>SHOULD UNDERTAKE TO WRITE</small> all I knew about war times and the boys in blue, it would require a large volume to hold it; but I will try to give you a few items.

I was born in Templeton, Massachusetts, but we had gone to the West, and were in Fort Madison, Iowa when the war broke out.

My eldest son felt he must go into the army, and at first it seemed to me that I could not spare him; but he went, and was in many battles during the four years he was in the service, and the Lord heard my prayers and returned him to me to tell what he had been through during the cruel war.

My other son was in school in Boston; but as soon as he was graduated he went into the navy on the steamer "Lillian." He, too, was in many battles, and sometimes sick, but God spared his life.

A mother can judge what were my feelings, with my husband dead and my sons engaged in such a perilous undertaking.

In 1862 I went to Keokuk to spend the winter with Mr. and Mrs. Samuel E. Miller; and whether it was in March or April I cannot tell, but the Government took a large hotel for a hospital. Mrs. Miller and I went in when the men first arrived; and oh, such suffering. It was fearful to see!

The surgeon-general came to me with a roll of bandages and a bundle of lint, and said, "Mrs. Jennison, will you go with me and help to dress the poor boys' wounds ?" I did not feel that I had the nerve to go through it; but after I had helped with ten or twelve brave fellows, and saw how much there was to do, and so few to do it, I felt it my duty to stay and help. I thought perhaps if I did what I could for them, some one would care for my sons.

I boarded with Judge Miller, but used to go every day to the hospital, and I found plenty to do there. I carried my tablet, pen, and ink, and often wrote letters for the boys who were too sick to do it for themselves, or had, perhaps, lost the right arm or hand.

I think there were a thousand men here. There were fifty in one large hall with only a chair between the cots. I have known fifteen to die in one day; but oh, they were so brave to the end!

I used to read to them a great deal when they were in such agony that nothing could do them any good, and that seemed to quiet them more than anything else. Many a night I have sat by sick and dying soldiers.

I went into the hospitals to try to help, not for pay; on the other hand, I spent time, money, and health, working with my head as well as my hands. In about six months I was taken with the typhoid fever, and was carried to my home in Fort Madison, where I was sick for a long time. I had a book in which I kept the names of officers and many interesting facts, but during my sickness it was lost.

Martha F. Jennison
WESTON, MASSACHUSETTS

Estelle Johnson

I HAVE BEEN REQUESTED TO WRITE what I can remember about my life as an army nurse, while in the hospital of the 4th Vermont Volunteers. I hardly know what to say, as it is new work for me to write for a book. When the war broke out I lived in a little country village shut in by the mountains of Vermont. One day in August 1861, Leonard Stearns came in search of recruits. My husband and his brother-in-law were among those who enlisted, and sister and I objected, naturally; telling the recruiting officer that if our husbands went we should go too, but not thinking that such a thing could be.

In the course of a week Mr. Stearns came and told us that the colonel said that although nurses had not been called for, he wanted us to go. The boys formed a company under Captain Leonard A. Stearns, and went into camp at Brattleboro. They were assigned to the 4th Vermont Regiment, Company I.

On September 18th we were sent to join them and on the 20th signed our names—Estelle S. Johnson and Lydia A. Wood—to the roll, and were sworn in by Lieutenant Higby, in the presence of the colonel, adjutants and major, the Governor of Vermont and his son-in-law. The Governor tried to persuade us not to go. The regiment started about eight o'clock that evening, and went by rail to Stonington, where they embarked for New York, arriving there the next day in the forenoon. Thence by rail to Philadelphia, where we arrived in the evening, and marched to Cooper's Hall, where a collation was prepared for us. I do believe it was the best meal I ever ate; we were very hungry. Late that night we went on board a train for Washington, and this time we did not get along very fast. It seemed as if we only crawled, so slow was our progress. A few miles beyond the Relay we found the rails torn up in a piece of woods; but they were soon replaced, and we proceeded on our way, reaching Washington about eight o'clock in the evening. The colonel found a place for sister and I to rest at the "Soldiers' Retreat," where we had supper, lodging and breakfast; then went to join the company. From the depot they marched to Federal Hill, where the tents were pitched September 23d. I had left a little girl at home, who was one year old that day.

We stayed there a week; then the 9th Wisconsin came on the ground. It was raining hard, and the colonel would not move his men, so sister and I took the seven ladies who were with the regiment into the tent with us over night. One thing I must mention before we leave Federal Hill. Away in the distance was stationed another regiment. One evening near sunset we were looking over there, when we saw some men drawn up in line to shoot a comrade for desertion. I did not see the shooting, but I heard the report of the guns, and knew another poor fellow had paid the penalty of desertion.

September 28th we again started on the march. We crossed Chain Bridge, and halted that night close to Fort Smith. Only one tent was pitched; that was for the women. When all had turned in and were nicely settled for sleep, an order came to go into the fort, as an attack was expected; but we stayed in our tent outside and slept soundly all night.

Next day we crossed the road, and pitched the tents on a slight elevation. This place was called Camp Advance. Here we were assigned to the 1st Vermont Brigade, Brig. William F. Smith commanding. We stayed here nearly two weeks. The 2d Vermont was not far away, and there were five women with them, and some of the boys were from our home. Once we visited them. Soon after we moved on, and pitched our tents at Camp Griffin. Here was a level strip of ground, with a large cornfield on one side. A day or two later the long roll was called before daylight. That day the camp was shelled by the rebels, but the shells did not reach us. The captain wanted sister and I to go back to Langley; but I told him if he thought we would run at the first fire he was greatly mistaken.

As soon as possible a hospital was established a few miles from camp in a deserted house. I went there as nurse, or, as Dr. Allen called me, "matron." There were three rooms and a kitchen on the first floor and three above; the one over the kitchen being a low room with roof sloping to the floor and no light. Some of the boys were lying with nothing but their rubber blankets under them. For some time no regular sick rations were issued. One day Robert Langdon came over to see us from the 2d Regiment. He reported to Gen. Brooks how the boys were situated. Things were made lively for a day or two. The old house underwent a thorough change. Cots were made, and ticks filled with straw, hay, or cornshucks; and soon the boys were comparatively comfortable. I occupied one of the upper rooms and kept there my hospital stores.

Many of the soldiers were sick with typhoid fever, and my husband soon had it. I slept very lightly, and often was called to get the necessary things in which to lay out some poor fellow who had died in the night. From my room I had to go down stairs by passing through a narrow hall just the width of a door. Here was where they laid the dead, and sometimes there would be two, side by side, and it would be hard to pass them in the narrow space. It gave me an awful feeling to crowd by them in the dead of night. We had been at the hospital about ten days when sister Lydia was taken sick with the fever, and died the ninth day. Robert Langdon brought Amanda Farnham and Mrs. Black to prepare her for burial; but the boys could not bear to have her buried as the soldiers were, so clubbed together and paid the expense of having her embalmed and sent home, and her husband with her. He arrived before the coffin did, and that night was taken down with the black measles. She was kept three weeks, then buried beside her little girl; her husband getting there just after she was buried.

After her death my husband was much worse, and for days it was doubtful whether he could live or not, but he slowly recovered. The care of him in addition to my other duties kept me busy and from being homesick. When he became convalescent, Dr. Allen wanted me to go to the Brigade Hospital in the same capacity in which I was serving there; but I objected to going so far from my husband, who would soon return to his company.

I remember many of the boys so well. One called Phillips would be up and around one day, the next would be very sick. Chaplain Smith came often to see him; but as he grew worse he was sent to the Brigade Hospital, where he lived only one week. There were two Bailey brothers, and the doctor said there was nothing the matter with them but homesickness. Nearly every day I would go to them and read, or perhaps write letters for them, but they soon died. Another, Charlie Persons, had black measles. I used to go to him every day and do all I could. One evening an attendant came to tell me Charlie was dying. It was only too true. There he lay, his hands clasped over his head, apparently sleeping, but, really, quietly passing away. I took from under his pillow the picture of his lady-love, and this with other things I sent to her,—all but her letters, which I burned, for fear curious eyes might read them.

I went to Washington twice with Surgeon Allen. The first time I stopped over night with Miss Dix. Her house was filled with supplies. I shall always remember that visit. The next time Amanda Farnham and I went to get some needed things. We went to Georgetown in an army wagon, then walked on from there. Being very hungry we went into a bakery for something to eat. When the German woman who had charge saw our uniforms, she invited us into her kitchen to have some dinner, and would not accept any pay.

In time, my husband went on duty again but it was too soon. The fever settled in his right knee, so I had him under my charge once more. March 21,1862, the sick were all sent away, as preparations were being made for an advance; my husband being sent to Alexandria. Dr. Allen said he would never be able to march again, and he had to get a discharge. After this I did not feel that I could stay; but they said as he had a discharge I should not need one. How I have wished since that I had it. This was just before the battle of Lee's Mills. I left the regiment March 23, 1862, and reached home April 3d, my service covering only a little over six months; and as our regiment was not in any battle during that time, I had no wounded to care for, and have no thrilling adventures to relate.

Estelle S. Johnson
Holyoke, Massachusetts

Lucy Kaiser

IN APRIL 1861, I LEFT MY HOME in Saint Charles, Illinois, and went to Chicago, and from there to Saint Louis, where I went to a hotel and watched all incidental affairs pertaining to the Rebellion, until the battle of Carthage. Then I consulted with prominent men as to how and where I could apply my individual work in the way that would be most acceptable; and soon found a place at Jefferson Barracks, Missouri, then the old United States Post Hospital. I left my name and address with the steward, who promised to send for me as soon as I was needed; then returned to Saint Louis, where I spent the period of waiting in visiting soldiers who came to camp in and around the old Fair Ground, and I found many in need of care, as well as articles of actual necessity, which I furnished by writing to prominent ladies, who always responded to the call with a supply of clothing, bedding, food, and many things that helped to make life more endurable in the unorganized condition in which the army was at that time.

During my work there I was paying my board at the hotel, as what I did was entirely a free-will offering prompted by my pity and sorrow for a condition of affairs that had already cost so much human life and engendered bitter hatred. I remained there until August 6th, when I started out for Wilson's Creek, intending to make the march from Rolla with the regiment, then preparing to reinforce General Lyon; but upon my arrival I found the officers slow to obey orders, giving as an excuse the fact that they had no wagons for transportation. While thus delaying the battle was fought, and Lyon and many of his men killed. I lingered until the wounded began to arrive; then knowing it was useless to go to the front at that late hour, I returned to Saint Louis and resumed my work, going the rounds of Benton Barracks. I found all in the hospital in the lower part of the city well cared for by the Sisters of Charity, so my assistance was not needed there. I found men from Bull Run, Springfield, and other places where there had been fighting, and kept busy doing with as little delay as possible whatever ought to be done. Here I saw Generals Fremont and Sigel, and noted the contrast. Fremont, large and portly,— the picture of a commanding officer; Sigel, exactly the opposite: small in head and stature, and wearing glasses, which hid the redeeming feature of a prominent man.

As the hotel where I was boarding was crowded with military men, I changed to the Saint Lawrence, August 29th. Then hearing that there were many soldiers in Rolla who needed assistance I started at once, taking with me a large basket of such articles, as I thought would be required. After a long day's travel I reached camp just at evening, and found many sick ones; some had measles, some fevers or colds, and still others were homesick. There was one lady there doing what she could without supplies or conveniences. I gave her the basket, and promised to send more. A regiment composed of men from our town and its vicinity was here, and I saw my brother and a cousin, besides many old neighbors. The next morning I returned to Saint Louis, where I rested over the Sabbath, then taking up the work at the Barracks again.

September 4th, I wrote Miss Dix, inquiring into the detail business; then visited some regimental tents, taking, as usual, a supply of whatever I thought would be most needed to supply their immediate wants. During that week I continued such visits, also applied to many ladies for supplies. Then came an order to report for duty at Jefferson Barracks. Here I saw that I was really needed, and I worked in the wards until late that night, getting things in shape so I could go back to the city for needed articles, and returned on the 8th. At this time I received an introduction to ex-Governor Stewart, who escorted me to the dining room, and acted the part of champion to the "Lady Soldier," as he chose to call me. On the 9th I again visited the city for supplies, and witnessed the first military funeral I ever saw. I was also made very anxious by hearing that there had been a skirmish at Arlington Heights. I went for supplies again the 12th, as I wished to report to those furnishing what we needed most. On this occasion I was present at the presentation of a flag to the survivors of the battle of Springfield, by the ladies of the city.

On the 15th, while at the hospital, I had a call from a mysterious person,—tall, and cross-eyed, otherwise passably good-looking. His errand was apparently to get a Republican paper I was taking, but he went away without it. Query: "What did he call for?" I never knew.

The 17th I went through the city to the Fair Grounds, to the hospital where I worked before going to Jefferson Barracks Hospital. That day I saw the need of good help. The 18th and 19th I worked with the sick in the wards, and my heart was saddened by seeing so many in the prime of life called to the other land by such a mistaken path. Why did this revolt ever occur? The next day Dr. Buel came to us, asking me to interest some lady in behalf of his sick men, suffering for want of attention and supplies. I referred this to ladies in Saint Louis, who promptly responded. The 21st I visited the Sanitary Commission, and in answer to my request I received from Mr. Yeatman, as an agent for Miss Dix, my coveted commission, and the 23d was put on the hospital payroll. I considered the situation thoroughly, and decided that let what would come, I would not abandon the soldiers so long as I was able to stay. I soon found that there was no clothing in the linen room, in fact no linen department, and was at a loss what to do, as we could not get "such things" from Government. We applied to the Sanitary Commission but they did not have anything. We next appealed to the Ladies' Aid who promptly sent a limited supply. I made an enemy of the steward's wife, by refusing to grant her request for clothing for herself and family; but I found she was in practice, and would have it dishonestly if she could not get it honestly.

My next work was to superintend the cleaning of the ward, so far as soap and water would do the work. By this time the sick were mostly convalescent,—all doing well; but we had another anxiety, in the fear that some of our men had been taken prisoners. Until this time I had been obliged to occupy a room with the steward's hired girl and her baby; and as I was very tired I greatly appreciated a room alone, which I was now able to have. Then, too, more supplies came, and that made the work easier. The 1st of October a few new cases arrived, and the doctor ordered that the shade trees be cut down, to let more air and sunshine into the hospital. Soon my health was much improved.

After this my first attendant was taken sick and had to be removed for rest and change. I was greatly troubled, wondering when the struggle would end, and my anxiety was increased by the privations that the men in the wards had to endure. Then new patients arrived, and I had to do much of the work that belonged to the doctor in addition to my own. Soon all the wards were filled, and I had about all I could do; still there were many calls for help that I so wanted to render, and all the time I was harassed by the steward's wife. I never saw the equal of that woman; I could only hope that sometime there would be "rest for the weary," though I feared that hope might end in despair. I had to change attendants often, and so watch them very closely, as they often made mistakes, and did great mischief when trying to do right.

The 1st of November a disagreeable experience came to me. Wright reported me for not giving him enough to eat, and I suppose it was true. The fact was I could not get enough food: butter out, sugar out, no crackers, poor bread, tough beef, no vegetables, no candles; in fact, the commissary was bare, and the officers in town on a drunk.

November 5th, Mr. Jordan called to see the patients. We had a genuine surprise party. All the pleasure–seekers in the city came out to celebrate the connection of the North Missouri and Iron Mountain Railroads. Four locomotives, with thirty cars decked in holiday attire, landed a full complement of men and women; at the same time the steamer "Louisiana" brought seven companies of troops from Texas. There was much excitement among the patients on hearing the firing of the salutes; many supposed the enemy at hand. To cap the climax, the hospital was found to be on fire; but it was put out with little damage,—no thanks to the officers who were having their "good time" in the city. All through the month we had very little to do with, and complaint was common. A new doctor and steward came, but paid little attention to the patients; so I had to do what I could of their work, besides superintending the kitchen and dining room as well as the wards.

The 1st of December there were some deaths in the hospital. Things grew no easier, and at length I applied to the Sanitary Commission for an easier place, but they would not let me go. I was disgusted with the way the hospital was neglected, and wanted some one else to see if she could not do better than myself.

About the first of February 1862, I was asked to go to Benton Barracks for a time. This I gladly consented to do, for I wanted to see how the "Banner Hospital" was run. I had to do battle as supervisor and nurse, as I was all alone; also to superintend the kitchens and instruct the half-sick soldier who acted as cook; look after the laundry, and, in fact, was "chief cook and bottle-washer." I knew there was an able corps of nurses there, and I determined to learn all I could. I reported to the surgeon; also to the supervisor, who was a lady from Keokuk. I was assigned to a small building containing smaller rooms, or wards. I think I had ten men. What to do, how to do it, or whether to do anything, I did not know; so I decided to visit my neighbors. I found a lady sitting by a bed reading a paper, introduced myself, and asked her to tell me what was expected of me. I learned that my duty was to see that the men had medicine, food, and clothing; also to keep the ward clean. So far, so good; and I returned to try to get acquainted with my patients. Everything went smoothly, only I must say that I felt out of place, after having had so much to do, to be confined to a room about fourteen feet square.

But I managed to exist there until the troops commenced to leave for Pittsburg Landing; then I told Mr. Yeatman I did not like my place, and would go to the front. He did not think I could, as women were not allowed there then; but I took my staff in hand and went to the major, asking him if I could go if I would run all the risks and pay my own expenses. He told me that he had no objections if I could get on board the boat and up the river, but it must be at my own risk, as he would be court-marshaled if found out. I went to the Provost Marshal and got a pass to cross the river, then had my things put aboard.

The gang-plank guard did not read my pass, and I went aboard and directly to the surgeon in charge of the boat, and told him the situation, asking him to ignore my presence until we were well on our way, also to keep a state room for me. Then I went immediately to the sick, and tried to make them as comfortable as possible for the night. Soon an officer came aboard and called out, "All females will immediately come ashore." I looked him square in the face and saw him go, but I did not choose to go with him. The boat swung out and headed downstream, and I was afloat. I found a room and took possession, then looked around me, and soon saw a woman with two little girls. Her husband had smuggled her on board, as they were in the city and destitute, and the soldiers had agreed to divide rations with them, and give her their washing to do. At length we arrived and disembarked, and I followed the regiment to camp through the darkness and wind, as I knew of nowhere else to go. A few days after our arrival there was to be a grand review. A horse was furnished for my use and I rode out to see the parade. It was very imposing —a sight that is seldom seen in our time and country. Yet in spite of the splendor I returned to sick soldiers, who lay on the damp ground, wrapped only in a blanket.

Early Sunday morning we were roused by the drum calling to battle. The men responded promptly, leaving me with only one attendant, to care for the helpless sick. I gave them some coffee and hardtack, with a smile and the assurance that I would get them out of the way of the flying lead. The camp was in range of the battle, and I knew the regiment had no ammunition, and must soon fall back, perhaps before I could even get the men ready to go. Several balls came tearing through the tent, creating almost a panic. We had gone there in the dark, and had not taken the trouble to find out our position, and what to do we did not know. Suddenly I thought of a lieutenant who had been sick the day before. I sought among the tents and found him, and he gave me the points of the compass, and told me of a ravine near by where we must try to get the men. Those who were unable to walk we carried on poles, and thus all were transported but one old man, who was delirious and would neither go nor be carried.

A captain came in, wounded in the left shoulder, and so once more I went to the camp and returned with what I could carry, then bound up the wounds to stop the blood. By that time an orderly came with the command to get the men as far down the ravine as we could, and an ambulance would meet us there. As soon as all was in order I took a rifle and started for the battleground. I crossed a cotton-field, and passed an old log house known as the Post Office. I met an aged couple, each with a large bundles and trying to reach the river, but going the opposite way. They were German, and did not understand my English. I was not a German scholar, but I spoke to them the best I could and set them in the right direction, then hurried on. When I reached the line I found our men in great numbers, and worked as long as I could find anything to do with. After using my own handkerchief and skirt, and everything I could get at, I went down to the river. There I saw such sights as I never want to see again: wounded men, mules and horses, tents and blankets, in the wildest disorder. The surgeon was attending to putting the men on a boat. He sent me aboard to do what I could. There were men wounded in all imaginable ways. Soon an amputation table was prepared; meanwhile I sat down on the floor with my back to the partition, trying to rest a moment, as I had been passing through so much since before daylight. A woman came out of a stateroom just in time to see me there, and walking up to me she said in sharp tones, "Why don't you go to work?" As I had been on my feet all that dreadful day, without food and working in blood, I thought her question called for a reply, and I asked, "Why don't you go to work yourself, and see how you like it?" She said, "I am at work taking care of my husband, who has had his thumb shot, and is in that stateroom." I quietly walked over the wounded men to see him. He had had his thumb well dressed on the field. I found the kitchen, interested those in charge, and was soon giving coffee and hardtack to men who had not tasted food that day. Then I went to dressing wounds, and worked with the surgeon all night, and all the next day.

Monday night I slept on the colored woman's bed for two hours, then went to work again. Thursday I went on board a boat loaded for Cincinnati, in order to get some clothing, as my trunk had been lost during the battle. I purchased the needed articles, and returned to beat up the Tennessee River. I was so exhausted that I paid little attention to anything during the trip. On our arrival I reported to General Grant, who gave me an order to remain on a boat in the harbor until the hospital boat arrived. This gave me a little spare time, which I utilized by visiting the old campground, and looking up all the regimental hospitals along the way, taking orders for such sanitary goods as they needed. I went to the lower landing, where Mrs. Bickerdyke was in charge, and offered to assist her; but she promptly declined my help in a way which to me was rather amusing. She did not ask me into the tent; but, undaunted, I passed on, taking the number of Illinois men and their condition, for I knew there would be a boat for them that afternoon. The boat came, with a supply of sanitary goods. This I boarded and went to the room I had left in the morning, a tired, hungry woman.

I gave the president of the Commission the names of the men, and their condition so far as my observations had extended, and he took the matter in charge. Then I rode thirty miles without leaving the saddle. The next day I went aboard the boat and to work in earnest, as the men had lain so long that they were in need of immediate attention. Soon after I returned to my old rooms at Jefferson Barracks and set about getting my ward in order. The enlargement of the hospital had made a change of management necessary, and there were now other women there, so my work was much easier. Here I received a new certificate as Miss Dix's nurse, as the other was lost in my trunk. This second one was dated June 26, 1862. So I continued to work and wait for the end of the war, until the siege of Vicksburg. On the morning of May 17, 1863, I left for that field. I went on board a boat used as a transfer, May 21st. Here I met Generals Grant and Sherman, and Inspector General Howard. He was sick and cross, but thought he was all right. Dr. Hodges said I was sarcastic, but I stood the rebuke, for I was apt to express my mind, let the remarks hit or miss; and I thought only of the men, who had done quite as well as could be expected.

I stayed on the boat in plain sight of Vicksburg, and could hear the cannon and feel the vibrations almost as plainly as at Pittsburg Landing, although we were much farther from the battle. We left with nine hundred sick and wounded, and on the 12th had an accident to the boat, by running into a snag, but it did not damage the hull or hurt any of the patients. The next day the boats were lashed together for protection, as the shores were occupied by the enemy. But we arrived in safety the 14th.

My lot was about the same as that of other nurses, so far as I know. I attended strictly to the sick, irrespective of rank or personal pleasure. I continued the work until June 1864; then being tired out, and knowing the war must soon close, I resigned. During the time I was on duty I had many pleasant incidents, as well as many very sad ones; and among the saddest was writing to wife or mother that the dear one was dead. This I found no small task, as the men were of all nationalities, and it required much thought to express what I desired. But I can simply say that in this, as in other things, I tried to do my best.

Lucy L. Campbell Kaiser
SAINT CHARLES, ILLINOIS

Louisa Kamp

IN RESPONSE TO A CALL FOR NURSES to go South, to care for the sick and wounded, I volunteered, and sailed from New York, somewhere between the 5th and the 10th of March 1863, under orders to report at Hilton Head, South Carolina, but upon my arrival I was sent to Beaufort, where a place was assigned me in a hospital, under Surgeon Merritt at first, then under Surgeon Hayden, who took his place. After serving there until the last of August, I became very sick with malaria, and returned home on a furlough, intending to resume the work soon; but I did not recover sufficiently to do so.

Louisa C. Kamp
MERRIMACPORT, MASSACHUSETTS

Mary Knowles

THERE WERE FIVE WOMEN in the Webster United
States Hospital, where I served in Manchester, New Hampshire, but
only three of us are now living,—Mrs. Buncher, Miss Dudley, and myself; I do not know where Miss Dudley is at present. Mrs. Buncher had
charge of the Diet Department and my work was to prepare food for
the sick and wounded who were not able to go into the general "mess
hall."

I went from Nashua, New Hampshire to the hospital in 1864, and
came out in 1865; was there just about a year. We nurses did what we
could for the "boys in blue" who were under our charge; but I have always been sorry that I did not follow a regiment, as I think that
perhaps, in that way, I could have made myself more useful.

Mary F. Knowles
DERRY, NEW HAMPSHIRE

Mary Livermore

MARY ASHTON RICE LIVERMORE was born in Boston, Massachusetts, December 19, 1821. Her father, Timothy Rice, of Northfield, Massachusetts, served in the United States Navy during the war of 1812–15. Her mother, Zebiah Vose Glover Ashton, was the daughter of Capt. Nathaniel Ashton, of London, England. Mrs. Livermore was placed in the public schools of Boston at an early age and graduated at fourteen, receiving one of the six medals distributed for good scholarship. There were then no high, normal, or Latin schools for girls and their admission to colleges was not even suggested.

She was sent to the Female Seminary in Charlestown, Massachusetts, now Boston, where she completed the four years' course in two, when she was elected a member of the faculty, as teacher of Latin and French. While teaching she continued her studies in Latin, Greek, and metaphysics under tutors; resigning her position at the close of the second year to take charge of a family school on a plantation in Southern Virginia, where she remained nearly three years. As there were between four and five hundred slaves on the estate, Mrs. Livermore was brought face to face with the institution of slavery and witnessed deeds of barbarism as tragic as any described in "Uncle Tom's Cabin." She returned to the North a radical Abolitionist, and entered the lists against slavery, and every form of oppression. She was identified with the Washingtonian Temperance Reform before her marriage; was on the editorial staff of a juvenile temperance paper, organized a Cold Water Army of fifteen hundred boys and girls, for whom she wrote temperance stories, which she read to them and which were published in book form, under the title of "The Children's Army." In 1857 the Livermores removed to Chicago, Illinois where Mr. Livermore became proprietor and editor of a weekly religious paper, the organ of the Universalist denomination in the Northwest. Mrs. Livermore became his associate editor. At the first nomination of Abraham Lincoln for the Presidency, in the Chicago Wigwam in 1860, she was the only woman reporter assigned a place among a hundred or more men reporters.

Out of the chaos of benevolent efforts evolved by the opening of the Civil War in 1861, the United States Sanitary Commission was born. Mrs. Livermore, with her friend, Mrs. Jane C. Hoge, was identified with relief work for the soldiers from the beginning. Mrs. Livermore resigned all positions, save that of her husband's papers, secured a governess for her children, and subordinated all demands upon her time to those of the Commission. She organized Soldiers' Aid Societies; delivered public addresses in the principal towns and cities of the Northwest; wrote letters by the hundreds, personally and by amanuenses, and answered all that she received; wrote the circulars, bulletins and monthly reports of the Commission; made trips to the front with sanitary stores, to whose distribution she gave personal attention; brought back large numbers of invalid soldiers who were discharged, that they might die at home; assisted to plan, organize, and conduct colossal Sanitary Fairs; detailed women nurses for the hospitals by order of Secretary Stanton, and accompanied them to their posts: in short, the story of women's work during the war has never been told, and can never be understood save by those connected with it. The war over, Mrs. Livermore resumed the former tenor of her life, and took up the philanthropic and literary work which she had temporarily relinquished. Notwithstanding, her many years of hard service, she is still in vigorous health. Happy in her home, and in the society of her husband, children, and grandchildren, she keeps steadily at work with voice, and poll, and influence, ready to lend a hand to the weak and struggling, to strike a blow for the right against the wrong, to prophesy a better future in the distance, and to insist on a woman's right to help it along. Since her return from Chicago, her home has been in Melrose, Massachusetts.

Mary Loomis

MY TWO AND A HALF YEARS OF SERVICE during the war I shall not soon forget. The privations and sufferings of our brave and noble boys will always linger in my memory.

At the time the war broke out, my home was in Coldwater, Michigan. I entered the service with my husband sometime in May 1861 as a volunteer nurse, and was not under authority of any one except the surgeon. Later I was appointed matron of Hospital No. 13, Nashville, Tennessee, and remained there from September 1862 until January 1863. This hospital was in charge of H. J. Herrick, M.D. of the 17th Regiment Ohio Volunteers. I then went to No. 20, Nashville, and stayed until May, as matron under J. R. Goodwin, M.D., surgeon in charge.

I was also in a hospital at Murfreesboro, Tennessee and at Huntsville, Alabama. In all, I was in hospitals about a year; the remainder of the time I was in camp or on the march with my husband, Capt. George W. Van Pelt, and I always found plenty of work to do there. My husband fell in the battle of Chickamauga in September 1863, and in November I left the service.

Mary A. Loomis
BURR OAK, SAINT JOSEPH CO., MICHIGAN

Elizabeth Lucas

I WAS BORN IN DARLINGTON, ONTARIO in May 1835. My father was a firm friend of William Lyon McKenzie, and both grandfathers were among the early settlers of Connecticut, and served with General Washington. Both were with him the night he crossed the Delaware. I was married to William Lucas, September 28, 1852, and we moved to Michigan.

He enlisted in the 4th Michigan Cavalry, January 5, 1864, and was sent to Atlanta. Late in the fall his regiment returned to Louisville to recruit. My husband was sick, and I went to him there; and when the regiment went to the front, I accompanied it, for I thought he would soon have to go into a hospital. About the 1st of January 1865, I went into Brown Hospital, where I served in the linen room. Then my husband had his leg broken and was sent to Tennessee; but I had him transferred to Brown Hospital, where I could care for him. He had a long run of typhoid fever, so he was under my care some time. My daughter was with me, but was too young to be allowed to nurse, so she served in the linen room.

When the hospital broke up, I was discharged in August 1865, and came to the little farm where I still live. I recall an incident that occurred when I has on a United States steamer going from Cincinnati to Louisville. Just at evening the guerrillas fired upon the boat, breaking windows and frightening every one generally. The soldiers on board returned the fire, but it was so dark that they could not see even the banks where the guerrillas were hidden. Then the captain ran the boat so fast that we were more afraid the boiler would burst or the boat run aground, than we had been of the enemy. We reached Louisville in safety, however, and remained on board until the next morning.

Elizabeth Lucas
SWAN CREEK, MICHIGAN

Margaret Mackey

I WENT FROM MILWAUKEE, June 10, 1863, and served until July 1865 at Hospital No. 2, located on College Hill, at Nashville, Tennessee. During the first year I was there, Major Lyon was surgeon in charge; then he was sent to the front to a field hospital, and Major Herbert took his place in No. 2. At the close of the war I returned to my home.

Yours in F., C. and L.,
Margaret Mackey
390 4TH STREET
MILWAUKEE, WISCONSIN

Ellen Marsh

EARLY IN THE YEAR 1863 I commenced my duties as nurse in a military hospital. On my arrival at the barracks I was shown by the surgeon in charge through several wards, and introduced to some of the nurses with whom I was soon to be associated. The long rows of beds on either side of each ward, upon which were so many sufferers, made a deep and lasting impression. I felt I had undertaken a responsible work.

On the first day my attention was attracted to a man past the prime of life, who was evidently near its close. I was told that he wanted a letter written, but I found him too weak to do more than give the name of a brother to whom he wished to have his last words sent. The chaplain had talked with him, and felt convinced he died a Christian.

For ten days I found very interesting work writing for some, reading to others, and finding books, papers, and tracts for others; and had an opportunity to become acquainted with the character of those with whom I was to be associated, and thus learned how to meet their wants, and also gained a knowledge of the daily duties of a nurse before I was assigned a ward. But when I received my orders in military form, to report for duty to the surgeon of Ward A, I felt,—I shall have my own little province, and my own patients, for whom I shall work with a hearty good will. I looked up and down my ward—two hundred feet long. There were the same two rows of beds as in the others. They looked even longer than they were to me, just commencing the work; but as day after day I passed from one end to the other, looking after the wants of my patients, the distance grew less and my ward a home,—the patients my family. It is not strange that one had the feeling of sister for men who had suffered so bravely for their country, and a sympathizing and encouraging word for the coarsest and roughest among them; remembering that many had not enjoyed privileges of home and education.

The ward always looked cheerful, for a dozen windows on each side let in the sunlight, and the curtains were rolled high, that none of its cheer or warmth should be lost.

The most of the patients were convalescing, as they had been cared for during the winter, and only needed nourishment to fit them for the field as the spring campaign opened, or to be sent home, having been found unfit for duty in the army. By the side of one bed (a fever patient) sat the wife to whom he was too feeble to talk, but resigned to death. The only hope was what most careful nursing and nourishment could do for him; but his system was too reduced and in five weeks we stood at his death bed. Death seemed more solemn in such surroundings. For a time quietness prevailed in the ward. Soon all was as usual, the bed removed, and our patient's body prepared for burial. Words of comfort and sympathy to the wife and such aid for her homeward journey was given as was in our power. Then others claimed our attention.

On the same side of the ward sits another very young wife, whose husband is suffering from gangrene in his foot, which had been frozen. It was thought amputation would be necessary, but nature did the work, aided by rest and courage, and a cheerful disposition which has done much for him. In a few weeks he is walking around the ward, with the aid of crutches, and eagerly waiting for his turn to go home.

On the opposite side of the ward lay a Massachusetts boy, pale, delicate, and seemingly not long for this world. Below him is a boy about the same age, who was transferred from the same hospital to ours a few days before I had taken charge. These were the greatest sufferers, and the ones to whom I should devote the most of my time. The little patient last named needs more than passing notice. His courage and uncomplaining disposition under so much suffering is remarkable, and shows him to be a true soldier. The little form, bent out of shape, is pitiable. The limbs are swelled, and the cords so contracted that he cannot straighten them. One arm, his right, entirely helpless, and so emaciated that it is like a skeleton, lies on his breast. Two abscesses formed on that side prevent his moving it; therefore his food must be so prepared that he can pick it up with his left hand. He cannot let any one feed him while he is able to do so much with his other hand. His appetite is fitful as a consumptive's; we must tax our minds to get him the delicacies that will tempt him. Visitors are interested to help us; so Charlie fares quite well. He says as I often write for him, "Tell mother I am doing well,—that I have not lost my courage." His father, at home, is dying, and the other children are younger than Charlie, so there is no one to come for him. I passed many hours reading to him, or listening while he told of his school days and his life in the army. He had deceived about his age when he had enlisted,—was younger than allowed. He had acted as orderly, and had the promise of a better position. He could not believe but he would get well;—would say, "I am too young to die," even with such helplessness that he must be turned by an attendant if he wanted to change his position, as he could not lie but a few minutes on his back.

Our short services Sunday consisted of reading a portion of Scripture, a hymn, and then the prayers. To these he looked forward, although he would not acknowledge a deep interest in spiritual things, and even disliked to have the chaplain talk to him. He enjoyed having the patients sit round his bed and sing hymns, and would select one after another, and often we could hear his feeble voice join in. "There is rest for the weary," was one of his favorites. He failed gradually, but surely. The Sunday before he died he asked the chaplain to pray with him; and as we stood by his bed it was a solemn thing to realize that as long as the poor sufferer had strength, he clung to earthly support; but in his weakness called on God. We cannot doubt but God in his mercy heard. His mother arrived just at the last. She had started after the funeral of her husband. One evening just after "taps" I had left the ward, when there was a knock at my door, with the announcement that "the sick boy's mother has arrived." I hastened to welcome her, and made her comfortable to watch by her boy that night.

A few days later we stood by his bed. His mother, too overcome, had left the room, when he said, "Call mother; I want to say good-bye." He said to her: "Tell them at home I die happy. I hope I am forgiven. I am going to father." At his request the patients stood around his bed and sang, "I'm going home, to die no more." At the close of the hymn he breathed his last. The spirit had gone to God, who gave it; and the widowed mother went home alone to mourn her oldest child.

My services as nurse commenced February 15, 1863, at Armory Square Hospital, Washington, D.C. and covered nineteen months, with intervals of absence to get recruits.

Ellen Marsh
LINGWOOD, PRINCES PARK
LIVERPOOL, ENGLAND

Elvira Mason

MRS. ELVIRA MASON WAS ASSIGNED TO DUTY in December 1864, at Dale, United States Hospital, Worcester, Massachusetts, upon application of C. N. Chamberlain, surgeon in charge; and received an honorable discharge, September 20, 1865.

She writes:—

I did not go into the field, so of course I did not endure the suffering and privation that others did. I went from the town of Spencer, Massachusetts, and returned there when my labors at the hospital were ended. If I were well enough to write, I should be glad to tell of many incidents that came under my observation. I consider the ten months in the hospital the most interesting part of my life. My duty was mostly to look out for the extra diet of those who were not able to go to the mess table. In spite of my weakness, I will note one little incident.

One day the orderly came to tell me there was a new patient in Ward 6, a prisoner from Andersonville, and that he was a mere skeleton. I thought I would take him a good dinner, so I went to the Extra Diet Kitchen and prepared a piece of beefsteak, some mashed potato, a slice of nicely browned toast, and a mug of tea. He was sitting about midway of the ward, and I went immediately to him, saying: "Good morning, my poor fellow! I have brought you a nice dinner." He gave it one glance, then turned his head away, saying, "Oh, don't, don't!" "Don't what? " said I. "Aren't you hungry?" "Don't bring me so much.

It makes me sick!" I understood the situation and carried the food away, bringing back only a little on a small plate. "I think I can eat that," he said. Every day I increased the amount until he could eat a full ration. His eyes began to brighten, and soon he could go about the ward with the other boys; but I shall never forget the look he gave that plate of dinner.

I wish I were able to write more but cannot.

Yours in F., C. and L.,
Mrs. Elvira Mason
WEST PULLMAN, ILLINOIS

Rena Miner

MRS. RENA L. MINER, formerly Miss Littlefield, is a granddaughter of old Squire Littlefield, who was widely known throughout Northern Indiana and Southern Michigan, in the early settlement of that section. He was a man of iron constitution, indomitable will, strong convictions, and gruff manners; yet possessed of a generosity so broad, and a sympathy so ready, that he was instinctively sought as a champion of the oppressed. With what he saw to be wrong he held no compromise, but was its open, bitter, implacable foe.

Albert Littlefield, his eldest son and Mrs. Miner's father, was a man of wide mental attainments, studious, conscientious, and of an exceedingly retiring nature. It was said of him, "He never wronged a fellow being; a poor man himself, he has often divided his last dollar with one poorer."

Mrs. Miner is a true descendant of this hardy and scholarly ancestry. In early girlhood she manifested to an unusual degree an interest in social problems. She was troubled by the inequalities in environments and opportunities, the unjust estimate placed upon worth as opposed to position, and probably more so from the fact that it became necessary, early in life, that she should fight its battles for herself. This she began to do when scarcely out of childhood, as mill operator, seamstress, and compositor. During this hard life she managed to become advanced in the textbooks of the schools so that a few months' discipline fitted her to procure a certificate for teaching. After this she taught and attended school alternately until she had graduated from the common school course at Sturgis, Michigan.

At the breaking out of the war she was enthused with a patriotic desire to aid in maintaining the Union. Her father being too much of an invalid, and her brother too young to enter the service, she determined to represent the family herself, and appealed to the president of the Indiana Sanitary Commission for permission to enter hospital service. This request was refused on account of her youth; but, nothing daunted, she applied again and again, until struck by the resolution manifested, and receiving assurances from the home physicians of her capability, the gentleman finally informed her that if she would secure six elderly ladies to accompany her, he would give her an appointment with the rest, as their services were much needed. She promptly did; but when the time for departure came all but one had deserted, having become faint-hearted from the dismal predictions of their friends.

With this one friend she proceeded to Indianapolis, and was immediately sent to Louisville, Kentucky, whence they were transferred to Jeffersonville General Hospital. Late in the autumn of 1864 the hospital was nearly emptied by transfers, and she returned to her home for several months, but was again assigned to duty at St. Louis, where they received the returned prisoners of war, who were more pitiable, if possible, than wounded soldiers; remaining there until the closing of the hospitals, in October 1865, making sixteen months of service.

She was married to Mr. P. P. Miner, a veteran soldier, in September 1866. She is the mother of three children, and has performed all of her own household labor. During all these years she has been a trusted comrade, inspiring genius at her husband's side, preparing his thoughts as well as her own for the press. For half a score of years she was a constant contributor to the Western Rural. She has also been a contributor to the *Courant* of Chicago, the *Chicago Express*, *Indianapolis Leader*, *Industrial News*, *Michigan Patriot*, *New Forum*, and many others. In company with Mrs. I. C. Fales of Brooklyn, she founded the *Sociologic News*. She editing the Western department.

Mrs. Rena Miner
SAINT CHARLES, MICHIGAN

Hannah Moir

AMONG THOSE WHOSE SERVICE in the hospitals during the war deserves special mention, one whose service commenced early in 1861 and continued until the close of the long and bitter struggle, stands the name of Mrs. Hannah D. Moir; a name near and dear to many a faithful defender of the Union who has cause today to bless her memory. She was one who made the last moments of many a dying hero more pleasant by her faithful care.

She was a daughter of Nathaniel Thomas, but married a man named Moir, who held a commission in the main army. He was severely wounded and died of his wounds in a Washington hospital, where his faithful wife ministered to his wants until the end; then felt it her duty to remain and care for other brave men who needed her attention. Here her noble, self-sacrificing nature could find full scope. All so blessed as to come under her care were made to feel the influence of her gentle words. Young, bright, and of a cheerful disposition, she cast only rays of sunshine in her pathway, cheering the boys who lay sick or wounded as only a woman can. Kind, sympathetic, taking the burdens of others on herself so far as she was able, going on errands of mercy from one place to another. She was a ministering angel to all within the reach of her care or influence. My pen is inadequate to the task of giving my readers any conception of her goodness; but the recording angel, I believe, has written her deeds, and the "Well done" has been pronounced for her in heaven.

The writer of this sketch can vouch for her good works, as, severely wounded he lay, for months under her tender care. I have been invited to tell an incident in connection with my faithful nurse, and have consented, as I feel it may be of interest to some of the readers of this book.

I had been in Harewood Hospital for several weeks, being ministered to by this faithful friend, before I was aware that only a few miles separated our birthplaces. In my possession was a case containing over one hundred photographs of my friends in the North. I had carried these three years and more, and they had been a great comfort to me. They lay on the table at the head of my cot, and the boys who were able to walk would come to look at them. One day while they were thus engaged Mrs. Moir, in passing, noticed one in the hands of a soldier who had been my roommate, in former years, at Brookline, Massachusetts. Stopping, she addressed me thus: "How came you by that lady's picture?" "She gave it to me," I replied, "as she formerly belonged in my town." "Where is your company from?" she asked. "Plymouth," I replied. "Why, I was from Duxbury, and that makes us neighbors, does it not?" From that time the friendship already existing strengthened, and my own dear mother could not have done more for me than did my nurse. I wrote my friend of the discovery of her old friend, and a correspondence was opened, which for some unknown reason stopped at the close of the war.

I was brought to my home, and for a long time was helpless; but as time wore away, and my wounds allowed me to travel, I proceeded to visit Duxbury in search of my faithful friend, but all my labor was in vain. Years came and went, and still my longings were not satisfied. I wished once more to meet her and reward her for her kindness. Years later the friend, formerly of Brookline, said to me, "I have got track of Mrs. Moir, and as soon as I locate her, I will write to you of her whereabouts; she is writing in some office in Boston."

Now comes the singular part of my story. As each Christmas came it made my desire to reward my nurse more earnest, for I felt that I owed my life to her care and devotion. One Christmas Eve I had made my usual presents, then I said to my good wife: "Only one thing remains to be done. Could I find her, I should make Mrs. Moir a present; then I should be content." In a dream that night I thought myself on the same battlefield where I was last wounded, with every stick, stone, and stump about me as of old. As I lay there a woman approached me, passed, and turning back, came and called my name as she grasped my hand.

I at once recognized Mrs. Moir, dressed in her deep black, as of old. I never saw any one more plainly than I saw her. As I looked, the form vanished; but the black-gloved hand remained, and for several moments I felt plainly the pressure of that friendly grasp. I sprang from my bed and told my wife the dream, the same as I have related it to you, my readers. Now judge of my surprise when on the way to my office, walking down Broadway, South Boston (an unusual thing to do), as I passed my uncle, J. T. Cole's, undertaker's rooms, he stood in the doorway and invited me in. I accepted the invitation, seated myself by his desk, and carelessly glanced at a burial permit, on which I read these words, "Mrs. Hannah D. Moir, daughter of Capt. Nathaniel Thomas, of Duxbury, aged 38." I fainted dead away as I read, and when once more I was myself, my uncle said, "What was it that so affected you?" I replied, "You have listened to the story of my nurse; that death certificate is for her, I am sure; I know by the way the name is spelled."

He said, "This lady wrote in the office of Lawyer Robb at 25 Bromfield Street, Boston, and boarded at 428 Broadway, South Boston." It was near my own home. I at once visited 25 Bromfield Street and there learned that my fears were too true. The recital by her of my wounds was retold to me. I saw her in her casket, and how I longed for those closed eyes to open, those sealed lips to speak as of old! But she had gone to her reward. The dream I had of her, and the time I sprang from my bed, was within five minutes of the time her spirit took its flight. Since then, all I can do is from time to time to decorate her grave with flowers; but I hope one day to express my gratitude to one of God's noble women.

I might speak of the faithful service of others who ministered to my wants in the Overton Hospital, at Memphis, or on the battlefield; also on the journey to Washington, when I was near death's door; but it is not mine to know their names, although their memory is engraved on my heart, never to be erased. May God bless the faithful nurses, living and dead, who served their country and did as heroic duty as did any general or private who wore a uniform of blue. May Heaven deal kindly by the army nurses, as they dealt kindly by us.

Samuel A. Wright

296 STATE STREET, BOSTON, MASSACHUSETTS

Mary Moore

I WAS APPOINTED HOSPITAL MATRON by Colonel Smith of the 58th Regiment, Illinois Volunteers, in November 1861 at Camp Douglas, Chicago, and served there until some time in February, when our regiment left for Cairo, Illinois; then went to Fort Donelson, Tennessee where I helped to care for the sick and wounded during the battle, and afterwards on a hospital steamer. I next accompanied a party of soldiers to Cairo, where I cared for them until all but one were able to leave the hospital.

While at Fort Donelson, I have sometimes gone two or three days without any sleep, and with only an occasional cup of coffee or some hardtack, which I would eat as I went in and out among the sick. At one time all the sleep I had for three nights was on the bare floor, between my husband and a sick soldier, and with my husband's arm for a pillow.

No one but the poor boys themselves can imagine as we nurses can what suffering they had to endure during the Rebellion. I recall one poor old colored man who had borne a great deal, having been shot several times. I took eighteen buckshot out of his back one day.

I was in the hospitals something over nine months; then my husband died, and I returned to my home.

Mary E. Moore
KING CITY, MISSOURI

Janette Morrill

I WAS COMMISSIONED BY THE COLONEL of the 6th Regiment, Michigan Infantry, August 28, 1861, and served in Baltimore, Maryland, until April 1862 when I was assigned by Miss Dix to the Judiciary Square General Hospital, Washington, D. C. On account of severe illness, I left the service November 1, 1863.

Among the many amusing incidents of hospital life was the case of a man nearly fifty years of age, who, with half a regiment, was brought in sick with the measles. I could not make him understand the nature of a contagious disease. He thought he was sick enough to die; and remembering my own experience when I was a child, I did not much wonder. When at last he comprehended that in order to take the disease one must come in contact with some one who has it, he wanted me to write to his wife immediately, and tell her to see that the children have the measles, all but the baby. Why he made that exception he would not say; but made me begin and end the letter by telling "Eliza to have the children catch the measles."

A very pathetic thing occurred at one time when a number of patients were brought into the General Hospital at Washington. I was busy here and there with those who seemed most in need of care, when something like a sob reached my ear. I heard it several times, and it fixed my attention. I passed slowly along the ward, among the fifty or sixty beds, and finally reached a youth who looked as though his place were in the schoolroom rather than as a soldier. When he saw me watching him he broke down completely, and cried like a child. My own tears mingled with his as I tried to comfort him. I learned that he was not sixteen when he left his widowed mother in Kentucky and started for the front, and that night was the first time in eighteen months that he had heard a woman's voice.

But to me the saddest of all memories, and the one that makes other sorrows seem lighter, is the search for the missing ones, those for whom it was impossible to account,—father, brother, husband or lover. The thought of the dreadful uncertainty hanging over so many lives all these years makes me very thankful that my graves are on the quiet hillside at home.

Janette Maxwell Morrill
LAWTON, MICHIGAN

Matilda Morris

Eᴀʀʟʏ ɪɴ ᴛʜᴇ ᴡᴀʀ I ᴄᴏɴᴄᴇɪᴠᴇᴅ ᴛʜᴇ ᴘʟᴀɴ of going into some hospital as a nurse; but my friends would not listen to my plan, saying there was work enough to do at home. In spite of this, I could not feel that making shirts, bandages, etc., was all I ought to do. My mother finally gave her consent, and I wrote to David Todd, then Governor of Ohio, to see if I could get a pass. In about a week came a reply, containing pass and transportation to Washington, D. C. I was not long in making my preparations, yet it seemed a great undertaking, as I was not accustomed to traveling alone.

It was one morning in August 1862 that I left my home in Randolph, Ohio, leaving my two dear little daughters in the care of their loyal grandparents, who bade me Godspeed in my undertaking, though it was a sad parting,—for God alone knew whether we should meet again on earth. I took the train at Atwater, Ohio, August 20, 1862 and at Wheeling, West Virginia, our trouble began.

A dispatch had been received before our arrival, warning the officers not to start any train for Washington until further notice was given, as the rebels were making a raid on every train on the B. & O. Railroad. One thousand soldiers were sent to clear the way, and the next morning word came that the train could start. We knew it was still a perilous undertaking, yet we were glad to take some risk rather than wait any longer.

Here I had been befriended by a family of Quakers, who were waiting for the same train. The gentleman had been over the road a great many times, so he could point out all the places of interest. He had been employed by President Lincoln as a scout all through those mountains, and was only taking his wife and sister to Baltimore, then would start on another scouting expedition. He gave much valuable information, and a letter of introduction to some friends of theirs in Washington. We did not see anything of the enemy, but heard occasional firing, and of course knew what that meant. We parted at Annapolis, never to meet again; and that evening I arrived in Washington, but it was too late to see my husband, who was wounded and in a hospital there. I was very tired, and glad of a good night's rest at the hotel. When I awoke I could scarcely believe that I was at the Capital of the United States (or, rather, Divided States, just then). At nine o'clock I went to Armory Square Hospital, and found my husband's wound much worse than I had expected. I will not try to tell you how we felt, to meet again after so long a time, although under such trying circumstances.

When the surgeon came to make his morning call, I told him why I was there, and what I wanted to do, and learned that there would soon be need of more nurses. The next morning I reported to Doctor Bliss, and we had a long talk, which ended by his engaging me to begin my duties as soon as more patients came. He told me to remain until he needed me, but I was not idle very long.

One day I saw Doctor Bliss coming up the walk in great haste. "Ladies," he said, "if you have anything in particular that you wish to have done, do it now, for your ward will soon be full, and there will be plenty of work for us all. The enemy are coming this way, and there will be a big fight to keep them from entering the city." This was August 27th. Then came the Second Battle of Bull Run. The excitement in Washington was intense. We could hear the cannonading constantly. There were only a few patients left in our wards, and we put everything in readiness. We were near both of the river depots, where the wounded would be landed. Soon we heard a great commotion outside, and looking, I beheld what I never wish to see again. A sadder sight one could not imagine than those loads of wounded men. That day my life as a hospital nurse commenced. Our hearts and hands were full, tending to so many. Some died before they reached the building. Each ward had fifty beds and two nurses; but at home we think it hard work to care for one patient. It was a hard day for us all. First we gave each a drink of cold water, as that was their only cry. I shall never forget one poor fellow who was lying near an old building. He looked as if he were dead, but I stooped to make sure, and thought I saw his lips move. The man who was carrying the pail cried: "Come along! He is dead, fast enough." "No; wait a minute," I replied, and began to wet his lips. Very soon I had him revived so much that he could drink out of my cup. He was a New York Zouave. The next time I saw him he was on his way to his regiment. After water had been given to all we went around with bread and butter and coffee. Oh, how the poor hungry fellows did relish it! I had many a "God bless you" that day. A great many had been carried into the wards while we were working outside, and we next procured washbasins, soap and water, and went to washing the blood from their faces,—a work that was very grateful to the men. This occupied the time until midnight.

I might write volumes about what happened in this one hospital, but shall have to pass over a great many events.

One battle followed another, and each furnished wounded soldiers. I remained until after the battles of the Wilderness and of Spottsylvania Court House. I have a little Testament that one of my boys gave me. He picked it up in the Wilderness. Poor fellow, he died on the way home. His father came for him, and stopped in Philadelphia to get another son who was so badly wounded that he was not expected to live many days. Another son was at the front. The father wrote to inform me of his boy's death, and he said that the mother's heart was almost broken. And so it was all through the war: fathers and mothers, sisters and brothers,—all suffering for the same cause.

After being in Armory Square Hospital a long time I was transferred to Findley Hospital, also situated in Washington, where I remained several months under Doctor Pancoast. We did not have much to do, and I made up my mind to go to the front. The doctor said he would like to have me stay, but finally made out my discharge papers. He also gave me a splendid recommendation. I feel very proud of these papers, as I do also those given one by Doctor Bliss.

In order to go to the front I had to enlist with Miss Dix. After going through with considerable red tape she employed another nurse and myself, and had us sent to Sandy Hook, near Harper's Ferry, where we reported to Surgeon Barnes, in October 1864. He told us there was not much to do, as he had just sent away a lot of wounded men; but we had better stay, and perhaps there would be more in soon. I said, "No; let us go farther down into the valley." So he gave us passes and transportations to Harper's Ferry. They were made out to take us to Winchester, Virginia but we could not go for several days, as General Sheridan was there with his cavalry. We all remember the battle, and the victories he achieved in the valley of the Shenandoah. In October, when things became a little more quiet, we started for Martinsburg. We had not gone more than half way when we had quite a thrilling adventure. Suddenly our train came to a standstill. The rebels had been there the night before and torn up the track for miles, and wrecked and burned the train ahead of ours. There we were in a barren country, not a house in sight, and with the enemy all around us. The rebels had made a mistake, and they were wild with disappointment. It was our train that had the pay-car attached, and that was why we had so many soldiers aboard.

Report said that a lady had been burned; and as Miss Evans and myself were walking along the track, I found a piece of partly burned hair that surely had come from some woman's head. There was melted glass and iron all around,—ruins everywhere; and we were glad when the road was repaired and we could leave that awful place, the sight of which made us nearly sick. We reached Martinsville late at night, very tired and hungry. The next day we started for Winchester, and oh, how it did rain! But we never stopped for rain in war times. At the station was an ambulance train to take us the remainder of the distance. I think there must have been a thousand soldiers to guard the stores, for an officer had said, "The rebs are thick as flies in August along that route." General Custer was with us, and several other officers whose names I did not learn. It was a dreadful march. The boys waded through mud and water the livelong day, but not a murmur could we hear. At noon we halted at a place called Bunker Hill. There was wood on one side and an open field on the other. It was a dreary looking place. Soon after the train stopped we saw two men riding into the woods, and supposed they had gone as scouts. In a few minutes we heard a shot at no great distance, and soon saw the same men returning with a pig across the back of one of the horses. I never saw anything prepared to cook as soon as that pig. They did not stop to scald it, as the farmers do, but pulled off the whole skin, and in a short time the animal was in slices. In the meantime a fire had been started, and soon the coffee-kettles and frying-pans were on. I told Miss Evans I was going to have some of that meat for our dinner. She skeptically inquired how I should get it. I took a can of condensed milk and some salt, and made a trade. The boys seemed to enjoy the fun, and some of them carried us some coffee.

It was a cold, dreary ride, but after a great many halts and skirmishes we arrived in Winchester about midnight. The next day we reported to Doctor Hayden, at Sheridan Hospital, which was composed entirely of tents, some so low that we had to stoop to enter; but they were all full of badly wounded men. If the scene at Armory Square was dreadful, this was a thousand times more so. Here the men lay on the bare ground, with knapsacks, boots, or anything for a pillow that would raise the head. Passing along, I saw things that made me sick at heart. A young man not more than eighteen had both legs shot off. He could not live, yet he seemed cheerful. We did what we could for them with our limited means; but finally our supplies gave out, and even hardtack became a luxury. We were told to care for the Confederates as we did for our own, and we obeyed orders; but deep in my heart I could not feel the same.

We remained there until it was safe to move the men to Baltimore. We had hospital cars, which are a little wider than ordinary ones, and are placed on springs. They have on each side three tiers of berths or cots, suspended by rubber bands, and so arranged as to yield to the motion. I made two trips with this train, and the men said it went like a cradle. It was a pleasure to take care of so cheerful a company. My journey lasted two days and nights, and I think I never passed forty-eight hours so fraught with both sad and pleasant memories.

We reported again to Miss Dix, who sent us back to Findley Hospital, where I remained until April 1865; then went into the city to stay with some friends named Edson. One of them was (Miss) Dr. Susan Edson, who with Doctor Bliss were prominent figures during President Garfield's sickness.

One day I saw an immense crowd gathered in front of the War Department. Secretary Stanton was reading a dispatch from General

Grant, —"Richmond and Petersburg are ours." This caused great rejoicing, which deepened when the news of the capitulation of the rebel
army was flashed over the wires. The next night we went to the White
House, to hear the President speak. I shall never forget how his face lit
up with joy. But ah, this was his last speech! A few brief days of wild rejoicing followed; then the bright future was suddenly overcast as
Treason guided the assassin's hand in its deadly work. The mighty had
fallen,—Abraham Lincoln, the noblest of martyrs, to a noble cause!

While I was at Armory Square Hospital, he visited it several times.
How the boys would rally if we told them "Uncle Abraham" was coming. He would go down one side of the ward and up the other, shaking
hands with every one, and speaking a kind word. He would then shake
hands with me, ask me about my work and my home, and charge me to
be good to "his boys." I have often seen the tears roll down his care-
worn cheeks while he was talking with some wounded soldier.

After the funeral I went with friends to Richmond, and visited many
places of interest. Among them, that terrible death-trap, Libby Prison,
and do not understand how any of our men came out alive. I saw the
basement floors paved with cobble stones, and a little straw was thrown
here and there. The floor was so slimy we could hardly walk; yet here
our men had to eat and sleep.

I saw Sheridan's army pass through the place on its way to Washington. The men had many strange pets on their shoulders. Some had
owls, others coons, and one had a bantam rooster, that crowed several
times in my hearing. It took two days for them to pass, and we carried
barrels of water for them to drink. The Secesh were surprised to see so
many left to go home. I was talking with one of Fitzhugh Lee's cavalry
men, and told him that was only a small branch of our army. He replied, "Madam, we are beaten, but not conquered."

May 18th I started for Washington. I reached the boat in good season, and supposed I was all right, but a colored man soon came to me
and said, "How came you on this boat?" I told him and showed my
pass. "Oh, you are all right, madam, so far as that goes; but we never
carry passengers on General Grant's private boat." I said I was exceedingly sorry for the mistake, and he could put me off at the next landing.
During the conversation a military-looking man had seated himself
near us, and seemed to be reading; but I knew he heard every word,

and I also knew very well who he was. He soon laid down his paper, saying, "Sam, what is the matter?" "Dis lady is on your private boat, sah." He came to me and said, "Madam, will you please to tell me all about it?" I did so, and he answered: "I don't see anything very serious about this mistake; there is room for us all. Make yourself perfectly at home. We only go to City Point, but you can change boats there." Then turning to the waiter he told him to "make the lady comfortable while she remains on board." This gentleman was our good General Grant.

At City Point we shook hands, he bade me good-bye, and I thanked him again for his kindness, then continued my journey. In the meantime my husband had secured his discharge papers, and we bade adieu to our associates.

Peace reigned once more. All that remained to be done was to go home and make glad the hearts of those from whom we had been parted so long. My father was at the same station where I left him almost three years before. Soon we met mother, sisters, and our own dear little girls.

This was a great many years ago, and those girls have children of their own now, and we are grandpa and grandma. They often coax me to tell a story of the war. My father and mother have long since gone to the home to which we must soon follow; but it is a pleasure to recall the fact that I had a part in the beneficent work in which it was woman's peculiar privilege to serve her country. I feel abundantly rewarded by the knowledge of having done something to alleviate the suffering of those who gave health and worldly prospects, ties of home, find even life itself in the perilous service. Sweet flowers and tender plants creep over the graves that were made so long ago on many a field and hillside; and thus tender memories arise to enwrap the gaunt figure, and veil the grim visage, of War, that must forever stand a central object upon the canvas that portrays the history of those memorable years. I thank God for all his mercies and blessings during all these years. It was He who led us through; and if we love and obey Him, He will take us unto Himself, where all will be joy and peace forever.

Matilda E. Morris
CLEVELAND, OHIO

Grandmother Newcomb

GRANDMOTHER NEWCOMB WAS NOT SECOND in many respects to Mother Bickerdyke. She also gave four years to the care of our wounded and sick soldiers. Although not present in so many battles, she labored bravely for our fallen heroes.

She tells us: "At one time while the boats were loading with wounded to go up the river, there was a boy who had his furlough and transportation, but when he applied for passage, the captain refused, as he had too many already. The poor boy called out to me: 'Take me, too! Let me go home to die!' I ran down the plank to him, and in some way I got him on the boat." How it was done is told in the following:—

Grandmother Newcomb of Illinois,
Known to hosts of the army boys
For numberless deeds of kindness done;
Widowed at bloody Donelson.
She took far more than her husband's place
In the conquering march of the loyal blue,
In deeds of mercy and motherly grace,
To the blue-coats first,—but the gray-coats too.

Grandmother Newcomb of Effingham,
That July day, when the great boats swam

At the foot of Vicksburg's yellow bluff,
When the stars and bars had fluttered low,
And the stars and stripes were fluttering high,
And for one day there was glory enough,—

Grandmother Newcomb, out of the glow
Of jubilant triumph, heard the cry
Of one of her wounded soldier boys:
'Take me back to my Illinois;
Take me back to my home to die!'

Onward swinging, the huge boat's prow
Slowly swinging, a moment more
Had left the agonized boy ashore,
In all the frenzy of wild despair,
To die in this far, hot land of sands;
And his cool green prairies even now
Stretching their myriad healing hands
To gather, and shelter, and heal him there.

No soldier can come aboard this boat,
Hoarsely its sullen captain said,
In a growl from the depths of his bearded throat,
With an angry shake of his vicious head.
'Dying or living, you stay ashore.
We have one load, and we'll take no more!'
And at his command the long stage plank
Slowly rose from the sandy bank,
And, rending the air with a pitiful moan,
The sick boy sank to the ground like a stone.

How she did it nobody knew,—
And nobody knew it less than she,—
But right in the face of the wondering crew,
Right in the teeth of the angry mate,
As the plank came up, she walked elate,
Bearing the wounded boy somehow,

In the burst of indignant ecstasy,
Into the midst of the cheering crew.
'There!' said she, as she laid him down,
And facing the mate with a threatening frown,
'You throw him out, and you throw me too.'

Cheer after cheer went up from the bank;
Cheers from the boats, crew after crew,
As the great boat, slowly hauling its plank,
Northward into the channel drew;

And happy visions of prairies bright,
Happy visions for one of the boys,
Taking his hopeful homeward flight,
Under the more than motherly care
Of the Dorian matron standing there,—
Grandmother Newcomb of Illinois.

Elizabeth Nichols

IN BEGINNING TO NARRATE THE SCENES of my army life I will state that I first entered the service at the request of my husband, who wished me to join him in Chicago, where his regiment had been sent on exchange, after having been taken prisoner at Harper's Ferry. My husband and many others were sick, so I started with as little delay as possible on the 17th of October 1862 at about 2 o'clock P.M. and arrived in Chicago at 2 A.M.

It was three miles to Camp Douglas, where our soldiers were quartered, and I rode that distance in the street cars. Alone in the darkness I found the gate, but it was closed. I rapped, and heard the "Halt! Who comes?" I gave the guard my name, told my business, and asked for admission, only to be told that he could not let me in. I must wait for the officer who would change the guards. But when he came he told me to stop at some hotel until morning, and then return. I replied that I was a stranger, and did not know where to go at that time of night. It seemed so hard to send me away that they at length admitted me, although it was against the rules: telling me not to speak aloud, they conducted me to the hospital, inquired for Stillman Nichols, and, leading me to his cot, asked him if I was his wife. Knowing how tired I must be, he soon asked them to find some place for me to rest. They led me to the baggage room, gave me a couple of blankets and a pillow, and I was soon asleep in spite of my strange surroundings. The call of the drum awoke me the next morning, and after breakfast I reported to the surgeon in charge, and entered upon my work. As soon as my husband became convalescent he was detailed with two others to assist me; the work was also made easier by Christian ladies who brought baskets of provisions. It was good to see how eager the "boys" were to get a share of the contents of those baskets.

At last we sent the sick to the City Hospital, to be cared for until they were able to join their regiments; then we broke camp and started for Washington, the journey requiring four days and three nights. Refreshments were served at several places on the road. Once some ladies asked me why I was there, and when I told them that my husband and I were nurses, they praised my patriotism.

We stayed in Baltimore about three hours, and while there our colonel received sealed orders for the regiment to go at once to Texas; but before we could embark the order was countermanded, and we were ordered to Washington, where we arrived at daylight, and marched to the "Soldiers' Rest." It being the Sabbath, services were conducted here by Chaplain Brown.

From there we marched to the Fairfax Seminary, crossing the long bridge. It was a beautiful place, a large brick building, with shaded lawn, where I saw the roses in bloom at Christmas time. Here we camped, and a large empty room was taken for a hospital, and as we had our stores with us we did very well.

While there I had the pleasure of attending a darkey wedding. There were about one hundred freed slaves present. A colored minister officiated, but as he could not read, our officer of the guard stood behind him and read the service out of the Episcopal Prayer Book, and the minister pronounced them man and wife. Then the bride and groom led the way to another room, where a large table was spread with as nice a supper as one need to eat. After the supper came the wedding dance. Two fiddlers furnished the music; and such music as I had not been used to hearing, to say the least. The party broke up about morning, all pronouncing it a merry occasion.

After our regiment had gone to Stockade Camp, my husband and I had to stay nearly two weeks with nine sick men. The only facilities we had for cooking were a coffee-pot, one mess-pan, a spider, and a fireplace. We got along some way and the time came when I started in an ambulance to join the regiment. I found a great many sick but we got them into a hospital tent as soon as we could and soon felt more at home, though one died that evening. Through the night my husband watched by the body, while, wrapped in my blanket, I slept on a pile of straw.

Soon there were many sick with typhoid fever and other maladies, and I have passed through scenes that I shall never forget. Often and often have I stood by a dying soldier to hear his last words. I had a habit of going through the ward to say good-night and speak a cheerful word, for I often knew that some would die before another day.

One morning as I was about to enter the hospital the doctor met me with the dreadful news that the smallpox had broken out but through the providence of God I was spared. There were eighteen cases and only one died.

After a time we were ordered to Centreville, Virginia; the regiment went first. We sent our stores to the General Hospital, then boarded a freight car; the cook, three doctors, my husband and myself completed the load of freight. We were in the last car, the one in front being loaded with hay. Sometime in the night, when we could not see where we were, we were left behind. I rested quite contentedly sitting on the car floor, and in the morning an engine was sent for us, so we reached our regiment at last.

I remained there two months, then went home on leave of absence; meanwhile our regiment was ordered to Gettysburg, so I did not return. Then my husband was very sick, and was cared for eight months in Philadelphia. I worked my board while there, so as to be near him, but the "Sisters" were nursing him. As soon as he recovered sufficiently he was ordered to Washington, where he was detailed as cook in the Invalid Corps Camp, and he sent for me to help him. I stayed there one year and four months; then my husband was discharged, and we went home.

Elizabeth B. Nichols
CLYDE, NEW YORK

Hannah Palmer

Hannah Lathrop Palmer was born in Peterboro, Madison County, New York, January 28, 1827. Her father was a lawyer, a man of fine education, conscientious and upright in his life and business relations; often filling positions of high public trust and responsibility. The mother was of the Eastern family of Lathrop, and affectionately seconded all her husband's plans for the education and welfare of their three daughters, of whom the subject of this sketch was the eldest.

In this family the principles of civil and religious liberty, and the practice of advanced thinking and living, were paramount, the father finding his place among the original Abolitionists, and taking his share of the obloquy and suspicion which fell to the lot of those who advocated the then unpopular principles of brotherhood and human equality. For nearly his lifetime he was associated with Gerrit Smith in the work of the "Underground Railroad," as a temperance worker, a neighbor, and friend. He died at the age of fifty-six years, leaving to the mother and eldest daughter the care of his property and family.

Miss Palmer's profession was that of teacher, and she spent many years in higher grade schools, finally carrying on for five years a boarding and day school of her own in Canastota, where she still resides. At the opening of the war her school was closed as were many others; and feeling sure from the logic of events, the records of history, and the current political indications, that the death-knell of slavery was about to sound, she went heart and soul into the work of helping on, were it in ever so humble a way, the giant task before the nation of casting off its bonds, and making itself free indeed before all the peoples of the earth.

At once she commenced collecting money and supplies, serving as secretary and treasurer of the Soldiers' Aid Society in her own town, and as soon as the Sanitary Commission was organized, sending to it whatever was collected, for more than two years. After the Proclamation of Emancipation and the virtual overthrow of slavery, Miss Palmer shared in the joy of those who saw a brighter future for the dear native land; and though that land was still overshadowed by the dark cloud of war, she never doubted the final result. But the cry of the prisoner was ever sounding, and the sufferings of the wounded were ever before her, and she felt she must give more efficient aid in the great struggle.

More nurses were called for, and a correspondence was opened with Miss Dix, which resulted in the acceptance of Miss Palmer's services; and Miss Dix, in her usual energetic manner, hastened her departure, writing, "I already have five good Miss Palmers in the service, and think you will make the sixth."

Leaving her widowed mother in the care of friends, she reached the residence of Miss Dix late on a dark night in the middle of April 1864, and was kindly received by the housekeeper, who said: "Miss Dix has gone on business to the surgeon-general's, but will soon return. She has been looking for you all day." Soon Miss Dix came in with cordial greetings, saying: "I am really glad you have come; we need help very much. We shall soon have severe fighting." Next morning after breakfast that noble woman attended prayers, beseeching earnestly that the terrible war-cloud might be lifted from the nation; that all who were working in the great cause of freedom might stand firm for the right; and that the one who had just come to help in the work might be aided and strengthened to do good service. It was like a benediction, serving as an inspiration, and fixing more firmly a determination to do all possible, in the midst of perils, to relieve the suffering and save the lives of our brave soldiers.

Miss Palmer was sent at once to Columbia College Hospital; Thomas R. Crosby was the surgeon in charge. All nurses going there held themselves in readiness to go wherever help might be needed. For a few days there was little to do, as nearly all the patients were convalescent; and in this interval of leisure, newcomers were directed to look about town, and visit the public buildings, sometimes helping to repair hospital garments, in anticipation of the great battle all knew was coming. Miss Palmer was retained in service here, and writes: "I had a great dread of seeing suffering, and early in May, after we knew that fighting had commenced, and the battle of the Wilderness was in progress, I could not sleep, but often sat for hours in the deep windows of my room, during the night, listening for the coming of the ambulances bringing the wounded.

"At length on one bright day they came,—eight hundred men,— some able to walk from the steamer upon which they had been brought up the Potomac; some were taken from the ambulances already dead, others bleeding and nearly exhausted. When the work was once before me I felt no more dread, but with a grateful heart that I was permitted to enter this service, I henceforth wished no rest nor ease."

Many of the wounds made at the battle of the Wilderness were of a very painful nature; the balls often striking against trees, and becoming flattened, glanced, and then, entering the flesh, tore their way with ragged edges, sometimes leaving in the wounds bits of bark or moss. And how tired the poor fellows were! Days and nights of weary marching with the excitement and wounds of battle, or severe sickness, had left many nearly bereft of strength and life.

At this time a large number of wall tents were erected on the college campus. As soon as they were in readiness Miss Palmer was placed in charge of the Seventh Ward, consisting of twelve tents, each containing ten patients. Mrs. Blanchard, of Syracuse, her roommate and co-worker, had been sent to the front with several others of long experiences.

From the battlefield of North Anna, in the latter part of May, and that of Cold Harbor, June 1st to 12th, many wounded were received. The heat having become intense, and the flies and other insects numerous, it was very difficult to make the sick and wounded comfortable. Those who had been longest in the service said it was the most fearful summer they had seen.

About July 10th occurred "Early's Raid in Maryland," and for several days it was feared that the enemy would take Washington. Every hospital turned out all its convalescents who were able to march; and the home guards, marines, department clerks, and citizens hastened to the front in defense of the city, and to the aid of the 6th and 2d Divisions of the 19th Army Corps.

Fort Stevens was then attacked. One night the danger was so imminent that Mr. Lincoln, who was with his family at his summer residence near the Soldiers' Home, was brought by his escort into the city for safety. Upon 14th Street for days there was constant marching of troops, and passing of artillery and ambulances. The women of this hospital filled the haversacks of their boys with every thing needful, and three hundred convalescents were sent to the front. Then with anxious hearts they listened to the booming of the guns; watching by night from the cupola of the college the campfires of the opposing forces, and by day the signaling with flags at the forts. A week after the battle, eight of the lady nurses were taken in an ambulance to the battlefield, which presented a scene of desolation undescribable. Rifle pits had been dug along the roadsides, and dozens of chimneys were standing solitary, where once had been happy homes,—their gardens desolated, and vines trailing in the dust. Among the residences burned was that of Postmaster General Blair. Several fathers, mothers, and friends were on the field, with ambulances or carriages, looking among the half-buried bodies for the remains of husband or son.

The weary summer passed in hard work, and anxiety for the sufferers in charge, and with wavering hopes for the country, as the tide of war surged onward. Many poor fellows, too badly wounded to live, passed from earth to their reward, as martyrs to their love of country; and often sorrowing friends came to bear away the remains of their beloved dead. There were many very painful and impressive scenes, but there was no time to stop and think. The sound of the "Dead March" seemed to be ever in the air as those who had passed away were taken to their resting places in Arlington. And as some poor fellow in his delirium, or in the weakness of his last hour, reached to take the hand of the nurse, with the cry, "oh, mother, mother!" she felt that it was indeed a great privilege to be permitted to minister to those noble defenders of the flag and of "the dear native land," in their suffering and last agony.

In October a large number of sick men were brought from the 19th Corps, one division of which had been for a long time detained in a malarious region in Texas; the Seventh Ward receiving among them a case of smallpox, but it was discovered before there was danger of contagion. In November all the men able to travel were allowed to go to their homes to vote, it being the time of the re-election of President Lincoln. Great enthusiasm prevailed, and the prospects of the country seemed to brighten. Thanksgiving Day was a joyful one for "the boys." Seventy-five turkeys had been sent from Massachusetts, and were prepared with the usual accompaniments for the great dinner. The unanimous verdict was, "This seems like home," with "Three cheers for Massachusetts!" On Christmas Day several visitors came in, some bringing flowers; the Sanitary Commission furnishing for the men, as they often had done before, supplies of pipes, tobacco, socks, mittens, fruits, stationery, etc. On New Year's Day, 1865, several of the nurses found time to attend Mr. Lincoln's usual reception at the White House, which always was a very popular occasion. In the evening an entertainment was given by the nurses to "the boys," which had been for several days in course of preparation, consisting of recitations, speeches, pantomimes, etc., interspersed with music.

About January 15th, Miss Palmer received a message calling her home for a time; and as there was little work to be done just then at the hospital, Miss Dix gave her leave of absence, stipulating that if there should be more fighting, and help needed, she should return. Taking an affectionate leave of her "boys," and the lady friends with whom she had been so long associated, she took, as it proved, a final leave of hospital life, having served there nine months.

In 1883 Miss Palmer was elected an honorary member of Reese Post, No. 49, G. A. R., Canastota, New York, and in 1891 was granted a special pension of twelve dollars per month. She helped to organize Reese Relief Corps, No. 77, in September 1892; was one of its charter members, and has been three times reelected president.

Looking back from this year (1895) upon those dark days of war, she can but be grateful for the happy and honorable ending of the strife, and for the past prosperity of the country, feeling sure that "righteousness exalteth a nation but sin is a reproach to any people."

Hannah L. Palmer
CANASTOTA, NEW YORK

Mary Perkins

I HAVE TO INFORM YOU that Mary E. Perkins is now deceased; but, as her husband, I will try to supply what you require regarding her services in the late war, having known her from childhood.

I assure you I am in full sympathy with all movements to perpetuate the history of whatever pertains to that struggle, having been a participant therein; but especially the memory of those noble, self-sacrificing women who left friends, and home with all its comforts, to endure the hardships of camp and hospital, and to minister to the wants of the sick, wounded and dying. It was through their heroic efforts that many are calling them blessed today.

Andrew F. Perkins
711 4TH STREET
SOUTH SAINT CLOUD, MINNESOTA

Mary E. Perkins (formerly Chamberlain) was born May 5, 1839, at Brewer, Maine, where she resided until she was seven years old; then removed to Enfield, Maine, where she lived until the breaking out of the war in 1861, when she volunteered her services to the 11th Maine Volunteer Infantry as nurse. She has accepted, and accompanied the regiment to Washington. After arriving there she entered Camp Stone Brigade Hospital, on Meridian Hill, where she remained attending the sick until the regiment went to the Peninsula, in March 1862. Following the fortunes of the regiment, she embarked with them for Fortress Monroe. On arriving there it was found that orders had been issued that no nurse be allowed at the front. She then sought and gained permission to enter Hygeia Hospital at Hampton, Virginia.

About two weeks after, Miss Dix arrived at the hospital, and seemed very loth to accept her as a nurse, on account of her age; but upon the earnest solicitation of the surgeons and nurses, telling of her qualifications and zeal in the work, Miss Dix mustered her into the service. Here she remained, attending the sick and wounded of McClellan's army during the Peninsula Campaign.

After the battles of Seven Pines and Fair Oaks, she was detailed on the hospital boat that went to White House Landing, to receive and care for the sick and wounded. Twice after this she was detailed on the same errand.

Sometime in September the Hygeia was broken up, and she was transferred to the temporary hospital near Fortress Monroe, where she remained until the last of October, when she went to New York to nurse an only brother who had been disabled in the service. When he could travel, she procured her discharge and went home.

Testimonials of her high character, her sympathy for the patients, and the efficiency with which she performed her duties while in the service, from all the surgeons under whom she served, show how much her efforts were appreciated. Hers was a nature that could see no suffering or distress without doing the utmost to alleviate it.

In April 1865, she was married to Andrew F. Perkins, of Saint Cloud, Minnesota. November 18, 1893, she died, beloved by all who knew her.

Adeliza Perry

ADELIZA PERRY, army nurse at Fort Schuyler and Balfour Hospitals, to the dear boys who are left, their old nurse sends loving greetings. And with those beloved comrades who went forth from our midst, over whom together we wept and strove, oh! so vainly, to hold back, hopefully we will look forward to a joyous reunion.

OUR HEROES.

Think of President Garfield,—think of Ex-President Grant! Words cannot express our admiration for the heroism and fortitude with which they endured their sufferings and met the end. But what have we for those others, the most of them mere boys, with all of life's promise and high hopes before them, far way from familiar faces and the ministrations of loving hands, bearing up under the agonies of mortal sickness, looking forward to, and meeting, the dread Messenger without a murmur? In my hospital experience I could number such by hundreds,—yes, think by thousands. I cannot recall a case, as long as the mind of the sufferer remained clear, where he was not bravely cheerful and intrepidly resigned to move on, obedient to the last call.

A Wisconsin boy, wounded, and suffering from malaria, was in a ward of half convalescents, of which, true to his fun-loving nature, he was the very life. We had thought he was on the road to recovery. I was busy in another part of the building, one morning, when word was brought that he was worse, and wished to see me. A hospital nurse learns to read the signs of approaching dissolution unerringly. The luster had gone out of his young, joyous eyes, but he was smiling. I laid my hand upon his forehead, already clammy with the damps of approaching death. "Oh, that is so good!" he said; "that is like my mother's hand." He stopped now to recover the gasping breath. "Couldn't you," he went on, after moment's struggling, oh! so pitifully, to keep up his voice, "bring me some—flowers?" I flew to the hospital reception room, and clipped every bit of bloom from our few window plants. "Thank you," he gasped, with his beautiful, boyish smile, as I laid them upon the fast-stiffening fingers. "Now— couldn't you get—get—something to tie—them together,—so I can—hold them?" The voice was hardly audible. I cut the tape that held my scissors, and secured them; then he looked entirely gratified. "Thanks!" I just caught the word before the smiling lips fell apart, and the labored breathing ceased.

In another ward, at this time, there lay a New Hampshire boy, quietly awaiting the last summons which he knew was surely close at hand. One day, as I was waiting at his bedside, he whispered: "Put your hand under my pillow. You will find a wallet with a ball of yarn in it; it is wound round a fifty-dollar bill. Please to hide it; it isn't safe here. As soon as I am gone, send it by express to my folks. The address is in the wallet." His manner was as composed, and his voice as calm, as though he were contemplating an ordinary journey. He was "gone" before the end of another twenty-four hours; and it was not until after I had expressed the parcel that I learned that I had violated a rigid rule of the service, which forbade every hospital attendant taking charge of property of any kind belonging to a patient.

At one time a large number of sick and wounded men were brought into our hospital, all in such a state of exhaustion that the surgeon in charge gave me permission to deal out among them some delicious homemade wine, which had been sent me from Massachusetts. How glad I was that it seemed to carry comfort and reviving energy, until I reached one more prostrated, I thought, than any to whom I had ministered. "What is it?" he asked, feebly, wistfully lifting a pair of mild brown eyes. I explained, and he shook his head, oh, I felt through all my being, so reproachfully! "I promised my mother," the poor lips had barely vigor to articulate, then rested. After a time the four noble words were repeated,—no more. Then the eyelids fell, and he dropped asleep. Before morning he was dead. How I wished then, how I wish today, that I could see that young man's mother and clasp her hand. How the memory of "mother" or some other beloved one at home, mingled itself with the last earthly thought. One day while passing between the cots the hand of a mature man clutched my dress. He was wildly delirious, and dying. "I have two beautiful little girls," he held me long enough to say. The expression of the wasted face seemed to radiate light,—a light that did not leave it even after the features had settled into the tranquility of death.

"Don't tell them how bad off I am," would be the entreaty when I wrote "the letter home." "It would worry them. Say I'm better,—getting on slowly." Oh how many, many times I have taken such letters to my room to add the grief-carrying postscript that it seemed to me a cruelty to withhold. On one such occasion I met the large-hearted surgeon, who counseled me not to do it. "Send it as it is," he said. "There may yet be a change; who knows?" But the "change" removed the sufferer to the spiritual world. Meantime the letter, speeding to its destination, summoned the anxious mother to the hospital, but, alas! only to see her son's grave. The remembrance of her agony wrings my heart today. She had brought slippers, in which to move lightly about the bedside of the loved one, and the photograph of his sister, to gratify the fond brotherly eyes. These she put into my hands. No, no; she could not take them back. The pretty home picture I still keep by me,—a sacred memento which admits me, as it were, into membership with a dear family circle.

But why multiply relations? We know that the records have all been kept. No individual has been overlooked; no iota of character, of aspiration, or affection, of all the throngs who were under my care, in the all-fostering Divine thought, has ever missed its quota of recognition and protecting love.

Adeliza Perry
15 GOULDING STREET
WORCESTER, MASSACHUSETTS

Rebecca Pomeroy

M RS. REBECCA R. POMROY, of Chelsea, Massachu-
setts, was a woman peculiarly fitted to minister to the needs of the
soldiers during the late Rebellion. At forty years of age she was left a
widow. Her life up to that time had been filled with sorrow, leaving her
almost hopeless; when at a gathering at which she was present, through
the earnest solicitations of her friends, she providentially met an aged
lady who spoke the word that proved the touch-stone to her life, and
she went from the place with renewed faith.

> Let thy gold be cast in the furnace,
> Thy red gold, Precious and bright,—
> Do not fear the hungry fire,
> With its caverns of burning light,—
> And thy gold shall return more precious,
> Free from every spot and stain;
> For gold must be tried by fire,
> As a heart must be tried by pain.
>
> In the cruel fire of sorrow
> Cast thy heart; do not faint or wail:
> Let thy hand be firm and steady;
> Do not let thy spirit quail!

But wait till the trial is over,
And take thy heart again;
For as gold is tried by fire,
So a heart must be tried by pain!

I shall know by the gleam and glitter
Of the golden chain you wear,
By your heart's calm strength in loving,
Of the fire they have had to bear.
Beat on, true heart, forever;
Shine bright, strong, golden chain;
And bless the cleansing fire,
And the furnace of living pain!

Ah! it was indeed a "furnace of pain" in which the heart of Mrs.
Pomroy had been purified; and now she had grown calm and strong.
The kind eye could look out upon the world once more, and see God's
providences in their true proportions. The Spirit of the Infinite had
met her troubled, world-weary soul after years of half-rebellious suffering and at last she had laid the burden down, and was willing to face
life,—only it must be a more complete and perfect life of service.

When the war broke out she had been a widow two years. One son
was all that had been spared to her by the cruel hand of death, and he
soon enlisted. It was not long before she prayerfully questioned, "Lord,
what wilt thou have me to do?" She felt that God was calling her to some
larger work. Back upon her soul surged a tide of assurance that she
should go as an army nurse. Knowing how frail she was, friends and physicians endeavored to persuade her not to go; but it was useless. She
answered, "I want to be a mother to those wounded and dying soldiers."
In September 1861 she started alone from Chelsea, Massachusetts.

Upon her arrival in Washington, Miss Dix went with her to visit the
places of interest in and around the city. When they entered the
Georgetown Hospital she found that a nurse had become exhausted,
and she decided to leave Mrs. Pomroy to fill the vacant place; so she assumed charge of a ward containing fifty typhoid patients.

At the close of that first day she found herself struggling against
such weakness that it seemed she must succumb to it. Excusing herself,

she managed to reach her own room, where she sank upon the rude cot, and poured out her soul in prayer for Divine strength and guidance. We cannot but believe that prayer was answered, for she soon was able to rise and resume her duties, working part of the night.

A boy had been in a dying condition for several hours, and as she bent to give him the last stimulant, he threw his arms around her neck, crying, "Oh my dear mother!" Death sealed that clasp, and it required two attendants to release her. This, and other strange experiences, marked her first night in the service of her country.

In a few days she was transferred to Columbia College Hospital, where we gleam from one of her letters that she became familiar with death and suffering, and could pass through all that was required of her by relying upon the unseen Hand that she felt fed her with the bread of heaven. Often during the long nights, she stood alone beside some dying soldier, soothing and sustaining him in those "last moments," so fraught with awe and sadness. The kind, motherly heart could not forget those scenes and many of her hospital experiences have become familiar household stories. Perhaps one of the most beautiful is that of the bugler of the 11th Maine.

The poor fellow had lingered week after week, becoming fearfully emaciated. At the very last he was conscious of his condition, and said to Mrs. Pomroy, "Mother, may I have my bugle?" She sent for it immediately but his poor, nerveless hands were too weak to hold it. An attendant, comprehending the unspoken, yet eloquent appeal, placed it to his lips. For a moment his face was transformed by something of the old-time enthusiasm, as he concentrated all the energy of that wasted frame for the supreme effort. Two or three quivering notes wavered and died upon the air, then the lifeless hands fell. The last bugle-call had been sounded!

Mrs. Pomroy was a friend indeed to the soldiers under her care, and her efforts met a grateful appreciation. But few realize how much we as a nation owe her for helping to sustain President Lincoln and his family at a time when that strong man was almost overcome by the sorrow that shrouded his home. The burden of the year's war lay so heavily upon his heart that he seemed almost crushed by the weight. Then Willie, his second son, died, after a short sickness. His youngest son was expected to die at any time, and Mrs. Lincoln, too, was very sick.

At this juncture Miss Dix called to see if she could render any assistance, and he asked her to recommend a nurse. She selected "Auntie Pomroy," who reluctantly left her boys, not realizing what an opportunity was hers in thus being permitted to learn, as few others could, the honest, manly faith of our great-hearted President, and at the same time to render the human sympathy and help he so much needed. His own words, and the strong friendship he ever afterwards manifested toward her, show how grateful to him were her ministrations.

While she was still a member of the President's Family, two young ladies offered to assist her in carrying on a prayer meeting in her ward. The Officers in the hospital were mostly Catholics, and her first venture in that line had been followed by strict orders that it should not be repeated. Now she obtained the President's permission, and by the aid of the Misses Rumsey and Mr. Fowle of the Soldiers' Free Library, the meeting was established.

At last she returned to her boys; but the sympathetic relations between her and the President's family could not be lightly set aside, and she was a frequent visitor at the White House. During one of these visits, Mr. Lincoln said he wished to do something for her very much, and urged her to be perfectly frank and tell him what she wanted most. She was surprised by so generous an offer, and could not think of any personal wants; but like an inspiration came the thought of his visiting her patients at the hospital, and she proffered that simple request, which he gladly granted, to the great delight of the boys, whose enthusiasm knew no bounds. She said that one poor fellow refused for days to wash the hand that had grasped the President's.

It was characteristic of Mrs. Pomroy that she sent to the kitchen for the colored help, as she wanted to share in this happy reception. They stood by her side as Mr. Lincoln was passing out. "And who these?" he asked. "This is Lucy, formerly slave in Kentucky. She cooks the nurses' food;" and Lucy received the same warm hand-clasp that had been given to others. "And these?" "This is Garner, and this Brown. They are serving their country by cooking the low diet." Their radiant faces attested their appreciation of the greeting they received. When he had gone, Mrs. Pomroy was severely criticized for introducing "niggers" to the President. So much was said that she felt saddened, though firm in her convictions of right; but the gratitude of the colored people did much toward healing the sting of the sharp words. "Lub ye, missus, long as ye lib! Nebber spec such a t'ing." At her next visit to the White House she asked the President if his feelings were hurt by being introduced to the colored help. "Hurt? No, indeed! It did my soul good. I'm glad to do them honor," was the hearty response. Later, when Mrs. Lincoln was severely injured during an accident to the carriage, caused by some enemy, he went for Mrs. Pomroy at once, and for three weeks she watched by her bed.

Then came a time when the President expected to be attacked personally any day. When the news came of the battle of Port Hudson, he walked the floor in an agony of distress, saying: "The Lord have mercy on those poor fellows. This is a righteous war, and God will protect the right. Many lives will be sacrificed on both sides, but I have done the best I could, trusting in God." "Mr. Lincoln," she answered, "prayer will do what nothing else will; can you not pray?" The tears were dropping over that worn face as he said, "Yes, I will. Pray for me, too," and he went to his room.

At midnight a messenger rode rapidly toward the White House with a telegram. Mrs. Pomroy was sitting in the sick-room when the President entered, crying: "Good news, good news! Port Hudson is ours! God is good!" Mrs. Pomroy answered, "There is nothing like prayer in times of need." "Yes, oh yes! But praise, too; for prayer and praise go together."

Occasionally a rebel would fall to her care; but she confessed to an inability to feel toward them as she did toward Union men. One who had been in her ward some days asked if he might call her "Mother" as the other men did. "No," was her reply; "not while you are cherishing rebellion in your heart." She spoke with him on the subject from time to time, and he took the oath of allegiance before leaving the hospital.

She served three years and seven months, then received an honorable discharge, April 1, 1865; and as she went to seek to regain her health after a serious illness, she wrote to a friend thus:—

"Taking all things, I have passed through trying experiences, but this morning the sun shines just as bright as ever. God is still good to us, and may it never be in my heart to complain or murmur while my experience is so full of God's unbounded love."

Mary Breckel Pringle

I WAS BORN IN COLUMBUS, OHIO, January 11, 1833. My maiden name was Mary Breckel. When the war broke out I was living in Keokuk, Iowa, and while at church one Sunday, volunteers were called for to go into the hospital at Quincy, Illinois and the next day I started alone. Upon my arrival I was introduced to Miss Orland, and went with her to Hospital No. 1, as her assistant, by appointment of Dr. Stanton. After about a month I was transferred to No. 2, as superintendent. I had been there about a year when I heard that my brother was sick in Columbus. I went to see him, and while there a hospital was organized on Broad Street, and I went as superintendent. I became sick from overwork, and had to leave the service, July 1863.

It would give me much pleasure to hear from any of the "boys in blue," who knew me while in our country's service.

Yours in F., C. and L.,
Mary Pringle
CHILLICOTHE, MISSOURI

Mother Ransom

I HAD BEEN APPOINTED AIDE to our physician, Doctor McClintock, in charge of a large number of sick soldiers, who were to be transported to their homes or to Northern hospitals. In making preparations I came to a poor fellow whose wan, appealing face touched a tender cord of my being, and I said, "Are you going to start North tonight?" He turned wearily, and said, "I fear I am too weak to endure the voyage, unless there were someone on whom I could depend." I said, "I may go." "Oh! then I will venture," his face beaming with gladness. The preparations were all made, and we sailed in the Government transport "North America," commanded by Captain Marshman of Philadelphia. We started on the evening of December 16, 1864, at six o'clock. The ship was manned by forty-four men. There were twelve passengers, and two hundred and three enlisted sick soldiers brought from Dallas, Hermitage, Manning, and Baton Rouge, and four women besides the stewardess: one a lady returning from New Orleans with her sick husband; another, Miss Fowler, with her brother; and one a passenger who had nothing to do with the army. We had pleasant weather until the night of the 20th.

We buried one of our brave soldier boys in the sea, little thinking that ere we reached New York one hundred and ninety-four of our dear soldiers would find a watery grave. On the morning of the 22d just off the coast of Florida, the steamer was reported leaking forward.

Effort was made to stop the leak, but in vain, and there seemed no hope. However, a soldier who had been a sailor before the war reported a sail. It proved to be the "Mary E. Libby," from Cuba, laden with molasses, for Portland, Maine. She answered our signals of distress, and when she came alongside, the seas were so heavy the vessels collided, and for a time it was hard to tell which vessel would go down first.

When the vessels struck, one of our firemen jumped for the deck of the "Libby," and was lost between the vessels. The fireman and the purser were the only men of the crew that were lost. At five o'clock on the morning of the 23d the first boat left our sinking steamer. The vessel was pitching and tossing about, and I was so sick I felt I could not utter one word, but in my heart I prayed, "Father, if my work is done, and Thou seest it best for me to find a grave in Old Ocean's bosom, Amen." I pulled myself to the deck as best I could, having a life-preserver on over cloak and shawl. I was confronted on the deck with that large number of soldiers, all crying and praying, and there I saw the soldier boy who said, "If you are going I will venture."

My dear soldier boys, God's power in the elements forbade me doing, oh! what my heart and hands would so gladly have done. They were taken and I was saved, which for months seemed to me such a mystery. Those noble young men who had been disabled in our country's interest, they represented fifteen regiments, the greater part of them from Illinois, but some from the East, and fifty men of Scott's nine hundred, of the Eleventh New York Cavalry. I asked Dr. McClintock, "Who is preparing our sick soldiers who are in the steerage?" I knew there were six or nine unable to get up alone. He replied, "We shall do the best we can for the soldiers." "But, Doctor," I said, "who is helping them?" I did not realize that two feet of water was at that time their winding sheet, which was the case, as I afterward learned.

I can never efface from my memory that great number of men crying and praying on the deck and stairway. The second boat to the "Libby" had on board Miss Fowler and her brother. She had refused to go in the first boat without him. Eight loads were attempted to be transferred, but one which was manned by the purser and two assistants was swamped, and all lost. The boat I went in came near being swamped. Two men manned the oars; a third gave the command, his voice so solemn and terror-stricken it was enough to pierce the hardest heart. The storm was so severe, and the waves rolling so fearfully, each word echoed over the sea and back into our hearts: "Row, boys, row, row, row!" I can never forget the solemnity of that hour while memory holds her seat, those words rolling up from the depths of the ocean, "Row, boys, row, row, row!" Captain Libby had a heart as large as a human body could hold. He and his crew did all they could do in their cramped condition to care for so many. Fortunately for us and the "Libby" a steamer from Hilton Head, bound for New York, overtook us on the morning of the 30th, and conveyed us to New York, arriving in the night.

Doctor McClintock sent me to the State Sanitary Commission, and as soon as they knew of the terrible disaster I had passed through, they presented me with fifty dollars and took me to the New England Rooms, a temporary hospital, where I was cared for as if I had been a princess. For weeks this terrible scene was kept fresh in my mind by one and another inquiring for friends. It was almost beyond my power of endurance to recount that heart-rending scene. Our dear soldiers on that sinking ship; one hundred and ninety-four went down with her!

Shall we meet beyond the river,
Where the surges cease to roll?
Where, in all the bright forever,
Sorrow ne'er shall press the soul?

Mother Ransom of Indiana

Pamela Reid

Wɪʜᴇɴ ᴛʜᴇ ᴡᴀʀ ʙʀᴏᴋᴇ ᴏᴜᴛ ᴍʏ ʜᴏᴍᴇ was in Farmington, Iowa. I began my nursing before I left home to go to the hospital. It happened in this way:—

One day I heard that a wounded soldier was at the station, too sick to proceed any farther on his way home. I had him carried to my house, and nursed him until he was much improved in health, when his brother came to accompany him the remainder of the journey.

My next experience was with my husband, who was wounded at the battle of Belmont, and I went to care for him until he needed me no longer.

After the battle of Shiloh, I saw in a newspaper that the Estes House had been taken for a hospital and female nurses were wanted. It was ten o'clock ᴀ.ᴍ. when I read the notice, and at four ᴘ.ᴍ. I was on my way, and the next morning commenced my duties under the direction of Mrs. Wittenmyer.

I served at the Estes House one year and a half, with the exception of a few weeks leave of absence to go to my husband, who was wounded again. At the end of that time a hospital was established at the Medical College, and I served there until my health failed.

Mrs. Pamela Reid
Gᴇᴏʀɢᴇᴛᴏᴡɴ, Mᴀssᴀᴄʜᴜsᴇᴛᴛs

Selener Richards

WHEN THE CIVIL WAR BROKE OUT my home was with my parents on a farm in Southern Wisconsin. My name was Selener J. Bray. We had but one brother at home, and it was not until the second call for "three hundred thousand more" men rang out over the North, that my brother felt it his duty to go.

In those days the love of country was as strong in the hearts of the loyal girls as in that of their brothers. We were proud to do as much of their work as possible, feeling that thus we were helping to put down the rebellion. But all work grew into mountains in those troublesome times, and yet we wanted to do more to help save the country. It was found that not only could women care for the sick and wounded but that they were needed to prepare food suitable for the sick. To meet this want, light Diet kitchens were organized and two Christian women placed in each kitchen with power to draw needed supplies from the Commission. It was their duty to see that the food was well prepared. The slaves were freed, and we had all the help required. My sister and I had charge of the light Diet Kitchen in McPherson Hospital, in Vicksburg, Mississippi. We went there in February, before the war closed, and remained until July. Our work before that was in Memphis, Tennessee. There my sister was very sick with fever.

As we look backward, over time in its flight, and remember what we did, we are glad to be able to place our names among the helpers in our great Civil War; and if we did not tend the boys in the wards, we feel compensated in knowing we made many of the poor, half-dead, exchanged prisoners feel new springs of life running through their veins from the food we prepared for them. Yet many of them were past recovery; no effort could bring back the natural look from the vacant stare of that glazed, wondering expression in the eyes of our starved boys who came to our hospital in such large numbers from Southern prison pens. The average death rate for many weeks reached six a day—poor, starved boys! Their coffins were white pine, and many of their names unknown. Here Mrs. Wittenmyer had the superintendence of Sanitary Christian Commission work, where she nobly performed her part. I have always cherished with delight the thought that I had done something.

Mrs. J. T. Richards
206 WASHINGTON AVENUE
MASON CITY, IOWA

[We congratulate Mrs. Richards upon the important part of her nursing; no less a nurse because of her superintendence of the Diet Kitchen.—*Mary A. Gardner Holland.*]

Ann Maria Schram

I WAS ONLY A YOUNG WOMAN THEN, but it seems but yesterday that the war broke out, and my husband was wounded, having responded to the first call for volunteers. Oh, what changes there have been since! Now I have two grown children; and other things remind me of the flight of time. Disabilities have come upon me, too, and I am no longer able to get around very well; still, I must not mourn, but accept whatever the Lord sees fit to send, as He knows best.

One of the surgeons under whom I served while in the hospitals, was Dr. Charles F. Haynes, now of Brighton, Massachusetts. He was a noble man, kind to every one under him, but especially thoughtful of the poor wounded soldiers. May God bless him and his family for his kindness during the cruel war.

I have never regretted that I went to nurse the soldiers in those dark days. I have stood by the bedside of many a dying man, and those scenes are fresh in my memory today.

The following sketch from a paper outlines my work:—

"The case of Mrs. Schram is familiar to many of the old residents of Amsterdam, as she resided here in 1861, when certain Patriotic citizens assisted her to proceed to the front, and carry out her noble purpose of rendering aid as a volunteer nurse in army hospitals. She first went to

Burkittsville, Maryland, but finding that the hospital had been removed to Frederick, Maryland, reported for duty there, and was assigned by the medical staff; as hospital nurse, to duty in Camp B outside of Frederick City, among wounded and sick soldiers, removed thither from South Mountain and Antietam. The service she rendered there is gratefully remembered by many a veteran and has probably been mentioned at many a 'camp fire' since the close of the war.

"Notwithstanding that her service was without pay, and her expenses, including her board outside of the hospital, at her own cost, she frequently bought and furnished to convalescent and other sick and wounded soldiers necessaries for which army regulations did not provide. The exposure incident to camp life and her untiring work impaired her health and necessitated her return, after eight months of service."

Yours in F., C. and L.,
Mrs. Daniel Schram
FORT PLAINS, NEW YORK

Harriet Scott

IN NOVEMBER 1861, I LEFT MY HOME in Irasburg, Vermont, going to Camp Griffith, Alexandria, Virginia. My husband, who enlisted in the 3d Vermont Infantry in the spring of 1861 and was transferred to Battery F, Fifth United States Heavy Artillery, was stationed in winter quarters at Camp Griffin. I secured board at a farm house nearby, going to the camp each day, caring for the sick boys as would a mother for her sons. On March 10, 1862, the Vermont Brigade and Battery F moved, as they then thought, for Richmond.

Calling on Mrs. James Glen of New York State, her husband also a member of Battery F, we went to Miss Dix. Telling her I was from the Green Mountain State, she said, "I know you are loyal, I want you." She engaged Mrs. Glen and myself, giving us our commissions as nurses, sending us to Fortress Monroe to report to General Dix. He said, "We are on the eve of a great battle, you must return to Washington." We reported to Miss Dix. She sent me to Union Hotel Hospital, Georgetown, which was filled with typhoid fever patients. I was detailed as night nurse; remained till June 1st, when at the request of Doctor Bliss was transferred to Armory Square General Hospital, when first opened, and assigned to Ward B.

My first hard work was for the wounded from the seven days' fight—McClellan's retreat from Richmond. I remained at Armory Square through the summer of 1862, where both heart and hands were more than full. Dr. Charles Bowen (ward surgeon) gave me especial charge of the worst cases on low diet, forbidding anyone else to give them a spoonful. Armory Square, being near the boat landing, was filled with the most severely wounded from all the battles of 1862.

During the sultry heat, when scarce a breath of air was stirring, not a friendly tree for shade, we worked all the day, and often through the night, caring for some boy who could not live till morning, who had begged me to stay with him till the end, that his last look on earth might rest on my face. Many nights, at the surgeon's request, have I remained with those who had suffered amputations, giving them quinine, and occasionally a spoonful of brandy, bathing foreheads and chests with brandy to stimulate and strengthen the little vitality left, singing low sweet hymns, soothing them to sleep. After commencing my work in Ward B, one of my boys, mortally wounded through the lungs, said inquiringly, "You are not a Catholic?" I answered by asking, "what do you want?" "A priest."

It was very early in the morning. I went to Doctor Bliss for a pass. Doctor Bliss said, "go after breakfast." "No, he may die, please write the pass while I get ready." Doctor Bliss directed me to a young priest (at this late day have forgotten his name). He returned with me to Ward B. The attendant placed the screen around the cot, and the sacraments of the Catholic faith were administered to the dying boy. Nearly every day through the summer, the young father came to my ward to know if any one wished to see him. I state this that all may know that the Catholic boys enjoyed the consolations and ministrations of their faith.

One day President Lincoln visited the hospital, bringing grapes (with two men to carry the basket), himself giving to all who were allowed to have fruit,—shaking hands, speaking kind words to each one. Noticing the small red flag at the foot of some of the beds, he said, "May I ask, nurse, what those flags mean?" "They mean low diet, sir." "What is low diet?" "Wine, whey, milk and water, rice gruel—always something very light." Walking with President Lincoln through the ward to the door, he said, "Well, nurse, we often hear the remark that these are days that try men's souls;—I think they try women's souls too. I shall remember you and all the noble women of the North when this land is at peace."

Peace to his ashes; all honor to his name !
Our beloved Lincoln, of glorious fame.

On Christmas, 1862, Miss Dix sent me on board the Government Transport Steamer, *Rockland*, Capt. Oris Ingraham commanding, to Aquia Creek, to care for the wounded *en route* to Washington hospitals. This first Christmas eve the boat had been loaded with wounded, when orders came to Captain Ingraham to anchor for the night in the middle of the river; on account of the sharp shooters it was unsafe to return. I found a young boy mortally wounded, and sat on the floor by his side. Looking up in my face, he said, "O! for just one hour with mother," and passed away still clasping my hand. I closed his eyes and folded his hands, knowing he was his mother's darling. I knew she wafted his name above, morning, noon, and night on the wings of prayer.

I served during the winter of 1863, often leaving the transport, going in the ambulance to pick up the wounded, carrying food and drink to those who must wait longer. I passed one night in the ambulance on the battle field, very near the enemy. We dare not make a fire or even light a match. I drank water dipped from holes made by the horses' feet in the mud; it tasted good and sweet. After lying all night in the mud and water, the infantry were detailed to cut logs and carry them on their backs to build a corduroy road; that the heavy guns and baggage wagons might be lifted out of the mud.

I have seen fourteen horses vainly trying to pull one gun from the mud, the wheels sunk to the hub. Seeing me, the famished boys came offering five dollars, or all the money they had, for something to eat—this was the hardest time of all my experience. I said to them, "Boys, I have only a few supplies for the sick, and wounded; but if getting out of this ambulance into the mud on my knees would bring you food, I would most gladly do it. I cannot give this to you; do not ask me, it will kill me to refuse you." Those are the boys who, if living today, often have to take a back seat. Tongue cannot describe, pen cannot write, what our boys suffered, always without complaint or murmur. God bless them every one; were I able, I would strew their paths with flowers and cry, "All hail ye noble of God."

In the spring of 1863 Miss Dix granted me two weeks of rest, with my friend Mrs. Glen; then detailed me to do what I could in the Washington hospitals, carrying supplies, helping the boys to get furloughs, and start them home. Miss Dix sent me to Gettysburg battlefield, where I worked unceasingly till the wounded were all cared for and carried away. I continued my hospital work till the last of August when, completely tired and worn out, went home to Vermont to rest, intending to return and work for the boys till the close of the war; but alas! that time never came. I have not been rested from that day to this; yet never a feeling of regret for nearly two years of service; I count the days spent in hospital work the most precious of my life. The suffering and untold agonies so heroically and patiently borne by the nation's heroes; my brothers; their calmness and serenity when the angel of death called to the camping ground beyond the river are all most blessed memories, and have lifted me up and above the suffering of sickness and weakness, for many years, and I can truly thank God that I lived in those trying days, and was enabled to do my little for my country's brave defenders.

Harriet M. Scott
CHARLESTOWN, MASSACHUSETTS

Hannah Sheppard

IT HAS BEEN SO LONG SINCE I PASSED through the sad scenes of the war, that they seem much like a dream to which it would be hard for me to give definite outline.

I went from my native place, Millville, New Jersey, July 6, 1864, and Miss Dix assigned me to duty at the Chesapeake Officers' Hospital, Fortress Monroe. The New Camp, Hampton and Chesapeake Hospitals, were all under one surgeon,—Dr. McClellan. They were not near any city, but were just above Fortress Monroe, on a point often called Old Point Comfort.

In the fall of 1864 I was assigned to the Hampton and New Camp Hospitals, where I remained until the following June; being discharged June 28, 1865.

I served under the name of Hannah Bowman, but was married a year later.

Yours in F., C. and L.,
Hannah A. Sheppard
PORT ELIZABETH, NEW JERSEY

Emma Simonds

MRS. EMMA L. SIMONDS WAS APPOINTED as a nurse by Mrs. Hoge and Mrs. Livermore, under the authority of Miss D. L. Dix, on August 26, 1863, and was assigned to work in Memphis, Tennessee, as chief nurse of Ward A in the Gayoso Hospital; Dr. F. Noel Burke, surgeon in charge.

She went from DeKalb, Illinois, soon after our marriage, to Memphis, where I was on duty as an army surgeon, United States Army, in Jackson Hospital. At the close of the war she returned with me to my home at Iowa Falls. In 1873 we moved to Fayetteville, Arkansas, where she resumed practice as a professional nurse; which work she continued until January, 1892. She died in May 1893. I think she was the most unselfish, most charitable in her opinions and in her demeanor toward others, the most forgiving in spirit, and the most truthful in all her expressions, of any woman I have ever known.

Yours Truly,
J. F. Simonds
WASHINGTON, D. C.

Ruth Sinnotte

I WAS COMMISSIONED BY MR. YEATMAN, in Saint Louis, as nurse at large, and sent on board the steamer "Imperial," a hospital boat plying between Saint Louis and Pittsburg Landing; Dr. Gove, surgeon in charge, and Dr. Bixby, assistant surgeon. I remained on board the "Imperial" until the Tennessee River had fallen so low the boat could go no farther, and went out of the hospital service.

I was then sent by the medical director on board the "Ella," and remained on that boat until she went out of hospital service, and became a transport boat. Then Dr. Douglass, the medical director, sent me to Monterey, in Tennessee, the receiving hospital of Corinth battlefield, in charge of Dr. Eaton; I think he was from New York.

While there I was sun-struck, and on the third day was attacked with yellow jaundice. I then obtained a furlough, and went home to Illinois. As soon as able, I reported to Governor Yates, who ordered me to go South with the 113th, or Board of Trade Regiment, Colonel Hoge.

The colonel put my name on the muster roll as matron for three years, or to the close of the war. I went to Memphis with the regiment, and we encamped at Camp Peabody, about two miles from the city. When they went on the Tulahoma raid, I accompanied them, by particular request of Colonel Hoge. The fourth day, was sent with all the sick to Holly Springs, Mississippi.

I was there a number of weeks, and before Bragg took the place, was ordered to Memphis. On the way I was told the troops had gone down the river, and General Wright advised me to keep on down to the fleet. I did so. While with the Vicksburg fleet, one day I noticed the boat I was on was dragging her hawser from the tree where she had been fastened. I reported to the captain. He said, "I know it." There was no steam on, and we were drifting down the river. The captain said we were going to Vicksburg, and were only a half mile from the line between the two armies. Among the sick was a captain of one of the companies of the 113th Illinois Regiment. I immediately went to him and reported the treachery on board of the boat. He could do nothing, as he was too ill to raise his head. He swore me, and gave me the necessary signal. I went on the hurricane deck; no one was there, no one on the pilot house. I gave the Signal as he told me. In a moment I saw it answered. Immediately the "Von Pool" came down and towed the boat to the upper end of the fleet, and put a stop to our going to Vicksburg. All of the crew, from the captain to the chambermaid, were so very angry they would have killed me had they known I was responsible for the change of programme.

We had several wounded officers among the load of sick and disabled men on my first trip from Pittsburg Landing to Saint Louis. Our transport was the "Imperial." Each officer had an orderly to wait upon him. The attendant of one, a colonel, came to me and said, "Are you afraid of the colonel?" I replied I was not. Then said he, "I wish you would see if you can do anything with him, but I really fear he will kill you." "Oh, no; I will go: where is he?" He pointed the way, keeping well out of sight of the officer.

When I came to the stateroom he occupied the door was ajar. I looked ill and said, "Good morning, Colonel." He answered, "What do you want here?" "I came to see if you have had breakfast." "No, and don't want any." But I said: "You must eat something. I will see what I can get that you may relish." I went to the kitchen, toasted a slice of bread, poached an egg, poured it over the toast, made a bowl of chicken broth, and a cup of green tea and apple jelly made up the breakfast. I put it on a waiter with a white napkin (these things were for officers only), went to his room, and said, "Now see what of this you can eat." "Can't I get rid of you? I wish I had something to throw at you, but I have thrown everything I can get at that Dutchman," meaning his attendant. I said, "You must eat; there is no other way for you." "I will tip over that cart of yours," and he made a spring toward the tray. I said, "Sir, stop such pranks, and take some of this food immediately." He then grabbed the toast, crammed it all into his mouth, the broth followed with a gulp, the tea and jelly in turn, all in less time than I am telling you. I said to him, "That was pretty good, wasn't it?" "Good enough." "Will you eat more if I get it for you?" "I suppose I can if I must." I prepared the same amount. He ate it all, using a knife and fork.

I then asked why he treated me so badly when I was only trying to help him. He told me this story: "I am from Marion County, Illinois. I was acknowledged to be the richest man in the county. I raised a whole regiment and equipped it. They chose me their colonel. I had a wife and child, a little girl. I settled all my business, made my will, appointed my wife administratrix and guardian of my child. I took my regiment, was accepted, and went to the front. As soon as I was gone, my wife sold everything I had and put the money in the Confederate cause, took my child and went to New Orleans, her former home. I was in the battle of Pittsburg Landing; had my leg shattered, and amputated at the hip. Now I have lost my property, my wife and my child, lost my leg, and what have I to live for?" I waited a moment, then said,—

> *"You must live for the good that needs assistance,*
> *For the bad that needs resistance,*
> *For the future in the distance,*
> *And the good that you can do."*

He was all right to the end of the trip, and ate his food as I gave it to him. He was left at Saint Louis. I think he was put into Benton Barracks. We went back to Pittsburg Landing for another load of the mangled human freight. On our return to Saint Louis I learned the colonel was dead,—had died because he would not eat.

On my second trip on the "Imperial" my ward was the cabin. One afternoon, having got my men made comfortable for the night, I thought I would go to the lower deck, and see what the conditions were there. I heard the surgeon say to an attendant, "You need not give him anything more; he won't live till morning." I asked the doctor what his sickness was "He has the typhoid fever, and is now in the sinking state." I said, "Can I do something for him?" You can do all you like; it will avail nothing." I said, "Will you give me an order on the drugstore?" (The bar of the boat was the drugstore.) He tore a leaf from a memorandum book and wrote, "Let Mrs. Sinnotte have whatever she wants from the drugstore."

I ordered a cup of brandy and some red pepper. I mixed them, dipped cloths into the mixture and bound them onto the bottoms of his feet, the palms of his hands, and over the breastbone. I tried a little of the brandy to his lips. He could not swallow. Then I tried a few drops of water. After a while the water ran down his throat without strangling him; then I got a little chicken broth, and alternated every fifteen minutes, a few drops of brandy, then of the broth. I stood over him for hours. After awhile I noticed a change for the better. He could swallow, and his pulse was quite perceptible. Finally it beat as quick as I wanted to feel it.

After midnight I became quite faint; I had not eaten and could not stop for supper. I called the best nurse on the boat to relieve me. I went to my quarters, but could not undress. I unfastened my shoes, then fell into a faint, or dead sleep. Did not awake until the sun called me, shining through the slats of my door. I went to my patient. He looked up and smiled. The doctor soon came along, and said, "Why, ain't he dead yet?" The sick man whispered, "She," pointing to me. The doctor asked me what I had done. I said, "I attended to him as though he were my own, and in our own home;" I asked if I could have him in my ward. He said, "Yes; you deserve to have him." When he got to Saint Louis he walked the length of the boat between two men, shook hands with me, and said: "God bless you always. You have saved me to my wife and five children."

Mrs. Ruth Helena Sinnotte

Sisters of Charity

THE ORDER OF THE SISTERS OF CHARITY was established by Vincent de Paul in 1634, on the lines of the ancient community of the Hospitaller nuns of Saint Augustine, but with some modifications, not only in respect of its vows, which are only yearly and inward, but in the spirit of their discipline, as formulated in his own memorable words: "Your convent must be the house of the sick; your cell, the chamber of suffering; your chapel, the parish church; your cloister, the streets of the city or the wards of the hospital; your rule, the general vow of obedience; your grille, the fear of God; your veil to shut out the world, holy modesty."

The sisterhood is spread over the continent of Europe in charge of hospitals, infant asylums, other infirmaries, and schools. In this country the Mother House is at Emmitsburg, near Baltimore. Many hospitals and asylums in this country are under the care of these Sisters, and more especially in the South and West.

Sisters of Holy Cross

TRIBUTE TO THE SISTERS OF THE HOLY CROSS, of Saint Mary's Convent, Notre Dame, Indiana; also, to the Sisters of Charity, by very Rev. W. Corby, C. S. C. of Notre Dame University, Indiana: —Three years Chaplain in the famous Irish Brigade, "Army of the Potomac."
(By permission of Mother General, Saint Mary's Convent, Notre Dame, Indiana.)

Sixty Sisters of the Order of the Holy Cross from Saint Mary's Convent, Notre Dame, Indiana, went out under the intelligent Mother Mary Angela as superioress. (Mother Angela was a cousin of the Hon. James G. Blaine.) These Sisters volunteered their services to nurse the sick and wounded soldiers, hundreds of whom, moved to sentiments of purest piety by the words and example of their angel nurses begged to be baptized in articulo mortis—at the point of death. The labors and self-sacrifices of the Sisters during the war need no praise here. Their praise is on the lips of every surviving soldier who experienced their kind and careful ministration. Many a soldier now looks down from on high with complacency on the worthy Sisters who were instrumental in saving the soul when life could not be saved. Nor was it alone from the Order of the Sisters of the Holy Cross that Sister nurses engaged in the care of the sick and wounded soldiers. Many other Orders made costly sacrifices to save life and to save souls, notably the noble Order of the Sisters of Charity. To members of this Order I am personally indebted. When prostrate with camp-fever, insensible for three days, my life was entrusted tò their care. Like guardian angels, these daughters of Saint Vincent watched every symptom of the fever, and by their skill and care I was soon able to return to my post of duty. I subjoin an enthusiastic eulogy pronounced by a non-Catholic officer whose enthusiasm on this subject is shared by all who came under the care of these daughters of Christ:—

SISTERS IN THE ARMY.
(from a speech made by Capt. Crawford; the 'Poet Scout.')

On all of God's green and beautiful earth there are no purer, no nobler, no more kind-hearted and self-sacrificing women than those who wear the somber garb of Catholic Sisters. During the war I had many opportunities for observing their noble and heroic work, not only in the camp and the hospital, but in the death-swept field of battle. Right in the fiery front of dreadful war, where bullets hissed in maddening glee, and shot and shell few wildly by with demoniac shrieks, where dead and mangled forms lay with pale, blood-flecked faces, yet wearing the scowl of battle, I have seen the black-robed Sisters moving over the field, their solicitous faces wet with tears of sympathy, administering to the wants of the wounded, and whispering words of comfort into the ears soon to be deafened by the cold, implacable hand of death. Now kneeling on the blood-bespattered sod to moisten with water the bloodless lips on which the icy kiss of the death angel had left its pale imprint; now breathing words of hope of an immortality beyond the grave into the ear of some mangled hero, whose last shots in our glorious cause had been fired but a moment before; now holding the crucifix to receive the last kiss from somebody's darling boy from whose breast the life-blood was splashing, and who had offered his life as a willing sacrifice on the altar of his country; now with tender touch and tear-dimmed eyes binding the gaping wounds from which most women would have shrunk in horror; now scraping together a pillow of forest leaves upon which some pain-racked head might rest until the spirit took its flight to other realms—brave, fearless of danger, trusting implicitly in the Father whose overshadowing eye was noting their every movement; standing as shielding, prayerful angels between the dying soldier and the horrors of death. Their only recompense, the sweet, soul-soothing consciousness that they were doing their duty; their only hope of reward, that Peace and eternal happiness which awaited them beyond the star-emblazoned battlements above. Ah! my friends, it was noble work.

How many a veteran of the war, who wore the blue or gray, can yet recall the soothing touch of a Sister's band, as he lay upon the pain-tossed couch of a hospital! Can we ever forget their sympathetic eyes, their low, soft-spoken words of encouragement and cheer when the result of the struggle between life and death yet hung in the balance? Oh! how often have I followed the form of that good Sister Valencia with my sunken eyes as she moved away from my cot to the cot of another sufferer, and have breathed from the most sacred depths of my faintly beating heart the fervent prayer, "God bless her! God bless her!"

My friends, I am not a Catholic, but I stand ready at any and all times to defend those noble women even with my life, for I owe that life to them.

The following tribute also, taken from the *Philadelphia Sunday Times*, I feel impelled to quote:—
"WHAT THEY DO WITH THEIR BEGGINGS."

During the late war, while Gen. S. was in command of the Department at New Orleans, the Sisters of Charity made frequent applications to him for assistance. Especially were they desirous to obtain supplies at what was termed "commissary prices"—that is, at a reduction or commutation of one-third the amount which the same provisions would cost at market rates. The principal demand was for ice, flour, beef, and coffee, but mainly ice, a luxury which only the Union forces could enjoy at anything like a reasonable price.

The hospitals were full of the sick and wounded, of both the Federal and Confederate armies and the benevolent institutions of the city were taxed to the utmost in their endeavors to aid the poor and the suffering, for those were trying times, and war has many victims. Foremost among these Christian workers stood the various Christian sisterhoods. These noble women were busy day and night, never seeming to know fatigue, and overcoming every obstacle, that, in so many discouraging forms, obstructed the way of doing good—obstacles which would have completely disheartened less resolute women, or those not trained in the school of patience, faith, hope, and charity, and where the first grand lesson learned is self-denial. Of money there was little; but food, fuel, and medicine were scarce and dear; yet they never faltered, going on in the face of all difficulties, through poverty, war, and unfriendly aspersions, never turning aside, never complaining, never despairing. No one will ever know the sublime courage of these lowly Sisters during the dark days of the Rebellion. Only in that hour when the Judge of all mankind shall summon before Him the living and the dead will they receive their true reward, the crown everlasting, and the benediction: "Well done, good and faithful servant."

It was just a week previous to the Red River Campaign, when all was hurry and activity throughout the Department of the Gulf, that Gen. S., a stern, irascible old officer of the regular army, sat at his desk in his office on Julia Street, curtly giving orders to subordinates, dispatching messengers hither and thither to every part of the city where troops were stationed, and stiffly receiving such of his command as had important business to transact.

In the midst of this unusual hurry and preparation, the door noiselessly opened, and a humble Sister of Charity entered the room. A handsome young lieutenant of the staff instantly arose, and deferential handed her a chair, for those somber gray garments were respected, if not understood, even though he had no reverence for the religious faith which they represented.

Gen. S. looked up from his writing, angered by the intrusion of one whose "fanaticism" he despised, and a frown of annoyance and displeasure gathered darkly on his brow.

"Orderly!"

The soldier on duty without the door, who had admitted the Sister, faced about, saluted, and stood mute, awaiting the further command of his chief.

"Did I not give orders that no one was to be admitted?"

"Yes, sir; but—"

"When I say no one, I mean no one," thundered the general.

The orderly bowed and returned to his post. He was too wise a soldier to enter into explanations with so irritable a superior. All this time the patient Sister sat calm and still, biding the moment when she might speak and meekly state the object of her mission. The general gave her the opportunity in the briefest manner possible, and sharply enough too, in all conscience.

"Well, madam?"

She raised a pair of sad, dark eyes to his face, and the gaze was so pure and so saintly, so full of silent pleading, that the rough old Soldier was touched in spite of himself. Around her fell the heavy muffling dress of her Order, which however coarse and ungraceful, had something strangely solemn and mournful about it. Her hands, small and fair, were clasped almost suppliantly, and half hidden in the loose sleeves, as if afraid of their own trembling beauty; hands that had touched tenderly, lovingly, so many death-damp foreheads, that had soothed so much pain; eyes that had met prayerfully so many dying glances; lips that had cheered to the mysterious land so many parting souls, and she was only a Sister of Charity—only one of that innumerable band whose good deeds shall live after them.

"We have a household of sick and wounded whom we must care for in some wayward I came to ask of you the privilege, which I humbly beseech you will not deny us, of obtaining ice and beef at commissary prices."

The gentle, earnest pleading fell on deaf ears. "Always something," snarled the general. "Last week it was flour and ice; today it is ice and beef; tomorrow it will be coffee and ice, I suppose, and all for a lot of rascally rebels, who ought to be shot, instead of being nursed back to life and treason."

"General!"—the Sister was majestic now—"Rebel or Federal, I do not know; Protestant or Catholic, I do not ask. They are not soldiers when they come to us: they are simply suffering fellow-creatures. Rich or poor, of gentle or lowly blood, it is not our Province to inquire. Ununiformed, unarmed, sick, and helpless, we ask not on which side they fought.

"Our work begins after yours is done. Yours the carnage, ours the binding up of wounds. Yours the battle, ours the duty of caring for the mangled left behind on the field. Ice I want for the sick, the wounded, the dying. I plead for all, I beg for all, I pray for all God's poor suffering creatures, wherever I may find them."

"Yes, you can beg, it'll admit. What do you do with all your beggings? It is always more! more! never enough!"

With this the general resumed his writing, thereby giving the Sister to understand that she was dismissed. For a moment her eyes fell, her lips trembled—it was a cruel taunt. Then the tremulous hands slowly lifted and folded tightly across her breast, as if to still some sudden heartache the unkind words called up. Very low, and sweet, and earnest was her reply.

"What do we do with our beggings? Ah! that is a hard question to ask of one whose way of life leads ever among the poor, the sorrowing, the unfortunate, the most wretched of mankind. Not on me is it wasted. I stand here in my earthly all. What do we do with it? Ah! some day you may know."

She turned away and left him, sad of face, heavy of heart, and her dark eyes misty with unshed tears.

"Stay!"

The general's request was like a command. He could be stern, nay, almost rude, but he knew truth and worth when he saw it, and could be just. The Sister paused on the threshold, and for a minute nothing was heard but the rapid scratching of the general's pen.

"There, madam, is your order on the Commissary for ice and beef at army terms, good for three months. I do it for the sake of the Union soldiers who are, or may be, in your care. Don't come bothering me again. Good morning!"

In less than three weeks from that day the slaughter of the Red River Campaign had been perfected, and there neared the city of New Orleans, a steamer flying the ominous yellow flag, which even the rebel sharpshooters respected and allowed to pass down the river unmolested. Another and still another followed closely in her wake, and all the decks were covered with the wounded and dying, whose bloody bandages and, in many instances, undressed wounds gave woeful evidence of the lack of surgeons as well as the completeness of the rout. Among the desperately wounded was Gen. S. He was borne from the steamer to the waiting ambulance, writhing in anguish from the pain of his bleeding and shell-torn limb, and when they asked where he wished to be taken, he feebly groaned:

"Anywhere, it matters not. Where I can die in Peace."

So they took him to the Hotel Dieu, a noble and beautiful institution in charge of the Sisters of Charity. The limb was amputated, and there he was nursed for weeks through the agony of the surgical operation, the fever, the wild delirium, and for many weary days no one could tell whether life or death would be the victor. But who was the quiet, faithful nurse, ever at his bedside, ever ministering to his wants, ever watchful of his smallest needs? Why only "one of the Sisters."

At last life triumphed, reason returned, and with it much of the old, abrupt manner. The general awoke to consciousness to see a face not altogether unknown bending over him, and to feel a pair of small deft hands skillfully arranging a bandage, wet in ice-cold water, around his throbbing temples, where the mad pain and aching had for so long a time held sway. He was better now, though still very weak; but his mind was clear, and he could think calmly and connectedly of all that had taken place since the fatal battle—a battle which had so nearly cost him his life, and left him at best but a maimed and mutilated remnant of his former self.

Yet he was thankful it was no worse; that he had not been killed outright. In like degree he was grateful to those who nursed him so tenderly and tirelessly, especially the gray-robed woman, who had become almost angelic in his eyes, and it was like him to express his gratitude in his own peculiar way, without preface or circumlocution. Looking intently at the Sister, as if to get her features well fixed in his memory, he said:

"Did you get the ice and beef?"

The Sister started. The question was so direct and unexpected. Surely her patient must be getting really himself !

"Yes," she replied, simply, but with a kind glance of the soft, sad eyes, that spoke eloquently her thanks.

"And your name is—"

"Sister Francis."

"Well, then, Sister Francis, I am glad you got the things—glad I gave you the order. I think I know now what you do with your beggings. I comprehend something of your work, your charity, your religion, and I hope to be the better for the knowledge. I owe you a debt I can never repay, but you will endeavor to believe that I am deeply grateful for all your great goodness and ceaseless care."

"Nay, you owe me nothing; but to Him, whose cross I bear, and in whose lowly footsteps I try to follow, you owe a debt of gratitude unbounded. To His infinite mercy I commend you. It matters not for the body; it is that divine mystery, the soul, I would save. My work here is done. I leave you to the care of others. Adieu." The door softly opened and closed, and he saw Sister Francis no more.

Two months afterward she received a letter sent to the care of the Mother Superior, enclosing a check for a thousand dollars. At the same time the general took occasion to remark that he wished he were able to make it twice the amount, since he knew by experience, "what they did with their beggings."

The beat of the drum, calling on the nation to arm her sons for the defense of the "Stars and Stripes," broke the stillness of the sacred seclusion even of Notre Dame and Saint Mary's. Then it was that our peaceful barge with its graceful figure-head changed into a swift companion of mighty ironclads, not freighted with guns but with Sisters, taking possession in the name of charity of empty warehouses, of unfinished barrack-like sheds, to which they gave the name of hospitals; and which became hospitals in very deed and in truth, by some transformation known only to the hand of Christian charity. The records of those years will be known only at the Day of Judgment, in their fulness and their beauty; but generations to come, the white-veiled novice of the Order of the Holy Cross will be allowed, we hope, to renew the zeal of religious aspirations, by perusing the story of those hospital Sisters, some of whom died and were carried to their burial over the flooded Mississippi in the hospital boats; others sank more slowly, but as surely, under the awful fatigues and hardships of their self-sacrifice, and lie in the peaceful burying ground at Saint Mary's; while others still labor, wise and valiant and steadfast, in the several vineyards of their Congregation.

From that record which our own hand penned from the stories of individual Sisters, sent in from kitchen and infirmary and classroom, to give what seemed a deposition more than a story, so scrupulous were they for the accuracy of each incident related, we shall draw from memory, without the ability or permission to give names or dates, one or two instances which bring out the characteristics of the subject of this sketch as no eulogy could do. We must be allowed to parenthesize that when the record was finished, after weeks of close labor, and we said: "What an interesting volume this will make; how eagerly it will be read:" we heard not one merry laugh only, but a dozen, and the exclamation; "A volume! Do you suppose this will ever go into print? No, indeed; but into the most secret drawer of the records of Saint Mary's!"

During the early days of the war and the hospital service we all know how inadequate were the supplies for the sick and wounded; how meager the equipments for the hospital nurses. A poor little circular stove-pipe, served the indefatigable Mother Angela on which to prepare with her own skillful hands the early cup of gruel for her patients, rising at four, or if need were, at three in the morning to answer the first call of the sufferers; and the character of the stores provided was such as few could realize one year later. At this time the Commissary Board sent a visitor to the camp and hospital where Mother Angela and her Sisters were stationed. During all these months nothing could exceed the courtesy of the officers, who always shared any choice provisions which came to them with the Sisters, as they supposed, while the Sisters as scrupulously passed on to their patients everything which could tempt the sick appetite, sharing, in fact, only the rations served regularly to the hospital wards.

When the Commissary visitor arrived he was duly escorted to the hospital, which excited his warmest approbation for its order, neatness, comfort of every sort; but as he was bowing himself out in the most complimentary manner from the presence of Mother Angela and her band of Sisters, she said to him: "But, Mr. ——, you must allow us to show you some hospitality. Pardon our lack of silver and porcelain, but take a cup of hospital tea!" "Thank you, thank you, Mother Angela, but I have taken dinner already with the officers, and need nothing." "Allow me to insist!" and before another excuse could be urged, a Sister appeared with a snow-white napkin and the tin cup and spoon of the hospital and—the anything than fragrant beverage of hospital tea. "Sugar, Sister," said the sweetly-ringing voice of the gentlewoman, Mother Angela, and before our Commissary visitor could waive off this fresh specimen of hospital luxury, Mother Angela had dumped into the tin cup what resembled the scrapings of the molasses-barrel more than sugar. Our Commissary visitor was a gentleman from the toe of his boot to the crown of his head, and he drank the cup of tea, well stirred,

to its dregs without a grimace, bowing as he handed the empty tin cup
to the Sister, while Mother Angela rubbed her little hands with unmis-
takable glee and the full merriment of laughing eyes, as she said: "I
knew, Mr. ——, you would wish a taste of our hospital tea!" The Commissary visitor vowed in his heart as he turned from the hospital door
that the next train, on his arrival home, should take, as he said in his
letter to Mother Angela, such stores to her own and to every hospital
under his charge as a Christian man could accept without shame from
the hand of any hospital nurse in the land.

One other incident. Among the disabled Confederates brought to
the Union Hospital at ——, was an officer of high rank, who had been
wounded in the lung, and his arm nearly torn from his body. Lashed to
his bed of suffering to secure his wounds from any loosening of bandages, he seemed like a Prometheus bound; only full of gratitude for
the care bestowed by surgeons and nurses. One day, while the Sister in
charge was in attendance upon the officer, a surgeon stepped in hur-
riedly, saying, in a low voice: "Sister, you must leave the room
instantly!" And as she showed reluctance to leaving her patient, who
needed her attention, he repeated: "Instantly, you must not delay!" She
obeyed, but went directly to Mother Angela, whose quick step, noise-
less as it was, brought her, almost in the same breath, to the officer's
room, confronting the astonished surgeon with the question: "Why
have you dismissed my Sister from the bedside of her patient?"

"Danger, immediate danger."

"Then she should most certainly have remained at her post."

"You do not understand me. There is an uprising of the troops who
have just heard of this officer's arrival, and although they are under a
mistake, no one can convince them that he did not, knowingly, fire
upon the scalded Union soldiers jumping from the exploded ironclad
——, into the Mississippi. They are resolved to shoot him in his bed."

As he said this, a hoarse yell broke on the ears of the surgeon and of
the religious, on the ears, too, of the patient pinioned to his cot.

"You must leave the room, Mother Angela! They are here already,
and too frenzied to listen to reason, or even to commanders."

"And you cannot protect your prisoners, your wounded prisoners?"

"Nor can we protect you, even Mother Angela, unless you leave this
room instantly!"

One look at the wounded officer gave her the face of a man who could have met death in battle bravely, now to die like a villain. His wounded lung was strained to gashing, his nostrils dilated, his eyes starting from the sockets, the large beads of perspiration rolling from his face—a veritable Prometheus bound to his hospital cot! Without a word in reply to the surgeon, Mother Angela stepped to the window, which was wide open, closed it and stood directly before it.

By this time the hoarse shouts of the multitude, "Shoot the coward, like a dog as he is!" with curses loud and deep, filled the air. No sooner; however, did the soldiers see the slight figure of Mother Angela, her white cap and collar standing out from the black veil and habit, than they cried out: "Go away, Sister, go away! let us shoot him like a dog!" But the slender figure remained immovable. Again rose cries and shouts: "Go away, Sister! Leave him—he deserves to die like a dog!" But not a finger of that little woman was raised, even in expostulation, until it was plain to them that they must shoot the Sister before they could harm her charge.

All at once came a lull, then a silence; then as the far rear urged forward the surging ranks, there was a turning at the front as if to pass some word along the lines; when one by one, then by tens and fifties and hundreds, the multitude moved silently away from the hospital precincts, and the very hush of death hung over the space where half an hour before clamored the infuriated soldiers of a noble Republic. Only when the keen eye of Mother Angela had seen the last man in his barrack, did she raise the window sash and turn to her patient. One look of gratitude, of unspeakable confidence, told her all that was in his heart; but she did not leave him, even to the care of a Sister, until his safety was guaranteed from headquarters.

The war over, Mother Angela and her Sisters returned to Saint Mary's to take up the old obedience wherever it had been; the only thing, even today, indicating their part in the national crisis, being the spiked cannon which a few months after were sent to Mother Angela and her community as a recognition of their services by the commander in whose division they had labored. The spiked cannon still lie on the green before Saint Mary's Academy, one of Mother Angela's unfulfilled visions; for she always said: "Wait! one day you will see them transformed into a statue of our Lady of Peace."

Helen Smith

M RS. HELEN E. SMITH was residing in Worcester, Massachusetts, when the war broke out, and with many others did what she could to assist those who were taking part in the great struggle. In 1862 she had married Woodbury C. Smith, who had enlisted in the 34th Regiment Massachusetts Volunteers, then in camp in that city. After the departure of the regiment for the seat of war she visited her home, and then accepted a position in the linen department of McDougal Hospital, Fort Schuyler, New York Harbor. Here she remained three months.

In July 1864 she was appointed as a nurse by Miss D. L. Dix, and ordered to report for duty at United States General Hospital, Hilton Head, South Carolina. She was placed in charge of the linen room until the matron went home, on account of ill health, when she was appointed matron, remaining in charge until the end of the war.

In June 1865 she joined her husband, Capt. Woodbury C. Smith, 35th Regiment United States Cavalry Troops, at Charleston, South Carolina, where he remained in the service for a year after the war ended. Mrs. Smith had two brothers in the war, also.

Her present address is Worcester, Massachusetts. She is a charter member of George H. Ward Woman's Relief Corps, No. 11.

Of her hospital experiences she writes as follows:

It is difficult to select incidents, as every day was so full of joy and sadness,—sadness that we felt on thinking of the suffering of those around us; joy that we could do something to help the soldiers.

One of the saddest things I saw was near the close of the war, when the "Andersonville Pen" was broken up, and some five hundred men who had been imprisoned there were sent to Hilton Head Hospital, to be clothed and await transportation North. How can I describe them? It is beyond description! Had my husband or my brother been among them I could not have recognized either. Emaciated, void of expression, clothed in rags, they excited not only the deepest sympathy but also the deepest indignation of all who saw them. It was a fearful thing that they should have been so inhumanly, so brutally treated.

They learned that we had some slippers at the linen room. The men were barefooted, and their feet were so swollen that they burst, and were sore with scurvy, so they almost fought for the slippers as there were not enough to go around, and we had only small sizes. But the men would not be contented until they had tried to put them on.

They asked for handkerchiefs; we had none, but we had several hundred print dressing-gowns sent by the Commission at home. Not a soldier would wear one if he could get one of Uncle Sam's blue and gray regulation gowns; and as the war was nearly closed, we should not need them, so we obtained permission to cut them into handkerchiefs for the men. We had enough for all, and the day they were to sail they marched to the veranda of the linen room, and colored boys and girls gave one to each of them. And how that piece of calico was appreciated!

It has been said of the war drama "The Drummer Boy" that the prison scene is exaggerated. It is not. It cannot be.

Our surgeon in charge, Dr. John H. Huber, was a kind and true friend to the soldiers, always thoughtful of their welfare. So, also, was his first assistant, Dr. J. T. Reber, and the executive officer, Dr. Wm. H. Balser. It seemed like a family. The chaplain, Mr. Van Antwerp of Pennsylvania, was always ready to do what he could to alleviate the physical suffering or minister to the spiritual wants of the soldiers.

One Saturday afternoon a woman came to my quarters with a permit to remain with me until the next steamer sailed. She was from Central New York, and this is her story: Word was sent that her son was very sick on Folly Island. She wanted to go to him at once, and soon procured the necessary pass, but there was a delay of weeks before she reached the place; then it was only to find that he had been sent to Hilton Head Hospital. When she arrived her son had been dead a week. Sick from the red-tape delays, and almost heart-broken at the loss of her boy, she was a sad picture to me; but I did what I could to make her comfortable. We visited the wards, where she talked with the soldiers, who strongly felt her motherly presence. She wanted to carry the body of her son home. On Sunday we drove to the National Cemetery, and when we showed her his grave she said, "No, no; I cannot disturb him!" and seemed content to leave him there in those beautiful grounds.

In the winter of 1864 and 1865 there were between two and three hundred rebel prisoners encamped in an open field a short distance from the hospital. There were many boys not more than twelve or fifteen years old among them. So as the sick from this camp were brought to our hospital, it chanced that one little fellow, not more than fourteen, sick with typhoid fever, came under my care.

He was delirious, and called piteously for his mother; so his nurse called me, and as I sat by his side he opened his eyes and exclaimed, "Mother!" then threw his arms around my neck. I soothed his few last hours, and allowed him to think that I was his mother. And thus such incidents might be multiplied.

Only those who have had experience in the hospital, or prison, or on the battlefield, can realize how barbarous and cruel a thing is war. With the increase of liberal thought, and the broader view of the value and responsibility of life, war between civilized peoples should be well-nigh impossible. "May we never have another!" is my earnest prayer.

Mrs. Helen E. Smith

Sarah Sprague

THE SUBJECT OF THIS SKETCH, Sarah J. Milliken, was born in Baldwin, Maine, August 3, 1830, and was the daughter of Josiah and Sally (Townsend) Milliken. At the age of twenty she went to Lynn, where her brother had preceded her, and remained until the breaking out of the war. During the first year of the Rebellion she was in Maine, where, in company with other patriotic women, she was engaged in making army clothes for the men at the front. But tiring of this, she wished to be of more use to her country. An opportunity came when Miss Dix called for volunteer nurses. With two other women she left her home in September 1862 and became a regularly enlisted army nurse. When she arrived in Washington, the city was crowded with sick and wounded soldiers, and every available building was used as a temporary hospital. She was first assigned a place in the courtroom of the City Hall building, where for nearly a month she ministered to the wants and relieved the suffering of the soldiers under her charge.

At the end of the month the wounded were removed to the Judiciary Square Hospital, which consisted of ten wards, each containing thirty-six beds. Miss Milliken was given charge of Ward Three. The surgeon was Dr. A. Hartsuff, and the chaplain, Rev. John C. Smith, of the First Presbyterian Church of Washington.

Miss Milliken continued in charge of her ward until the spring of 1863, when she was retained as the only female nurse, and given charge of the whole hospital. At this time the work of caring for the sick was performed by convalescent soldiers, and she directed these men in the performance of their duty. In her enlarged field of action she had ample opportunity to display that womanly kindness and sympathy which made the army nurses so dear to the hearts of the soldiers. She had under her charge the wounded from many a famous battlefield, and could relate many interesting and touching incidents which came under her immediate notice. After sixteen months she retired from the service, January 1864, receiving the following recommendation from the surgeon in charge:—

U. S. A. GENERAL HOSPITAL,
JUDICIARY SQUARE, WASHINGTON, D. C.,
JANUARY, 1864

This certifies that Miss Milliken has been employed in this hospital, as nurse, for many months. She has always been found faithful to her duties, kind to the patients, and strictly honest; thus combining all the qualities of a good nurse and estimable woman.

A. Hartsuff

In 1872 Miss Milliken married, and her present address is

Mrs. Wm. N. Sprague
LYNN, MASSACHUSETTS

Adelaide Spurgeon

ALMOST BEFORE THE ECHOES of the guns which marked the commencement of hostilities between the North and the South had died away, Hon. Henry J. Raymond, of the *New York Times*, with that keen foresight which marked his career as a newspaper man, had formed the idea of organizing a band of ladies to proceed to Washington to act in the capacity of nurses, should they be needed. Several meetings were held, either at the Cooper Institute or the Woman's Library, under the auspices of Miss Elizabeth Powell, who was selected for this purpose by Mr. Raymond.

At the final meeting, many of those who were confidently expected to go, declined; their enthusiasm, which had worked itself to fever heat at the commencement, having died out, and they decided to remain with the "home guard." Six names were called as they had been selected, and when my own, Adelaide E. Thompson, was pronounced and I arose (I being very slightly built at that time), a gentleman in the hall inquired what she expected to do with that little creature; to which Miss Powell responded, "That 'little creature' is one of the reliables."

On the morning of May 3, 1861, we boarded the train at Jersey City. It was loaded with troops on their way to defend the flag. Our progress was very slow. At Havre de Grace we embarked on board a steamer for Baltimore, thinking to hasten our journey in this way, as it was expected the train would be detained some time at that place. I shall never forget that journey. The boat, which was small, was crowded with the roughest class of citizens of "Maryland, my Maryland," whose sole amusement was playing cards, expectorating huge streams of tobacco juice, and cursing the Yankees.

A terrible storm came up, and, to make it more interesting, all of our party except two were affected with that ailment which must be felt in order to be fully appreciated; viz., seasickness. One other lady and myself escaped, and we were obliged to leave the close, dirty little cabin every few moments, to obtain a breath of fresh air; preferring to be drenched by the spray which washed over the deck, to being stifled by tobacco smoke.

On the evening of the third day we reached Baltimore, and proceeded to Barnum's Hotel, where every attention was paid to us; as the rails, which had been torn up during the riot when the Massachusetts troops passed through Baltimore, had not yet been relaid. The next morning an omnibus was chartered, and at about sundown on the evening of our fourth day from New York, dirty and weary, we reached the Mecca of our hopes, Washington, then, comparatively speaking, a mud-hole, but now transformed by Northern enterprise and industry into one of the most beautiful cities in the world.

We took apartments at the Kirkwood House, remaining there three days, and then removed to a boarding-house kept by Miss Bull, a daughter of Judge Bull, located on Twelfth, between E and F Streets.

But here a new trouble arose. Our baggage was somewhere between Washington and New York, but just where no one could tell; and all inquiries, both verbal and by telegraph, failed to solve the mystery. After all this travel we were with absolutely nothing except what we stood in; but at this crisis a good genius appeared, in the person of E. Z. C. Judson, better known as "Ned Buntline." I had known him in New York, and learning that I was in the city, he had searched me out.

Some years before, when he was imprisoned on Blackwell's Island for alleged complicity in the Astor House riots, I assisted him in hauling up the Stars and Stripes to the top of the boat-house, having been invited over there by him for that purpose. I sometimes think that people love the old Flag better since they have had to fight for it. Mr. Judson succeeded in unearthing the baggage, and we were enabled once more to endorse the declaration that "cleanliness is next to godliness."

Our leader, Miss Powell, then started out on a tour of inspection. The Union Hotel, in Georgetown, was being fitted up as a hospital, but was not yet ready to receive patients. The surgeon-general finally informed her that there was only one hospital open in the city, and that was the smallpox hospital; and as they could get no one to go there, a nurse was badly needed.

Miss Powell returned almost in despair. She related the situation to the ladies, but no one responded. One pretty little woman, the youngest of the party, whose husband was here in one of the regiments, declared she could not think of such a thing, for if she took the disease and got her face all marked up, her husband would never forgive her. It is but justice to say that she proved herself very efficient in another place. The oldest lady said she could not think of such a thing for she had not felt well since she left New York and she only felt able to read the Bible; and thus poor fellows must be so sick that reading would only weary them. The others being of the opinion that "silence is golden," remained silent. To me, anything was better than inaction, and I volunteered my services. They all endeavored to point out to me the risk I was running, and the hard work before me; but I was firm, and after a mournful dinner with my comrades I took my little bundle of clothing, and, accompanied by one of the ladies, departed for the hospital. My friend bade me good-bye on the opposite side of the street, and with some little trepidation I crossed over and entered the building. I was met by the physician, Dr. Robert I. Thomas, from Iowa. I handed him the letter from the surgeon-general, appointing me a nurse in the smallpox hospital; and thus as the first nurse in the District of Columbia, on the 16th day of May, I entered upon my duties.

The hospital was a small two-story and basement brick building, located on First Street east, between B and C north. It contained six rooms and a medium-sized closet, which was fitted up as a sort of dispensary. The front basement was used as a dining room for the steward, a rattle-brained Southerner, who had taken the place as he had nothing else to do. The doctor remained but a few hours daily, and as soon as he left, the steward generally started for the city, and returned somewhere in the small hours, grossly intoxicated. The only other inmates who were able to walk around were an Irish woman, who pretended to wash the clothing, and another to cook. The cooking and washing were both carried on in one room, by means of a small stove, which one of our Yankee housewives would have considered fit only for old iron.

Fortunately there was not much to cook. I say fortunately, because the old woman could not be persuaded that sick men did not like greasy food, or that broth would be more palatable without the huge piece of fat bacon which, in spite of all my remonstrances, she would persist in putting into the kettle. But one day the doctor happened in when the boys were being fed, and saw them putting the greater part of their soup into the cuspidors. He called her up, and in terms more emphatic than polite, informed her that if he saw any more such cooking he would throw it out of the door, and then throw her after it. This was too much for the old lady, and she stood out upon the order of going, but finally went.

My first move after her departure was to consign the laundry work to the stable, at the back of the yard. We had plenty of flour, and I proceeded to make up a large batch of bread, which was greatly relished by the boys; but as to the meat,—here words fail me. Never before, or since, have I seen such meat. It would have required the power of a Hercules to masticate it. The sugar was of the consistency of mud, and about the same color, and tasted more like salt than sugar. Butter was not to be thought of, and vegetables of any kind were out of the question. No dishes; nothing but tin cups and tin plates, and so few of them that the food of two or three men had to be served up on one plate. There was no money. No hospital fund had accumulated, and the entire building was the picture of misery, with nothing to make the boys comfortable. Of course nothing could be done. For about ten days I did the cooking, in addition to my other duties. At the end of that time our old cook, whose injured dignity was somewhat more serene, decided to come back, and leave the bacon out of the soup,—as the doctor hinted that he might place her under arrest if the offense was repeated.

At this time I determined to take a trip to New York, and get contributions from my friends. I accordingly applied to Judge Holt, who referred me to Hon. Edwin M. Stanton, who, in turn, gave me a note to General Mansfield. With some nervousness I stood before the old general at his headquarters on 17th Street. He looked up from a desk at which he was writing, and said in a sharp tone, "Well?" I handed him the note from Mr. Stanton, and at the same time said, "General, I want to get a pass to go to New York." "What do you want to go to New York for?" "To get some things for the boys." "What boys?" "The boys in the smallpox hospital." "Are you the nurse there?" "Yes, sir." "Get paid?" "No, sir." "Volunteer nurse?" "Yes, sir." "Afraid of taking the disease?" "No, sir." He wrote a few lines, which he handed me, remarking: "Well, you are a plucky little woman. Here is your pass, good for three days, and you ought to ride over any railroad in the country free of charge as long as you live." He shook me by the hand, and said, "Good-bye; don't forget to come back to the boys." That night, with a large, empty trunk, I started for New York. The train was filled with soldiers going home; some discharged for disability, some returning from sickness; one poor boy, crazy from fever, declaring that he could whip the whole Southern army, individually or collectively, if he was given half a chance. I returned in three days, my trunk well filled with needed articles; also a large box, and a bottle of powerful disinfectants prepared for me by Mr. Green.

I found many additions to our number on returning. As the doctor did not come I placed a cot in a corner of his office, where I could obtain two or three hours' sleep during the night. I have passed many nights entirely alone in the building, except for the sick men; sometimes three or four bodies lay in the adjoining room, waiting for the morning light to bring the undertaker. The first man died from blood-poison, caused by impure vaccine put in his arm before he left Michigan. The weather was warm, and before his comrades arrived to bury him, the body burst. We were obliged to remove all the sick men to a tent in the adjoining lot, while the house was flooded with water. Every train that came in brought more; and as they came pouring in after the first battle of Bull Run, we were obliged to take another house a short distance away. A large mansion was secured on what is now known as Washington Heights. One of the convalescent patients volunteered his assistance, and we were constantly alternating between the two houses.

It is impossible to describe the horrors of that long, hot summer. There was no Potomac water in the city at that time, and the pump near the house would become dry every few days. Then a new difficulty arose. The authorities refused to allow any more bodies to be buried in Potter's Field, as they were fearful of spreading the contagion. Three coffins were placed on trestles some distance from the house, where they remained a day and part of the next night. Some colored men were then hired to carry them over into a gully, and one of our hospital men held a lantern while the graves were dug; and there amid the silence and darkness of midnight they l were laid to rest. I believe some arrangement was made later by which they could again be buried in Potter's Field.

I do not know the date of our removal, as I paid no attention to anything but the wants of the sick, relieving in the Scripture injunction, "Whatsoever thy hand findeth to do, do it with thy might." Time passed unnoticed, and I never supposed any of those hinge would be noticed, except by the recording angel.

The same old laundry woman moved with us into our new home, and died at her post from overwork; but the cook was replaced by a man.

At last I broke down, and contracted blood-poisoning, from which I have never fully recovered. The Doctor ordered my removal, as it was impossible for me to be any better while I remained in that poisoned atmosphere. I went to the home of a friend, and commenced a course of arsenical treatment, which gave me great relief. I still held my commission as a nurse, and was sent for repeatedly, but the medical director thought it unsafe in the diseased condition of my blood; so I reluctantly abandoned the vocation I loved so well.

I then entered the secret service at the provost marshal's headquarters. I was sent for one day by the judge advocate, who wished me to interview two parties who had been taken out of the ranks as a regiment was marching up the avenue. I went into a back room, where I saw two boyish-looking persons in uniform.

After a short conversation they owned up to being of the gentler sex; but the deception was perfect. One was the wife of one of the men, and the other was engaged to one. They had traveled hundreds of miles with the regiment, and would probably have gone to the front but for the rascally behavior of one of the lieutenants, who was in the secret. He offered some insult to the young wife, which she resented, and in a spirit of revenge he signaled the provost guard, and had them taken out of the ranks. They both wept bitterly, not only at the disgrace but at being obliged to return to their homes, leaving their loved ones, perhaps never to meet them again. With some difficulty clothing was procured, and they were sent home very much wiser women that when they left.

I have not space to recount all of my adventures while I was in the service; wherever I was requested to go I went. Once I managed to get into the Old Capitol Prison, by order of a stripling army officers but was promptly released on his being told by the judge advocate that I was entitled to enter any place of confinement in the discharge of duty. I kept no dates, but was given credit on my papers for two years.

Before closing I will relate a little incident, one of the laughable things which occurred among so many sad scenes. One day I went into the Central Guard House to identify some of our boys who had overstayed their passes and been arrested as deserters. While there, six Zouaves, who were the terror of the city, were brought in for some breach of discipline, and ordered to be shower-bathed. Now, this shower-bath was no light punishment, the hose being about the size of the ordinary street hose.

A young lieutenant, who was strutting about in all the dignity of a new uniform and untarnished shoulder-straps, said he was going to see the fun. In about ten minutes he came out thoroughly drenched, and the most demoralized-looking man to be found. The Zouaves had overpowered the guard, and turned the hose on the lieutenant. He had seen the fun to his heart's content.

In conclusion, I will state that my eldest brother responded to the first call for troops at New Haven, Connecticut, went through the war until the army disbanded, but died of consumption shortly after. Two sisters, one having two little children, the other a bride of a few months, bade their husbands Godspeed, and never saw them again; while my fair-haired "baby brother," as we called him at home, died from a disease contracted from infected clothing at Newbern. They will all sleep sweetly in Southern soil, with thousands of others, until the Great Commander shall order the last roll-call, and the grand army of this famous Republic shall hear from His lips the welcome words, "Well done, good and faithful servants."

Adelaide E. Spurgeon
WASHINGTON, D. C.

Hannah Starbird

I ENLISTED IN AUGUST 1864 under my maiden name
of Hannah E. Judkins, from Skowhegan, Maine, under Miss Dix, who
had charge of all the regularly enlisted nurses. I reported at her house
in Washington, and was sent to Carver Hospital immediately, where I
first ministered to the wounded and afflicted soldiers. I remained there
only three weeks, and was then transferred to Saint John's College
Hospital, Annapolis, Maryland, where Dr. G. S. Palmer was surgeon in
charge. I was there until the hospital was broken up, July 15, 1865. It
accommodated about twelve hundred patients, and sometimes there
were fourteen nurses. It was a post for paroled prisoners, who were our
patients. Pen cannot describe the first boat-load of half-starved, half-
clothed, thin, emaciated forms whose feet, tied up in rags, left
footprints of blood as they marched long to be washed and dressed for
the wards. In many cases, their minds were demented, and they could
give no information as to friends or home, and died in that condition,
their graves being larked "Unknown."

The stories related by sick and dying soldiers of their suffering in
prison, corroborates what I have seen in print, only one half cannot be
told! The patience, bravery, and fortitude of our soldier comrades will
ever be cherished in my memory.

Hannah E. Starbird
DENVER, COLORADO

Mary Stinebaugh

I WAS BORN IN GALION, OHIO. My mother's health was poor, and at an early age I was her trusted nurse and overseer of the children, and preferred this loving service to play. I attended school at Galion, Oberlin, and Cleveland, Ohio, and was a student at Oberlin College when the war broke out. We were not blind to the fact that blood must be shed. One of the professors and two students had already been imprisoned at Harper's Ferry. Many of the students had friends in the Kansas and Missouri troubles, and we were all wide awake.

My brother, George Stinebaugh, then only twenty-one years of age, while on his way home from Kansas, stopped in Illinois and enlisted. He was wounded at Shiloh, and left on the field until our men retook it; then was sent to Mound City Hospital, Cairo, Illinois. We received a letter telling us that he had lost a limb, and asking me to go and nurse him. My father thought this unsafe, and so he started, but was not allowed to pass the lines. Later came the news of his death.

More than a year passed. I expected soon to begin to teach in a Ladies' Seminary, when an invitation came to go South under the leadership of Rev. S. G. Wright, who had been a missionary among the Indians for twenty years. After a sleepless night spent in prayer I was ready to give up my chosen work, feeling that I could teach after all this was over, if I lived to return. My father objected to my going, but I said, "You have given your boys to die for their country; now you can give your girls to nurse them."

My aunt came while I was packing my trunk. "Oh!" she said, "they have all gone! The last one has enlisted, my five dear sons and my son-in-law. I have packed the satchels for six. I could not stay at home, and have walked three miles to see you and forget!" "Yes," my mother replied; "all our boys have gone, too, and Mary Ann is going!" Then the brave Spartan mothers tried to forget their anxiety while packing my trunk.

The youngest son soon returned, one limb shot off; his cousin, without his right arm; and some never returned.

Father said: "Mother, can't we send some butter and fruit? They will need it." Soon forty pounds of butter and half a barrel of dried fruit was ready, together with bandages and other supplies. We took the boat at Cincinnati for Vicksburg, and stopped at Cairo, to see if I could find my brother's grave. We visited the hospitals at Memphis, and found everything in as good order as war would permit, the hospitals well supplied with women, both colored and white.

Here I met a doctor, who said: "Did you not have a brother in Ward D, Mound City Hospital? I see a striking resemblance." I told him that I did, and he replied: "Well, Madam, if you had been there you might have saved his life. I assisted in amputating his leg, and he was doing well, until high water compelled us to move the sick upstairs. The artery opened while they were moving him, and the attendant did not know enough to put his thumb on and stop the bleeding. When I reached him he was dead."

We were assigned to Milliken's Bend, twenty miles above Vicksburg, where General Grant dug the canal, and where the mortality was so great. The army had been removed, leaving one company to guard the hospitals, containing the sick.

The next day after our arrival I was informed that I was chosen matron. Many of the men had chronic diseases, that seemed to baffle the skill of the most competent doctors; yet the soldiers were hopeful now that Union women had come to care for them.

The men in charge were familiarly called the old and the young doctors; but their names the finger of Time has erased from my memory. We commenced our duties with plenty of Government rations, a large brick oven, a negro baker, an Indian cook, and any amount of colored people asking for something to do. All went well until the old doctor sent an order for the sick to have only two meals a day. This did not meet my approbation, but what was I to do? I was only a volunteer; so, also, was the acting chaplain. The old doctor outgeneraled us for a time, for "a soldier's first duty is obedience." The men complained, and at last we thought of a plan by which the Golden Rule could be obeyed if only we could find trusty help. An old colored preacher, who came timidly every Saturday for help in preparing his sermon "fo' de bredren de Lawd's day," assured us he could find "niggers 'nuf what could be trusted?" So while the doctor was in his office, or taking his afternoon nap, the sick had their supper.

Christmas Day the commander drew the soldiers up in front of the hospital, and invited the chaplain and myself to address them. I congratulated the men on their temperate habits, emphasizing the advantage of such a course. In a few days the men rolled a great barrel up the hill from the boat. Could it be pork? Was it something nice for the sick? Ah! it was nothing less than Government whiskey. Drunkenness became so common that the officers were alarmed. I proposed a temperance pledge, and much good resulted.

The smallpox hospital was only a mile down the river, and the disease was spreading rapidly. One day we saw some men with shovels hastily leaving a newly-made grave beside the road along which we were passing. "Whom have you buried there?" the doctor inquired. "Oh! a small-pox patient," was the reply. The doctor told me I was in danger, and warned me to keep out of the road. Fortunately I escaped the disease.

The troops had been removed, and there were constant rumors of guerrillas, but we stood our ground. Northern people went on with the schools and calmed the fears of the freedmen until shortly before Christmas. Then we saw the fire the outlaws had kindled to destroy us. The commander advised all who could do so to cross the river, and take refuge in the canebrake, or with a friendly family; the young doctor, with the help of the colored assistants, would care for the sick.

While we were away a real blizzard came up, and large snowflakes filled the air. How frightened the children were! They had never seen snow before, and running into the house they tried to hide, and were terrified to see us go out and enjoy it. The third day we attempted to return, as Chaplain Wright had planned a Christmas tree; but when our little boat got into the current, the gale was so strong that it was impossible to cross the boisterous river, and we were dashed back to shore. Another lady and I jumped overboard and waded to land; the others followed. When the sun went down we crossed safely.

All was quiet for some time; then came a lady on horseback with her husband and brothers. They had been attacked by the guerrillas, who killed one man, and swore that they would make a raid on Milliken's Bend the next night, and the "Yanks would lose their heads, women first." Again we fled, as we were assured that they would not harm the sick. We were none too soon in taking the road to Vicksburg. As we passed the graveyard, where about two thousand of Grant's men now slept, the fire met us, and the chaplain pointed to a hickory tree, near which a volume of fire and smoke was issuing from the ground. He told us it was buried cotton burning.

We found Vicksburg overrun with troops, and fasted one day, if never before. I had suggested taking a box of hardtack with us, but every one assured me we should be supplied. Not so. "Where are you from?" demanded the officer. "Milliken's Bend." "Well, you have drawn your rations;" and not a loaf of bread could be bought. One of our number had some tea and a few hardtacks, and these she divided for our breakfast. We found a vacant room, and rested until the next morning.

Before daylight we sent to the bakery, but the soldiers had been there first. They promised to have some bread soon, and we anticipated what a breakfast we should have, with some lovely hot bread and a few dried fish. But, oh, that miserable baker! I wondered if the soldiers met the same fate. The bread was not baked an inch deep. We had a good laugh; then toasted it on a stick before the grate.

We learned that help was needed at Natchez, and were soon on our way, passing the plantation of Jefferson Davis, and other places of interest. We often saw bands of guerrillas at a distance, but were not molested. The prejudice against Northerners was great in that city. The fort and white tents were seen in the distance, but where were our men? We had a letter of introduction to Mr. Wallace, and but for that, we should not soon have found out anything. We learned that there was not a female nurse in hospital or camp, and that there was much suffering, and need of workers.

So the labor was divided. Some were to look after Union women and children whose husbands and fathers had gone into our army, been robbed of their all, and left to die; others were to teach the freedmen, others to care for the sick. A confiscated mansion was turned over to us, with the injunction to be no "respecter of persons," but to welcome all who came, "in the name of the God of the universe."

It was here that Mr. Wright's experience and sagacity, acquired in the Indian service, became of great value. He soon canvassed the entire field, and reported the condition, and Miss Henry and I offered to nurse in the Marine Hospital. The doctor coolly informed us that they were not in need of female nurses, but that there was a hospital for colored women, and we might be of service there. Heavy-hearted we returned to the city, to await further developments.

Soon we decided to visit the wards after the doctors had made their morning calls. How glad I was of this opportunity to give an encouraging word, to soften a pillow, or fan a fevered brow.

One day I noticed that the men were watching us very closely. Finally one asked, "Are you not a Northern woman?" "Why, to be sure I am." "Do you have the papers? Where are they fighting? We should so like to see a paper." I told him he was too sick to read; he said, "But you can read to us, and if you are a Northern woman you can write home." Oh! what an avalanche of questions followed; but I took no step until I had spoken to the chief attendant.

In the spring of 1864, Rev. Mr. Brown and lady, he seventy years of age and she sixty-five, established a branch of the Christian Commission within the fort. As I did not always have the company of a lady, I thought it wise to call and take Mother Brown with me. She was a mother not only to me, but also to the boys in blue. Her presence made my work much easier. One Sabbath morning in the spring of 1864 everything was quiet. Soldiers and citizens were attending church. The gunboat had dropped down the river a mile; the fort was a mile above the landing, and Camp 70, U. S., colored, still a mile beyond.

Suddenly we heard firing, and the answer. The church was soon emptied, and all was excitement. The Southerners ran to their homes or places of safety, the Northern people to the bluff overlooking the river. We could see the Confederates on the edge of the timber, about a mile away. They were commanded by a dashing German general, who rode a white horse, and wore a large white plume. They had attempted to cross the river and take our commissary stores in Natchez, under the hill. All our men were gone but some new recruits, and they were ex-slaves. Would they fight, or would they cower at the sight of their old masters? See I see! How they rush forward, hardly waiting for orders. They do better than the guns that fire on the enemy from the boat. In two hours they are driven from the field, leaving their dead and wounded.

Three rebel officers were brought to our hospital to be cared for. In a few weeks they were able to be in the sitting room. Our men eagerly read the papers, but they shook their heads. "Gentlemen," I said, "have you been well treated here?" "Very well," was the reply. "Don't you think you were on the wrong side?" "We do not wish to talk of this matter with a Union lady." "Yet I have a request to make of you," I answered. "When our men fall into your hands, will you not use your influence to have them treated as well as you have been?"

The sultry days came, and every time I entered the ward I would miss a cot here and there. At last it was deemed best for us to take a furlough. Our trunks were packed, and the boats would be up the river the next day; when, oh, dreadful news! Two boatloads of soldiers would soon arrive. We hastened to the Marine Hospital, but one load was there before us; every ward was filled, and they were laying them on the verandas, those dying, blood-stained men, and there were one hundred and fifty more to arrive. "And is this war?" we questioned. Oh, horrible sights I could not bear it.

When the other boat arrived, the men were stored in a rude building on a bluff overlooking the river. Soon we learned that the men were suffering for food and clothing. I procured a basket full of needed articles, and on my way saw an old colored woman coming out of her shanty. She asked if I was going to see the Union soldiers, and said: "I's gwine, too. My ole man says they's starving an' I's takin' em some dinner." Then she lifted the snowy cloth, and I saw beefsteak, butter, warm bread, and vegetables. I feared the doctor's frowns, but many of the men relished just such a dinner. As we walked toward home I said:

"Aunty, how can you afford this? Butter is fifty cents a pound, and beefsteak but little less." "Yo' see, honey, I does washens, an' de ole man gets jobs, an' us is free."

I must tell you how I came to adopt beautiful twin boys. I had often heard of them, and how unlike other colored children they were. One night I dreamed I was going alone to see the sick, when I discovered that I was two. I let my parasol fall, and my other self quickly dismounted and handed it to me. What could it mean? On my way to the hospital the next time, while talking to their teacher, the boys came up, and one touched my arm, then ran away, frightened. We reassured them, and finally they returned and said: "Aunty is going to die, and uncle is in the army. He marched by yesterday, and we ran after him to tell him aunty is sick, but he did not stop, and we cried. Please, ma'am, won't you take us to live with your father?" I went with them to see their aunt. On the way I dropped my parasol. One of the boys picked it up; the other said, "I will tote it for you." There was my dream, and I saw my duty. Their father was the son of a judge in Tennessee, and was treated as a son until he was seventeen years of age. Then he wished to go to school with his half brothers, and this enraged their mother, who said: "You are a negro. You cannot learn." "Have I not learned as much as my brothers, and do I not stay in the office with father?" he cried. In a short time he went, unsuspectingly, with a stranger on an errand, as he supposed; but he never saw his home again.

As I passed to and fro, I often noticed a little yellow girl perched upon a fence. One day I said, "See here, little Topsy, do you know you are free?" "No, missy." "Well, you are, and there is a school at the Baptist Church for you. Now go and tell your mistress to send you there, or she will lose you." The next day she was at the same place watching the "Yanks." "Why are you not at school?" "My missy say you 'Yanks' better go home an' let our city 'lone, or de break-bone fever will notch yo'."

Thus the work went on, with many interruptions and drawbacks, for about a year, while we did what we could for both patients and freedmen. Then I returned to my home.

Mary A. Stinebaugh-Bradford
MILLER, SOUTH DAKOTA

Vesta Swarts

ABOUT THE SIXTH OF JULY 1864, and at the age of twenty-three, I resigned my position as principal of the High School at Auburn, Indiana, where I then lived, and started for the South. I expected to join my husband, Dr. D. J. Swarts, assistant surgeon, 100th Indiana Volunteers, then on duty in a hospital at Altoona Pass, Georgia, and to assist him in the care of the sick and wounded at that place.

When I reached Indianapolis I learned that communication was cut off, and that it would not be possible for me to get through. While hesitating, and wondering what I should do, Governor Morton suggested that I report in person to the Christian Commission agency at Louisville, Kentucky, as he thought that Annie Wittenmyer, who was doing grand work for the soldiers, would find a place in some hospital where my work would be needed.

This I decided to do, and in a few days (about July 15th) I began work at Brown U. S. General Hospital, near Louisville, being employed by surgeons in charge under the auspices of the Christian Commission.

About October of the same year, I was transferred to Crittenden U.S. General Hospital, at Louisville, where I remained until March 27, 1865, when being unfit for duty on account of poor health, I was honorably discharged and returned to my home. Among the army nurses with whom I was associated, I recall the names of two most excellent women who are numbered with the dead,—Mrs. Underwood of Brown, and Mrs. Alling of Crittenden Hospital.

The war for the preservation of our Union evidently did much to advance the best interests of woman. It created a necessity for her labor in new and untried ways. It gave her an opportunity to prove her ability, and also to cultivate that true courage without which the most capable person may utterly fail of success. No women appreciate these facts so well as do the active workers of those days, among whom are the army nurses.

Fraternally yours,
Vesta M. W. Swarts, M.D.
CORNER MAINE AND SIXTH STREETS
AUBURN, INDIANA

Elizabeth Thompson

I ENLISTED at Plattsburg, New York, under Captain Moore and served under him for three months at Sackett's Harbor, where I was the first matron, having my daughter with me as an assistant. Here we had to work very hard, cleaning the hospital as well as caring for the sick, and trying to make everything as homelike as possible under the circumstances. The beef and the bread were an especial trial. At last my husband, who was the hospital steward, told the doctor about it, and at his request a loaf of the bread was brought for the doctor to see. He stood looking at it for some time, then said, "Well, there will be more sick ones than there are at present if they have to eat such stuff." We told him we could make the bread if only we had the material; and in a short time a barrel of flour arrived. As I was sick my daughter made the bread. When the doctor came the next time he inquired how we managed, and my husband showed him a loaf. He looked very much pleased, and said, "Oh, we can get along nicely, now that we have that little baker." From that time we made the bread, in addition to our other duties.

On leaving Sackett's Harbor, we went to Fort Niagara for three months, making in all six months of service; then, the war being ended, we were discharged.

Mrs. Elizabeth Thompson
VILAS HOME, PLATTSBURGH, NEW YORK

Fanny Titus Hazen

I WAS BORN IN VERSHIRE, VERMONT, May 9, 1840.
Lenox Titus, my great-grandfather, was a soldier in the Revolutionary
War.

At the outbreak of the Rebellion in 1861, when the whole country
was alive with patriotism, it seemed the greatest misfortune of my life
that I was born a girl. My eldest brother, then only seventeen, enlisted
in the 4th Vermont Infantry. I went home to bid him "good-bye" and
"God bless you." The people of the town gathered in the town hall to
receive their citizen soldiers on the evening before the departure of
Company K to join the 4th Regiment. As the boys in blue marched
through the hall, I would have given years of my life could I have taken
a place in the ranks with my brother.

Two years later, in 1863, two younger brothers, one eighteen, the
other not seventeen, enlisted. I could not rest; it seemed that I must go
to help care for the brave defenders of our country's flag.

I went to both Sanitary and Christian Commissions to go as nurse
under their auspices, but the answer was the same, "You are too
young." I also went to Doctor Hayward, in Hayward Place, Boston,
who sent nurses to Miss Dix. He also said: "You are too young; it will
be of no use to send you. Miss Dix would send you right back."

Believing if the wish of my heart was ever accomplished, I should
have to do it independently, I decided to go to Washington, and was

soon ready. Thinking letters of reference might be of service to me, I received one from Rev. George H. Hepworth, pastor of the Church of the Unity, West Newton Street, Boston (whose church I attended); also one from Doctor Steadman and from Doctor Willard. Thus equipped I went to Washington, the last of March, 1864. I called on Surgeon-General Hammond, who told me it would be of no use to go to Miss Dix, but if any surgeon in charge of a hospital would give me a position as nurse, he would endorse my name, which would place me on record as a regularly enrolled army nurse.

First of all I visited Armory Square Hospital, in charge of Doctor Bliss. He would give me a ward as soon as the new barracks were built, each ward then having a nurse. Doctor Bliss sent me to Doctor Cald-well's, on the "Island," where Sanitary Commission people, army nurses, mothers, and wives of soldiers could remain a short time free of expense.

I remained at Doctor Caldwell's two weeks. During this time I had an opportunity to go to the Demar (officers) Hospital; also to work in the linen rooms of several hospitals. The surgeons would tell me, "Miss Dix is the proper person for you to go to, but it will be of no use; you are too young." However, I went to Miss Dix; she received me kindly. I spoke of my brothers,—the eldest had given his life for his country, the other two were with the Vermont Brigade in Virginia; that I was most anxious to serve my country by caring for the sick and wounded soldiers; told her my age, regretting that I was not older, and gave her letters of reference.

She inquired where I was stopping, how much baggage I had, etc. I said, "A large and a small valise." She commended the good sense evinced in taking so little baggage, and said: "Child, I shall not say no, though it is entirely against my rules to take any one so young. I believe your heart is in the work, and that I can trust you. I shall send my ambulance tomorrow morning, at ten o'clock, to take you to Columbian Hospital, there to remain in quarters till I send you to Annapolis. In the meantime you will be under the training of Miss Burghardt. I have so instructed Major Crosby." (She wrote while she was talking.)

April 19, 1864, I went in Miss Dix's ambulance to Columbian Hospital, Fourteenth Street, Washington, in charge of Dr. Thomas R. Crosby, formerly professor of surgery in Dartmouth College. Doctor Crosby asked me to take charge of the linen room; but nothing less than active work in a hospital ward would satisfy me. Miss Burghardt needed rest; a furlough was granted, leaving me to care for her ward. The ward surgeon, Dr. F. Marsh of Michigan, will ever be remembered, not only by the nurses, but by all the boys who knew him; so bright, cheerful and breezy, his coming was like sunshine: just a walk-through the ward would make the boys feel better. Doctor Crosby, in the meantime, requested Miss Dix to let me remain at Columbian Hospital and on Miss Burghardt's return gave me Ward 2, left vacant by the resignation of Mrs. Russell, where I remained till June 27, 1865, when the hospital was closed.

My experience through that dreadful summer of 1864 cannot find expression in words. The hospital was filled in May with wounded from the Wilderness; then came the battle at Spottsylvania, and June 1st the battle of Cold Harbor. From the latter battlefield my youngest brother was brought to my ward. At the time I was so rejoiced to see him alive, I did not feel sorry that he had been wounded.

After each arrival from the front, all who could be moved were transferred to hospitals more remote, to make room for the next arrival from the battlefields; till at last the wards were filled with very badly wounded men, some soon crossing to the other shore, others lingering for months, suffering untold agonies, ere the longed for rest came; still others lived to carry through life crippled bodies. Many were the letters written for those unable to write to the dear mother, father, brother, sister, or sweetheart, and many the letters received with thanks from the absent friends.

The bodies of some were sent home for burial. I never failed to place by the heart of each silent soldier a bouquet of the florist's choicest flowers that the dear mother might feel assured that an earnest, sympathetic heart had ministered to her son. One young boy, from the Pennsylvania "Bucktails," was shot through the left lung at Spottsylvania. He lived four months. The bulletins of President Garfield's sufferings were the exact counterpart of Eddie Mullan's. I often spoke of it during the dreary days of watching and praying for the restoration to health of our beloved President. Eddie Mullan had a most beautiful and noble face; visitors passing through the hospital would stoop and kiss his fair forehead, saying, "For your mother."

During the summer, June, July, August, and September, our heads, hands, and hearts were taxed to the utmost; so much to do, so many claiming our sympathy, so many to tell that soon they must answer the last bugle call, and cross to the beautiful shore. Then it was, I realized how utterly insignificant were all my greatest efforts. I seemed like an atom, or drop of water; ten pair of hands could not do what one pair would willingly have done.

Telling one boy that he could never go home, he said: "Why? I shall get well." I asked, "Would you be afraid to die?" He hesitated, then said, "Yes;" in a moment, "No. Does Doctor Marsh say I can't get well?" I answered, "Yes." "Please pray for me." I knelt by his cot and prayed with him; he became reconciled. In the morning he called Doctor Marsh, saying, "O doctor, Miss Titus told me I could never get well, and prayed with me just as my sister would!" Every night for the three weeks that he lived I knelt by his cot and prayed. There were many deaths at this time, each one as the last hours came, saying, "O please, Miss Titus, stay with me; it will be but a short time;" and, "You seem so like a sister!"

So, hour after hour, through those nights of death, as I watched the life-light flicker and die of many noble men whose lives were a sacrifice for their country. Weeks seemed months, and months like years, that ages had passed since my hospital work commenced; and yet the day was not long enough to finish all one would like to do. Later we had our bright days, too, when wit and song prevailed, and occasionally had time to make (as the boys said) "pies and other things like what we had at home." The boys would bring the tables from the rooms, placing them end to end through the haul, making a long table, where all the men able to leave their beds sat down to a home-like meal.

In the spring of 1865 we had a boy, Sergeant Eli Hudson, of Sheshequin, Pennsylvania, a veteran volunteer, having served over four years, who was wounded in the left knee. He had been several months in the ward. The surgeons held many examinations; he was failing rapidly; could not retain anything, even cold water causing hemorrhage of the stomach. One morning I asked, "What is the verdict, doctor?" He replied, "He can live but a few days, and may die in a few hours." "Then, doctor, please let him have what he wants while he does live." "I give him into your hands, Miss Titus; do what you please for him."

The bandages were at once removed, as he had complained that they were uncomfortable. As soon as the patients were all cared for, I went to a market garden and bought a head of cabbage. He had often said he wanted something green, if only "boiled grass." When the cabbage was cooked I carried him some with cider vinegar, and fed him. He ate all on the plate, asked for more, which was brought, and still a third and fourth plate, till he ate the whole cabbage. From that dinner in May he began to improve, and the 14th day of June I started with Sergeant Hudson on a stretcher for his home in Sheshequin, Pennsylvania, as his life even then depended upon his diet, and such meals as he ate would make a well man sick. He recovered, but had a stiff knee.

In the winter of 1865 we had but few wounded men, and the hospital was filled with sick men from Point Lookout.

We needed lemons, cordials, farina, arrowroot, corn-starch, jellies, in fact everything, for the sick list had nearly every disease. The demand was such throughout all the hospitals that the Sanitary and Christian Commissions' supplies were exhausted. Remembering what Rev. Hepworth said, "If ever you need hospital supplies, let Mrs. Bird, chairman of the Aid Society, know what is needed, and we will send direct to you." I wrote Mrs. Bird, who received my letter Saturday evening, and it was read in church Sunday morning. Before night three (3) large boxes were filled and started for Washington, containing $300 (three hundred dollars) worth of supplies; enough not only for my boys but for all the wards of Columbian Hospital. The Aid Society also sent beautiful flannel shirts, socks, towels, and everything to fit out all my boys when able to return to the front; a mother could not more carefully have provided for a son. The girls of the Everett School in Boston sent two barrels of books through one of the teachers, Mrs. Emma F. W. Titus; many of them new publications, purchased expressly for the soldiers. After the close of the war the books were given to the chaplain in charge of the Freedman's Camp, as a nucleus for a library. Friends in Lawrence sent all the popular periodicals and magazines; also several leading weeklies. They were eagerly welcomed by the boys, and passed on from ward to ward.

Miss Dix visited the hospital every month, calling all the nurses to meet her in the matron's room. She always came for me, saying: "Child, go quickly as possible; tell the nurses I wish to see them without delay."

She was kind and thoughtful for all, but very strict in enforcing all her rules and regulations. She never wasted a minute, and had no patience with those who were slow. I shall ever remember Miss Dix with the warmest love and gratitude, and with the greatest reverence decorate her grave in Mount Auburn every Memorial Day. My hospital memories are among the most pleasant of my life,—pleasant in that I was doing what the Master would approve; "Inasmuch as ye did it unto one of the least of these, ye did it unto me."

Mrs. Fanny H. Titus Hazen

Julia Tompkins

My war record is much shorter than it would have been had I been able to carry out the earnest desire of my heart. From the time the first call for volunteer nurses was issued, my heart burned with patriotic longings to do something for our country and the dear old flag; and why not? My ancestors on both sides were descendants of the Puritan and Revolutionary stock. My husband was at the front, and I kept writing for his consent to go where I could help the sick and wounded; but as we had a little boy, and no one with whom to leave him, he would not hear to any such proposition until he was left in a hospital with most of his regiment, as they were returning to the front from Camp Douglas where they had been taken prisoners.

After he became convalescent I visited him at Benton Barracks, where he had been assigned to take charge of the kitchens and procure supplies. Again my very soul was stirred with longing to do something for the patient sufferers, and I begged to stay. When the soldiers learned of my desire, they added their entreaties to mine, as they had become very much attached to our little boy, who took the place of those "left behind," and enlivened many lonely hours. My husband at last consented, and I received my appointment. I went on duty in Ward A, Amphitheatre Building, at Benton Barracks, where I served until prostrated by a nervous fever, caused by my sympathy for the "brave boys who wore the blue," who were never heard to utter a complaint, no matter how badly they were wounded or how match they were suffering, but were ever ready to express gratitude for all we did for them.

On my recovery I was placed in charge of the linen room, and served in that department until I left the service.

Dr. Ira Russell was in charge of the hospitals when I went there, but was relieved by Dr. John H. Grove, August 10, 1863. He remained until February 12, 1864, when Dr. Russell returned. He was still there when I left the work.

When my husband was discharged from active field service, on account of disabilities, there was no one with whom to leave my boy, and I had to request that my connection with the hospital be severed, as I could not look after my child and do my duty as a nurse. My request was reluctantly granted, and I returned to my home.

One little incident connected with my work there gave me much pleasure. Miss Emily E. Parsons was "Superior Nurse" at our hospital. My sister's son had been wounded at Vicksburg, and was very low. She had him placed in my section of the ward, where he would be under my immediate care. I could not but feel complimented, as no nurse was allowed to be on duty in a ward where she had relatives, or even former friends, lest favoritism should be shown. She never had reason to feel that her confidence was misplaced.

Julia S. Tompkins
418 2ND AVENUE
CLINTON, IOWA

Mary Venard

I WENT OUT under Governor Morton's first call for nurses, commissioned by Mr. Hannaman, Sanitary Agent for the State of Indiana. This was February 4, 1863. I was then forty-one years of age. I was first sent to Nashville, Tennessee, for three months, but stayed six. I was in the Howard High School Building and had charge of the Diet Kitchen, but at the same time I did a great deal of nursing.

As a compliment to my cooking I received a very beautiful and practical cookbook, which I never felt that I deserved.

From Nashville I returned to my home, where I remained ten weeks; then received strict orders to go immediately to Natchez, Mississippi. I was in the Marine Hospital, and the fort was built up around us. This was the fall after the siege of Vicksburg, and for days and days we expected to be attacked, and had everything in readiness to be removed at a moment's notice. General Thomas came down the river with his regiment, and sent out his soldiers to reconnoiter, and that stopped it. The surgeon in charge proposed that if we were attacked, I should leave immediately with him in the ambulance. His very kind offer I declined, telling him if I had to leave, it would be at the last moment; then I would run down the hill, and, if necessary, defend myself. I was at Natchez one year and six months then returned to my home. I received a telegram the next day calling me to Indianapolis, Indiana, where I took charge of the Refugee Home jointly conducted by the Sanitary Commission and citizens, and had the name of being one of the best houses on the line. When warm weather came we secured homes for those who wished to stay; others were sent wherever they wanted to go. This home was closed immediately after the assassination of President Lincoln.

I next went to the Ladies' Home in Indianapolis, and remained until fall, when I went to Camp Morton, to help close that. In three months more, the war being over, I was honorably discharged by Mr. Hannaman, and returned to my home in Terre Haute, where I have lived ever since. I receive twelve dollars a month pension, and this is very acceptable, as I am not able to do much work. Two years ago I received from National Headquarters of the W. R. C. a beautiful nurse's certificate, which I appreciate very much. I am a member of John P. Baird Corps.

On Christmas Eve a number of members of Morton Post, G. A. R., called at my home in a body, and the commander, in a very nice speech, presented the pin I have on in the picture. It was an honor of which I am justly proud.

During my service as army nurse I received from my patients many tokens of friendship and esteem, among them three pieces of poetry, one thanking me for a bouquet of rare wild flowers I had gathered on the bluffs. The following is a part of another:—

To A Stranger.
    Your generous acts and noble deeds,
    Like fragrant flowers 'midst noxious weeds,
    Have won my admiration:
    Your care for one who's far away
    From those who for his safety pray,
    Inspires my veneration.

    Like angel visits, deeds so rare
    Awake our inmost, earnest prayer
    For blessings on the stranger;
    And oft we breathe the prayer of love
    To Him who reigns in heaven above,
    To shield you from all danger.

And though, perhaps we never shall meet
Till summoned to the Mercy Seat,
Your image I will cherish.
Amid the memories of my heart,
Sweet thoughts of you will share a part,
Till earthly dreams shall perish.

Miss Mary Venard
673½ WABASH AVENUE
TERRE HAUTE, INDIANA

Elizabeth Ward

I LEFT MY HOME in South Bristol, Wisconsin, on September 22, 1864, for Louisville, Kentucky. My first period of service was in Foundry Transfer Hospital of that place, under Surgeons Prescott and Phelps; where I remained until January 28, 1865, when I left under orders for Nashville, Tennessee. I was the first woman in charge of the light Diet Kitchen in Wilson Colored Hospital, and served there under Surgeon Russell, until I was taken dangerously ill with typhoid fever about the 25th of March, from which I recovered sufficiently to be removed by easy stages to my home the last of May 1865.

My period of service was short, when compared with that of many who entered in the earlier years of the war. I was too young at that time to be accepted, yet I feel very grateful that I was enabled, even in so short a time, to relieve, comfort, and cheer many sick and wounded soldiers.

Sincerely yours,
Elizabeth S. Ward
PLEASANT PRAIRIE, WISCONSIN

Mary Watson

AFTER THE BATTLE OF STONE RIVER, there came a call from Governor Morton of Indiana for twenty-five nurses, fifty surgeons and ward masters, and a large supply of sanitary goods of every description. I was the second one to put my name on the list of nurses to go to Nashville, Tennessee, to help take care of the sick and wounded in Hospital 14, which was a five-story building, a female seminary; but now full, from basement to attic, of sick and wounded soldiers. There were over five hundred there at one time, so I was told. I think it was true, for every bunk was full, and men were lying in the aisle with nothing but their blankets under them, and each waiting for some poor soul to die or be sent away, so he could get a bed. That looks hard, but it is true.

I could not go up or down stairs but I would often meet the men nurses carrying some poor fellow to the dead-house. For the first two weeks after the battle they averaged from twenty-five to thirty deaths a day, the ward master told me. Oh! it was terrible to hear the poor fellows, some praying, some calling for wife and children, others for father, mother, brother or sister, while the death damp was gathering on the brow, and they knew they would never see home or friends again. But I must not allow myself to think, or I shall write too much.

I remained at the hospital from January until some time in March, when I was taken sick with typhoid fever, and had to leave for awhile.

Then Governor Morton and William Hannaman sent me down to Murfreesboro, Tennessee; to nurse in the field hospital in the fort. I went in July 1863 and stayed until the last of February 1864. When I went, my husband was lying at the point of death in the fort. I was the only white woman there for two or three weeks, though there were several colored women, to do the cooking and washing.

I drew sanitary supplies for the sick, and did everything in my power for them. I stayed with the brigade until it was ordered to the front to join Sherman in his march to the sea; then I came home, as I needed rest.

Yours in F. C. and L.,
Mrs. Mary J. Watson
77 N. Liberty Street
Indianapolis

Margaret Edgar Weed

MARGARET A. EDGAR WAS BORN in 1838 and reared
and educated at Lockport, Illinois. When the Rebellion broke out she
felt it her duty to do all she could for her country; when the call came
for nurses she immediately offered her services, and, with her sister
Ellen, started for her first field of labor, October 9, 1861, and soon arrived in Jefferson City. Mrs. Livermore and Mrs. Hoge gave these two
girls commissions, and Doctor Beck assigned them work in different
wards under an older lady as matron.

The hospital was a large, four-story building which had formerly
been used as a ladies' academy. Here were wounded men, cases of
measles, typhoid fever, scarlet fever, and indeed all the diseases that followed the army. There were from thirty to forty men in each ward, and
the work was not as systematic as it was later in the war. Surgeons,
nurses, and soldiers were alike ignorant of hospital service, and it is a
wonder that so much was accomplished when we think that they did
the cooking, kept the wards and patients clean, superintended the entire housekeeping arrangements, beside having the responsibility of
preparing the diet.

The hospital was always full, and in spite of all that could be done,
many died. The summer was hot, the autumn pleasant, and the winter
severe,—the changes greatly affecting the patients. Occasionally an incident would occur that greatly amused the boys. One day a soldier

from Missouri came in from camp very sick, and as he grew worse and worse, we sent for his wife. She was dressed in a linsey-woolsey suit, and rode an old white horse. She had lived in the backwoods all her life, and of course saw many strange things at the hospital. Soon after she arrived, an engine came puffing up the track, hauling a train. "Oh my! What is that?" she cried. On being told she replied, "My! I never seed a car in my life before!" This amused the sick men, and did them as much good as a dose of medicine. She would sit by her husband's cot and smoke hour after hour. Finally he died, and she went home.

It would take a volume to record the suffering and death, the joys and sorrows, and the many interesting incidents which occurred at this one hospital, where Miss Edgar remained until it was closed, in 1862, and the nurses ordered to other places, wherever they were most needed.

After the battle of Fort Donelson there was a great demand for help, and the medical director ordered her to report at Paducah, Kentucky, where she was detailed to service January 23, 1863, and assigned to Hospital No. 1, under Major H. P. Stearnes. This hospital was a large, four-story structure, that had previously been used as a warehouse. She was placed in a surgical ward, where she had men from Corinth, Vicksburg, and second Donelson; and here she found all she could possibly do, day and night. It would be impossible for her to say how many passed through her ward during the two and a half years she was there, as she kept no record. The hospital had been conveniently fitted up at great expense to the Government, but it came to sudden destruction.

On the 26th of March 1864, the enemy, under Generals Forrest, Harris, Buford, and Thompson, made an attack on Paducah. The rebels tore down the fence around the hospital, took possession, and filled the building with sharpshooters. As the hospital stood on higher ground, this gave them a chance to shoot our men in the fort.

Miss Edgar relates her experience there in the following words: "As I was leaving the hospital I met a rebel soldier, who brought his gun down with authority, saying, 'Halt,' and then ordered me to fall into line. On going a little farther, Miss McLeary was ordered to fall in, and he marched us onto the open field between the rebels and our fort; but the balls flew harmlessly above our heads. Meantime our guns were under the necessity of shelling the hospital, in order to rout the rebels, who were killing the men in the fort."

While we were in the field a rebel officer rode up and asked, "Ladies, how came you here?" we told him it was the order of one of his men; whereupon he told us to get down on the ground, or we would be killed. We met a rebel soldier, and Miss McLeary said, "I thought my time had come." He replied, "You should always be ready to die." We were so frightened that we could tell nothing about time. Near by us a cow was grazing. A ball struck her; she jumped high in the air, and with a loud bellow retreated in good order. We momently expected the same fate, but in spite of our fears we laughed at our strange condition. This was my first experience in raid or battle. Soon we saw the rebels retreating, loaded with plunder; but they carried many dead and dying men, among them the lifeless body of General Thompson, covered with blood.

As we were moving off the field a rebel, carrying a flag, said, "Have you many Yanks?" "Yes, sir," I replied. "Reinforcements are coming down river." This was repeated, and passed along line, "Reinforcements are coming!"

Forrest sent in a flag of truce for a surrender of the fort. Meanwhile we escaped as best we could, made our way to the Ohio River and crossed into Illinois. We were not allowed to return until next day; then it was to learn that the hospital, with all its contents, had been burned.

Miss Edgar was next assigned to Hospital No. 4 and found all she could do there, as there were more victims from the attack on Paducah. Forty-six Union men and a thousand rebels had been wounded The work continued until late in August 1864. Then she returned to her home for a short time to rest; but was soon requested to report to H. Stearnes, surgeon in charge of the Joe Holt, United States General Hospital at Jeffersonville, Indiana, when she was detailed to service October 3, 1864, in the linen department. This hospital was a little city in itself. It was usually crowded, and fifteen hundred men were in it now. There was a diet kitchen, convalescent dining room and kitchen, commissary, bakery, and a large, elegant drug store. The laundry was run by machinery, and a Mr. Hamilton did the heavy lifting and kept the books. The linen room was on the plan of a large dry-goods store.

While in this hospital Miss Edgar was married to Alexander G. Weed, who was hospital steward of the 24th Wisconsin Volunteer Infantry. She was honorably discharged in the fall of 1865, and returned to private life.

She has many letters dating from 1862 to 1892, which express gratefulness and appreciation for her services.

Thirty years have flown since those days; she is now "gray," and inclined to live in the past, and think over the scenes of war-times. She has been a widow since 1891. Her address is

Margaret A. Weed
RUSSELL, KANSAS

Modenia Weston

I was born in Albany, New York, August 3, 1816. I went from Iowa into the army September 1, 1861. My labors were varied. I was first connected with the 3d Iowa Infantry Hospital. I was called the mother of the regiment. In October there were a great many sick with the measles, but soon the disease abated somewhat, and the regiment was ordered to Quincy to recuperate. We went to Benton Barracks next, where those who had not already taken the measles now had them. I was the only woman connected with the department and had my hands full. My labors were made much easier by having a good supply of sanitaries sent to me.

In February the regiment was ordered to Mexico, Missouri; the hospital department, containing thirty patients, to be left behind. As soon as the sick were able to travel we followed the troops, and had no sooner established our hospital than small pox broke out. In March all the able-bodied men were ordered to Pittsburg Landing; as soon as possible we followed, only to find most of the regiment sick with diarrhoea, from drinking surface water. The ladies of Quincy supplied us with sanitary stores, and with them a large box of tea. So I had tea made for those in the hospital department, and all got well.

I was with the regiment the first day at the battle of Shiloh, and we did up wounds until eleven o'clock. Then went to River Landing and aboard the steamer, on which were four hundred wounded. Here, too,

I was the only woman. They had no food, so I first sent for coffee, sugar, and hardtack. Tuesday the boat was ordered to Savannah, where we occupied an unfinished building. After we had been there a few days we received some supplies; then we did very well.

About the first of May four lady nurses were sent to us, and as soon as possible the wounded were removed. The sanitary stores were sent to Farrington. We found twenty-two hundred wounded, and some fever cases; all were in tents. We stayed until September; then the patients were sent North, the hospital was broken up, and the supplies sent to Corinth. Three other nurses and myself were sent to Jackson, where we remained until March 1863. Then, all patients having been removed, the nurses, twenty-two in number, were ordered to report at Memphis, Tennessee. From there we went to Washington. All this time I was a volunteer nurse, without pay.

April 20, 1863, I received my commission from Miss Dix. In January 1864 I was ordered to report to J. D. Erwin, Superintendent of U. S. General Hospital of Memphis, Tennessee. He sent me to the Small-Pox Hospital as matron. I remained there until October 1866.

When I volunteered, my name was Modenia R. McColl. Now it is

Modenia R. Weston
WAVELAND, HANCOCK CO., MISSISSIPPI

Elizabeth Wheeler

AFTER LOOKING OVER SOME OLD ARMY LETTERS, I find my memory so refreshed that I have concluded to try to comply with your request that I write a sketch of my experience as an army nurse.

When the first company enlisted from Worcester and my brother went with them, my whole soul was aroused, and had I been a man I should have counted one of the number. Soon word came that the 6th had been attacked while going through Baltimore, Maryland and that one of our men was killed. This caused great excitement, for that was not supposed to be rebel ground. I think all the women felt like learning to use firearms. I did the next best thing, which was to offer my services in case the men should be sick or wounded. It was a three-months' regiment, as that was supposed to be a long enough time in which to end the war; and my services were not needed by them.

But after the battle of Gettysburg, when so many wounded were sent to McDougal Hospital, Fort Schuyler, where several ladies from Worcester had already repaired, I received a summons and pass to go thither. It admitted of no retreat on my part; if it had my courage would have failed, so much did I shrink from going amidst such suffering. However, there was nothing for me to do but go forward; and I think it was July 5th with only one day's notice, that I started, feeling very weak in myself, yet "strong in the Lord."

When we arrived at the fort it was a strange sight to see so many scores of men in white garments lolling on the ground and fences. They had been ordered to exchange their woolen clothing for cotton, which seemed almost murderous, as they had worn nothing but woolen all through their term of service. This resulted in colds, coughs, and inflammation of wounds.

Each nurse had a ward of about fifty men. I tried to put on a brave front and imagine all as brothers, and in that spirit commenced my duties. That night I heard sounds that told of ague chills; and the next morning went to inquire who it was, and found it to be a young man who had lost his right arm in battle. He asked me for a woolen shirt, and I succeeded in getting one, although they were very scarce. But it was too late; the chill had done its work.

As I went around with the doctor to see the patients, I noticed his arm, which was unbound. The loosely hanging flesh looked very dark, and the bone could be seen. I thought it was gangrene, and asked the doctor if they would not have to amputate again in order to save his life; but received no answer. I showed that I was green by speaking to a doctor in that manner. He was a young cadet, put there for practice, the men said; and it was very hard for them to submit to being treated by one who did not know his business. The same wash-basin and sponges were used for all, and as a result gangrene got into the wounds, and that with the colds made quick work with the most of them.

When I next went to the young man who had lost his arm, he was restless and in a high fever. He told me how his twin brother had been killed in battle two weeks before, and that his father was dead, and he was all there was left to his mother. He was only twenty-four years old, but said, "I have been a very wicked young man." Then I spoke of our Heavenly Father's love, and asked him if I might read him the story of the Prodigal Son, telling him that God comes to meet us as soon as we have a desire to return from our wanderings, and that he was just the one Jesus died to save. I saw that in a few hours the end would come, so I repeated some of the precious promises, and asked him if he could not trust in Jesus. "Yes, I do; I will," he replied. I tried to comfort him with the assurance that the Lord will forgive all who repent, and he seemed satisfied. Later in the day he became delirious. The night watch came. In the morning I found that he had lingered through the night, but at 10 A.M. he died, and was buried with four others that afternoon. Oh, it seemed so sad when I thought of the friends at home! The men said he was a brave soldier, and that he would have lived if he could have been sent home, which would have cost the government no more than to keep him there.

It is dreadful to see so many die, and be buried in a few hours, and know that somewhere there were friends who loved them. And it was truly surprising how the men could be so cheerful, joking and throwing their crutches at each other, while they longed to be at home or back on duty. Those who could read spent much time in that way; others played games. Some had a habit of sitting at the head of the ward and playing cards. It was near my room and as I went in and out I would often hear an oath.

One day I said, "Boys, I never knew people to pray so much over their cards as you do." They looked up in astonishment, and said they did not know they prayed. " Well," I replied, "if I should ask God to bless as much as you do to curse, I should call it praying." I think I never heard swearing there again, except from visitors from other wards.

I had a rich experience one Inspection Day. It always came Sundays,—I suppose, to give the men more to do. There was a new order for "no boxes or books on the tables," so all such things were put in my room, as there was no other place. I had long wanted to get hold of those boxes, and now was my time. The reason was this: the boxes were often open when I went to dust, and on the lids were cheap pictures. I had ready many pictures of battles and generals, which I pasted over the ones on the lids, and they were all dry by the time they were carried out. When I went around the next morning it did me good to see the queer looks, though nothing was ever said.

I will close with two letters written while in the hospital:—

FORT SCHUYLER, SEPTEMBER 27.
DEAR MOTHER:—

I have received the boxes. That drum of figs from Mrs. Eldred it did not take me long to dispose of. I so much enjoy having a luxury to give the men. Please to tell the lady how much it was appreciated. I received a letter from Mrs. G. in behalf of the Sanitary Commission, saying she had that day forwarded two boxes of jelly. It is so good of them! I like to be the almoner of their bounties and show the soldiers how Massachusetts gives. I hope the next will be a box of woolen shirts.

The men in my ward are all getting along nicely, and until today I have had no very bad cases for a long time. One poor boy had his leg amputated. He is from Pennsylvania. He was wounded at Fort Wagner, and taken prisoner by the rebels. His foot was taken off by disjointing it at the heel. He had suffered terribly all the time, and now has to go through it all again. His groans are dreadful to hear; he does not bear it like many, still, we know it must be hard.

I have spent the day in my ward instead of going to the chapel. This man's name was John Conners. He was a little fellow, under twenty years of age, and very active, but he can neither read or write. I have been trying to teach him both, but he will suffer much that there will probably be a pause in the reading. It would have done you good to see the interest he manifested when I read to aim in the Testament. I read nine chapters right along. If I went to stop he would say: "But there is more yet; keep on. It seems like an interesting story." I presume he had never heard it read before. I explained as I went along. Today when he was in so such pain he would become quite quiet as soon as I commenced reading, and go to sleep. Tonight I told him to think about Jesus suffering for us (I had read the crucifixion to him), and asked if he could not try to bear it silently. He said he would, and now he is sleeping quietly. I never had such satisfaction in speaking or reading to any one. It all seems new.

DEAR FRIENDS AT HOME:—

I have ventured to do another thing. There is a young man by the name of K. I'm afraid he has been a bad young man. He was sick awhile ago,—the result of having a ball cut out of the side of his neck. I took care of him; he had hardly got well, when I was walking out, and saw him sitting on the ground with four others, playing cards. I was satisfied they were gambling. While he was sick, I opened a letter for him from his mother, in which she sent him five dollars, and one of the men said she sent him a letter that morning with ten dollars in it, telling him he should have the last cent she had. I thought I would make an effort to save him. I invited him to come into my room this Sunday morning, telling him I wished to talk with him for his good, and hoped he would take it kindly. He promised, and when I asked about his home friends, he told me he had a mother, one sister, and two little brothers. His father was killed in battle, nearly six months before.

I asked if he did not feel that a great deal devolved upon him to help to be a guide to those little brothers, and his mother's stay. After talking seriously with him of the effect upon his life, I asked him to spend the Sabbath in thinking what he would do. I told him I thought there was no one thing that would so harden the heart toward all one's friends as gambling; that I thought it would lead one down until he would take the last cent from a widowed mother, or from a hard-working sister; that it made one break all of God's commandments, and hate His laws. "Every word you say is true," he said. I gave him an interesting book to read, and asked him to think it all over and tell me, when I came to the ward that night, what he had decided,—whether to leave it off or keep on. When I passed through the ward at noon he was busy reading, and I think he was all day. As I went to my room at night, I said, "What is your decision?" "I have decided to leave it off," he replied. "I think it best for me." He remained two or three weeks, then was sent to the front. God only knows whether he was able to keep his promise.

Miss Elizabeth Wheeler
48 ORCHARD STREET
WORCESTER, MASSACHUSETTS

Cecelia White

I HAD TRANSPORTATIONS furnished me by Mrs. Wittenmyer, to go to Saint Louis. Then President Yeatman provided me with transportations to Memphis, Tennessee, where I was assigned to Washington Hospital, going on duty about the 15th of September 1863, and remaining until September 1864.

After I had been there a couple of weeks Doctor Wright came to me one morning to know what I was doing for the sick in my ward. "Doctor, I am doing all there is for me to do. You restrict us so that there is nothing for us to do." "In what way, madam?" "We are not allowed to prepare anything nice for the very sick ones, and they cannot eat the food from the kitchen." He made no reply; but that afternoon the steward put a nice cooking stove into an empty room, also the necessary supplies. In the morning the Doctor said, "Come with me, and I will show you your kitchen." I assure you we made good use of it, and it was very pleasant to hear the soldiers say, "That makes me think of home and Mother," when they ate the little delicacies we prepared.

I often think how little the people at home knew of what was going on in the hospital or on the battlefield. It seemed very sad to me to see men carried to the deadhouse day after day, and know that some poor mother, wife, or sister would mourn for each dear one.

One day the doctor told me of a young lieutenant at the hotel, and asked me to carry him something, and try to comfort him. He had been badly wounded through the right lung, in a skirmish the day before. I went as the doctor requested, bathed the poor fellow's face and hands, and combed his hair; but he was too sick for me to talk to him much then. Later, I said to him one morning, "War is a terrible thing!" "Yes," he answered. "If it hadn't been for that —— man who was put in the chair, we should not have had this dreadful war." "I beg leave to differ with you," I replied. "I believe he was a man of God's own choosing; he raised him up for this very purpose." I never enjoyed visiting him after that, and was glad when his friends came, a week later.

Our nurses did nine months' hard work, cooking in the kitchen in addition to their other duties; then Mrs. Wittenmyer and her assistants established a branch of the Christian Commission, and we soon went home.

I was forty-six years old when I went into the hospital, and now I am rapidly nearing the time when my years will number fourscore.

Mrs. Cecilia White
868 NORTH STREET
BURLINGTON, IOWA

Rebecca Wiswell

I ENLISTED in Boston, the first week in March 1862 and was in Government employ three years and four months. Miss Dix sent for me. I used to do up bandages, and carry them to the State House every day. They said mine were the best of any. One day they asked me if I had ever nursed. I told them I had for twenty years in Boston. They asked if I had any recommendations, and I told them I had plenty at home. "Will you please bring them up here and let us see them?" they said. Then after looking at them: "No one who has gone from this part of the country has had such high recommendations. You ought to be out at the front; and with your consent we will telegraph." So they immediately sent for me to go to Washington, and I spent the first night with Miss Dix.

Next day she took me up to Seminary Hospital. I stayed there a little over two years; then went up the Shenandoah Valley, and was there over four months; then was sent to Fortress Monroe, where I stayed four months more. Was very sick the last fortnight. I had a young man in my ward who would not tell where he belonged until the afternoon before he died; then he told me, and asked me to sing to him, and read a little from the Bible. I asked him where I should read, and he said, "Where you open; and sing, 'My heavenly home is bright and fair.'" After I had done this he said, "Now I want you to tell me just how long it will take me to die." "My dear, I can't tell you that," I said.

"None but God knows. Are you in a hurry to go?" "Yes; I long to be gone." He soon passed away, I trust to that bright world above where there is "rest for the weary."

I had one man who had six little boys and a wife. "Oh, how I long to see them!" he would say. "But that can't be; I must leave them to God's care." There were men there who were shot through the bowels. They were very hard to take care of. The worst case no doctor ever dressed but three times; then he was left in my care, and I did it five months. God does many wonderful things. We have great reason to bless and praise Him. I met one of those men in Washington at the Grand Army, a dear general, who said: "You saved my life. The doctor said I would die; but you said, 'You will live.'" The Lord does wonderful things that we poor creatures can't do.

May 20th I went to Annapolis, to see my nephew. There were about five thousand troops getting ready to move on to Richmond. The next week they were on the way.

In September we had left at our door a baby boy, about three months old. I took him into my room and kept him two days. I don't know what has become of him; he was put into the poorhouse. I saw him when he was two years old, and he was a smart little fellow.

After we had been in the Shenandoah Valley about four months, we nurses were ordered farther South; but rested in Washington three weeks before going into such hard service.

We had in the ward a young man who belonged in New York. He was brought in about eight o'clock one morning, and lived only until half past two P.M. He was very happy. I sang to him about two hours while he was dying. The officers would look at him and say, "How that man suffers!" "No, I don't," was his reply. "Jesus suffered it all. I shall soon be at home with him, and what a glorious meeting that will be. Jesus can make dying easy. There is something in my haversack I should like to look at once more." I opened it, and found photographs of his mother, his sister, and the lady to whom he was engaged. He kissed them, and said: "I hope they will be prepared to meet me in heaven. I shall soon be there." Oh, what a glorious death-bed scene to witness!

I often used to look at the troops, and the sight reminded me of the Day of Judgment, so many on the march.

We had some grand meetings during the war. President Lincoln used to say: "We need less talk, and more praying. God will hear and answer prayer." I often sang for my patients when requested to do so, and I have stood by some of the most blessed death-beds I can imagine. There were a great many praying men in the army,—a great many I hope to meet on the other shore.

I can't write well, my hands tremble so very much. I was eighty-eight years old the 24th day of last September.

With love to all,
Rebecca Wiswell
9 SPRING STREET
PLYMOUTH, MASSACHUSETTS

Jane Worrall

AT THE COMMENCEMENT of the late Rebellion, I resided with my husband and two children in Southwestern Virginia, but the feeling of the Southern people toward Union sympathizers was such that we returned to Boston, Massachusetts, the journey requiring two weeks.

Business soon called Mr. Worrall back to Virginia, where he was taken prisoner. After undergoing many hardships he escaped, and made his way to Boston, where he at once enlisted in the 24th Massachusetts Volunteers. In 1863 he re-enlisted for three years more; serving in all four years and eight months. I then decided to enter the service as an army nurse, commissioned by Miss D. L. Dix. I was first assigned to the Columbia College Hospital, Washington, D. C., and immediately took charge of a ward of twenty-five cots, some of the patients very sick, some badly wounded. The hospital stood upon a little eminence, and as I wended my way toward it, I met a funeral procession. Instantly the tears of sympathy stole to my eyes as I thought of the brave heart now cold and still. He had fought and died for his country. Suddenly I dried my tears, saying: "If I am to be of any use I must learn to control myself. I am here to cheer, not to sadden, the lives of my patients." After I arrived the matron escorted me through the ward of suffering, dying men. I shed no tears, and when we had completed the round the matron said: "Mrs. Worrall, of all the nurses we have had, you are the only one who has refrained from crying when going through the ward the first time. I know you will make a good and true nurse."

At the expiration of my term of duty here, there was a call for nurses at Fortress Monroe, and I learned with pleasure that I was to go there. We were met and escorted to Chesapeake Hospital by a delegation of convalescent soldiers. I was assigned to Ward 1, containing sixty-five cots. All were officers, some suffering greatly; but I felt that with the help of my Heavenly Father I could do the work. I remained there about six months, and during that time acted as special nurse to the Confederate General Walker of South Carolina. He was badly wounded, and was taken prisoner by Mr. Worrall's company. On the way he asked for water, and as Mr. Worrall gave it to him he said, "Is it possible that you, a Northern man, will show kindness to a Southerner?" "Certainly," was the reply. "You are now a wounded man." I did what I could for him, and assisted in dressing his wounds for about three months; then he was exchanged.

I was also special nurse to Captain Small and Captain Babb, both Union men. There was only one death in my ward while at Fortress Monroe; that was a lieutenant from Connecticut, shot through the body. He was a great sufferer, and died of internal hemorrhage! I did not leave him day or night, only to attend to the wants of the other patients. I sent for his father, who was with him when he gave up the "battle of life."

At last my health began to fail, and I told the surgeon in charge I should have to go home for awhile or be assigned to lighter duties; but Doctor McClennen said I could not be spared, so for a week I gave up my work. Then came a call for nurses at West Building Hospital, Baltimore, and I went there to take Ward 4, of thirty-five cots. I remained until the hospital closed. There were some severe cases of shot and shell wounds, but after a time my ward became convalescents, and were assigned light duty. Then the cots were filled with rebel prisoners, badly wounded, who in turn were exchanged for Union men from Libby Prison. A more distressing sight could not be imagined. They were in a dying condition, nearly starved. Five died within twenty-four hours. Those who could talk told me they had not had water to wash their faces and hands for three months; and if a bone was thrown to them they would fight for it like dogs. They were all brought on stretchers, and it was only with the best of care that any of them were saved.

While there I had a very singular case. The surgeon said he had never seen anything like it. A Confederate boy only sixteen years of age, and very ignorant so far as book-learning was concerned, was brought to the ward with a field amputation; but his doom was sealed. He had the lockjaw, and lay for twenty-four hours, when all I could do for him was to wet a piece of linen in brandy and lay it across his mouth, so he could breathe the moisture from it. He came out of that dreadful state perfectly rational, and after taking some nourishment, asked me to pray with him. I did so, and read the fourteenth chapter of Saint John, which I read to all my patients who would listen to me. Then he talked about two hours,—using the most beautiful language about the Bible and the glories of heaven. He certainly was inspired. Everybody who could do so came to hear him. At last, addressing me, he said: "Mother, don't you see the angels coming? They are holding out their hands to take me home." Then he dropped away like a child going to sleep.

Just before the hospital closed, five typhoid fever cases were brought to the ward. One died, and I contracted the fever in its worst form; and although everything was done for me I barely escaped, and have never been well since. I feel that my Heavenly Father blessed me all through my work, and carried me through my sickness. I was in the service a year and a half, and have the honor of being breveted major.

Jane M. Worrall
9 WARREN PLACE
ROXBURY, MASSACHUSETTS

Index